OUTLAW JUSTICE

Cultural Memory
in
the
Present

Hent de Vries, Editor

OUTLAW JUSTICE

The Messianic Politics of Paul

Theodore W. Jennings, Jr.

STANFORD UNIVERSITY PRESS

STANFORD, CALIFORNIA

Stanford University Press
Stanford, California

Printed in the United States of America

Library of Congress Cataloging-in-Publication Data

Jennings, Theodore W., author.
    Outlaw justice : the Messianic politics of Paul / Theodore W. Jennings, Jr.
        pages cm. — (Cultural memory in the present)
    Includes bibliographical references and index.
    ISBN 978-0-8047-8516-7 (cloth : alk. paper)
    ISBN 978-0-8047-8517-4 (pbk.   )
        1. Bible. N.T. Romans—Philosophy. 2. Paul, the Apostle, Saint—Political and
social views. 3. Justice—Biblical teaching. 4. Justice (Philosophy) I. Title.
II. Series: Cultural memory in the present.
BS2665.6.J8J456   2013
227'.106—dc23

                                                                    2012033120

ISBN 978-0-8047-8599-0 (electronic)

Contents

Acknowledgments

I was initiated into the complexities and pleasures of reading Paul by Hendrikus Boers, with whom over the course of forty years I had the pleasure of long-night conversations about Paul, and Romans in particular. It was with him that I learned the challenges of a "humanistic" interpretation of the New Testament (even though our theological perspectives were quite different). The first fruit of that interest was my book *Reading Derrida / Thinking Paul: On Justice*, which interrupted work on the current project and also reoriented it. The former book was published before Hendrik's untimely death.

This book could not have been written without the critical and enthusiastic engagement of many students in seminars on Romans beginning in Mexico in 1984 and continuing for many years at the Chicago Theological Seminary. In addition, students in my seminars that engaged contemporary continental philosophy have made many important contributions. I am as always grateful to them and for them.

I am grateful to Adam Kotsko, who graciously agreed to cast his expert eye over the manuscript, to the anonymous readers for the Press who made several helpful suggestions, and to the editors at Stanford, Emily-Jane Cohen and Hent de Vries, who encouraged the publication of this book. Tim Roberts and the editorial team have made invaluable contributions to the readability of this book.

The book is dedicated to all those I have been privileged to meet in many parts of the world who are engaged in the struggle for a new society, a democracy to come perhaps, in which exclusion and exploitation are ended and all enter into the messianic radiance.

Introduction

GETTING READY TO READ ROMANS

Why another book on Paul's letter to the Romans? Since the early third century, when Origen wrote his extensive commentary, this letter has been the most commented-upon text in the New Testament.

Romans is generally read as an exposition of Christian doctrine or (more recently) as a window into early Christianity. Here I will propose another way of reading the text. I will read it as a text that deals with the most fundamental questions of what might be called political philosophy, that is, a thinking of the political, a thinking of the way in which human life is to be ordered as a corporate or common life. Specifically, I will argue that Paul may be read as developing a messianic politics that stands in contrast to the political order established by Rome and as an alternative to the polity of "Moses" or of the "Judeans." In Paul's day there had already been attempts by Jewish intellectuals to argue for the superiority of Judean or Mosaic political order to the political order of Rome (Stowers 35). Both Judean and Roman polity had in common that they conceived of the political in terms of the basic law that structured common life. In this they were in a certain continuity with the thinking of the political that had characterized the approaches of Plato and Aristotle, who approached the political as a question of providing a legal order that would produce a just arrangement of social life. Thus, Aristotle, after famously affirming that the human being was the political life-form (*zōon politikon*), maintained that "justice is the bond of men in states. For the administration of justice, which is the determination of what is just, is the principle of order in political society" (*Politics* 1253a.37–39). His teacher, Plato, had offered reflections on an ideal political organization oriented toward justice in texts such as *The Republic, The Statesman*, and *The Laws.* Indeed, it appears that Plato attempted to put his ideas into practice in terms of developing a constitution for Syracuse. This attempt was based in part upon the notion that the principal exemplars of political order represented by Cyprus, Sparta, and Athens all had their polity derived from a lawgiver (Solon of Athens, Minos of Crete, Lycurgus of Sparta) who had provided a wise constitution or basic set of laws to govern the common life of the people (Plato, *Laws* 1.624–631). Given this notion of the lawgiver and the attempts of Plato and Aristotle to offer ideal constitutions, it is easy to see how Moses also could be understood as the founder of a sort of political or constitutional order.

At least since the time of Augustine, theologians have known that Paul is concerned in Romans with the themes that were the common currency of political thinking: law and justice. But it is also the case that most readings of Romans have deflected attention away from this political question in order to focus upon the situation of the individual believer in relation to God. This has also meant that the text has been read primarily as a religious rather than a political text. Of course, this dichotomy would probably not have been intelligible to Paul (or to Plato or Caesar Augustus for that matter), but the political and philosophical character of Paul's argument has receded from view. The result is that the text is read as a book of the church that concerns narrowly religious issues. Indeed, in English this process has been exacerbated by the disappearance of "justice" (and "injustice") from the translation of the text. Terms like "righteousness," "unrighteousness," and "wickedness" have been substituted to make the political significance of what Paul is up to disappear behind a fog of religiosity.

The reading of this text that I propose here breaks with this tradition of reading Paul. The reading begins by restoring terms like "law" and "justice" to their basic political significance. So dominant has the apolitical reading of Romans become that it will be necessary to introduce a number of unfamiliar translations into this reading. In part this is necessary to help the reader encounter a text with fresh eyes not blinkered by the tradition. A strategy of defamiliarizing is almost always necessary to allow a fresh encounter with the text. But in this case it is even more important if the text is to be liberated from its cloying confinement in the cultlike enclave of traditional religious reading. Much of this is simple substitution warranted by the text itself: Judean rather than Jewish, messiah rather than Christ, justice rather than righteousness, fidelity or loyalty rather than faith, generosity or favor rather than grace, Joshua rather than Jesus, and so on. The significance of these changes will become apparent as the reading progresses.

In terms of the reading of Paul's letter itself, it will be necessary to see that Paul is concerned with the most basic issues of political thinking: law and justice. However, Paul is proposing a radical rethinking of the political by insisting that justice should be thought in contrast to law. While agreeing with the tradition of political thought that the basic issue has to do with justice, Paul deviates from that tradition by offering a fundamental critique of the supposition that justice is to be achieved through a legal structuring of society. For Paul, I will argue, the political question of justice is to have a completely new basis: the act of God in the messiah. Thus, a new messianic political thinking is introduced that has radical implications for the way human social history is to be understood, a way that contrasts both with the Mosaic social order and with the Greco-Roman social order, especially that which is made concrete in the Roman imperial order (or disorder).

One of the things most often hidden from view in traditional readings of Paul is his fundamental critique of the Roman Empire and its conceptual underpinnings. Thus, the question of "law" has most often been restricted to the "religious" law of Moses, with little or no attention given to the critique of Rome. As long as Christians have sought to ingratiate themselves with the politically powerful, it has been necessary to deflect or ignore Paul's critique of the Roman Empire. Only in recent times has Paul's opposition to Rome become something that biblical scholars have recognized. Here the Paul and Politics working group under the leadership of Richard Horsley continues to be decisive. The books by Neil Elliott have also greatly deepened this perspective. More recently Brigitte Kahl has argued, in her *Galatians Re-imagined*, that Paul's concern with law must always be read in connection not only with the question of Torah but also in connection with Roman law (5–11).

The emphasis upon Mosaic or Jewish law and corresponding silence about Rome have permitted a deeply anti-Jewish reading of Romans. If one of the most important developments in the reading of Paul, and indeed the New Testament, in recent times has been the growing awareness of Paul's critique of the Roman Empire, another has been the growing recognition that Paul always remained a deeply Jewish (or Judean) thinker. Rescuing Paul and Romans from the anti-Judaism of much of the Christian tradition of reading Romans has been of immense importance in gaining a new understanding of the New Testament, of Paul, and of this text in particular. For, as we shall see, and as Barth already recognized, anti-Judaism is ruled out in principle by Paul in this very letter.

That Paul can be read as one who deals with the most basic issues of political thinking is not a complete innovation in theological reflection. Augustine, whose reading of Romans did so much to depoliticize its themes, nevertheless could also read it as providing basic clues to the contrast between what he called the city of God and the human city. The city or *civitas* was, of course, the basic unit of Latin political thought, as was the *polis* for Greek thought. Augustine recognized that the *civitas* of humanity had in the meantime become not a city-state but an imperial state. And he sought to contrast the human (Roman) empire with the city of God, the divine society inaugurated in Christ. Unfortunately, Augustine found it difficult to think the *social* character of the city of God, at least this side of "heaven," thereby rendering its political significance tenuous at best. Without adopting the specific ways in which Augustine sought to relate these basic political orders, we can nonetheless find a certain common ground in his recognition that in any case what is at stake is a *civitas*, a political ordering of the human world. (Our terms "civics," "civil society," and so on all stem from the Latin *civitas* as a basic political notion or category.)

Certainly Calvin was also aware of some of the political implications of what Paul had been up to in this text, even if its political relevance was fatefully focused on the infamous reference in Romans 13 to the idea that the political order derives from God. But it was at the end of the First World War, with the apparent collapse of Western social order, that Karl Barth in his Romans commentary recognized that what Paul is up to is articulating a radical critique of any existing sociocultural order. Certainly my reading of Romans owes a good deal to Barth's insight that this text can and should be read as an indictment of the social order (or disorder) of Western civilization. But it is in Latin American liberation theology that the relevance of Paul's argument for an understanding of the basic political structures of the world comes into sharpest focus. Above all I am thinking here of Jose Porfirio Miranda's *Marx and the Bible*, in which Paul is read as offering a fundamental critique of Western civilization—a civilization that entails a political economy that impoverishes the masses while securing the privileges of the few.

Although reading Paul as a thinker of the political is not without precedent in some theological circles and although it may be anchored in certain developments in the historical critical work of contemporary biblical scholars, the most dramatic developments in this way of reading Paul come neither from theologians nor from biblical scholars but from contemporary intellectuals who may be regarded as secular or even atheistic readers of Paul. Contemporary continental thinkers have increasingly turned to the basic questions of the political as they attempt to think the world as a global society dominated by forces that seem to be destructive of human flourishing. Many of them have been deeply influenced by Karl Marx's critique of the political economy of capital and by the ardent desire for the emancipation of the impoverished and the oppressed. In disillusionment with both capitalist globalization and the failures of certain forms of "communism," they have sought to find a way to think of a radically new political economy. In so doing they have increasingly turned to the Bible and especially to Paul, not as "believers" in a doctrine, or practitioners of a cult, or members of an institution that calls itself Christianity, but simply as intellectuals in quest of a radically new way of thinking about human society oriented toward justice. They offer opportunities for reading Paul outside the confinement of specifically religious or even theological commitments. In this they follow a trail blazed at the beginning of the Enlightenment by Hobbes and Spinoza and soon followed by Locke. Although these earlier thinkers saw Paul as a kind of political philosopher, their issue had more to do with the possibility of emancipating the political from the hegemony of religious institutions and from the straitjacket of confessional commitments. Thus, at the early stages of the Enlightenment Paul was of considerable help in the program of what might be called secularization of the state and was therefore regarded also as a champion of religious liberty.

Even in the nineteenth century, Friedrich Engels, Marx's friend and constant collaborator, had recognized the relevance of Paul for an emancipatory political project. He recognized certain affinities between the project of international socialism and the work of Paul in establishing communities of social justice among the oppressed masses of the Roman Empire. In his *History of Early Christianity*, he writes: "So it was with early Christianity, so it was in the beginning of the socialist movement" (330). He cites with approval the suggestion of the radical biblical scholar Ernst Renan: "If I wanted to give you an idea of the early Christian communities I would tell you to look at a local section of the International Working Men's Association" (318). This even extends to the frustrations of both movements in collecting resources from the masses for the purposes of the movement (318)!

But it was really in the years following the collapse of the Soviet Union that the reading of Paul as what we now call a "public intellectual" gained momentum among European intellectuals seeking a new way to think the global political reality that had emerged with the dominance of capitalism and American hegemony.

While what is now called the Great Recession has cast into relief the excesses of global capital, and the bare new beginnings of the transformation of US polity makes clear in retrospect the bankruptcy of a crusade for freedom advanced through preemptive war and torture, the question of a fundamentally new way of thinking about global political arrangements has if anything become only more urgent.

In the rereading of Romans that I pursue in these pages, I will seek to read Romans in dialogue with these "secular" and even nonreligious intellectuals. Of course, my reading is informed by some of the developments in theology and biblical criticism to which I have already referred. But in order to read Paul as a radical thinker of the political, I find it most helpful to call upon those who read Paul outside the religious or even the scholarly ghetto of professional, academic, or ecclesiastical readings. It is the insight of Nietzsche and Heidegger, of Derrida and Nancy, of Badiou and Žižek, of Benjamin and Agamben that I think will most helpfully enable us to see how Paul may be read not simply as a theologian of the church but as one who is seeking to illuminate the most basic issues of our common life as human beings who dwell together on a planet in peril.

One way of justifying such a rereading of Romans in companionship with contemporary philosophers comes from a story about Paul found in the Acts of the Apostles. There he was met by "some also of the Epicurean and Stoic philosophers," who we are told "brought him to the Areopagus, saying may we know what this new teaching is which you present?" (17:19). We are then presented with a speech that the author of this text attributes to Paul in which much of what Paul says is fairly straightforward from the perspective of many philosophers of the day. For example: "The God who made the world and everything in it, being Lord of heaven and earth, does not live in shrines made by human hands . . . and he made from one every nation of men to live upon the face of the earth . . . that they should seek God in the hope that they might . . . find him" (17:24–27). All of this is in keeping with then-current philosophical common sense, as is the rejection of "idolatry and superstition" of various kinds. Paul then turns to something that might be a bit more controversial: "The times of ignorance God overlooked, but now he commands all men everywhere to repent" (17:30). Yet this might also be conformable at least to the philosophical vocation of calling people to leave off superstition as well as vice and to enter upon a life of reason and virtue. But it begins to become gradually more difficult to accept: "Because he has fixed a day on which he will judge the world in justice"—this too may be made agreeable to the sense that God is a God of justice who will condemn the world for injustice that we will find echoed in some of the historians and poets of this period—"through a man whom he has appointed"—here we are moving further away from the common sense of the matter, even though new emperors were often enough supposed to be the ones who would finally usher in a new era of justice—"of this God has given assurance to all by raising him from the dead"—and it is this last that the cultural common sense of the Greco-Roman world cannot abide (17:31). For good reason, then, the author says that "when they heard of the resurrection of the dead, some mocked" (17:32). This seems to good philosophical sense to be what Alain Badiou calls it: a fable. The text continues: "But others said, 'We will hear you again about this'" (17:32). Despite the puzzlement over some of the seemingly outrageous aspects of this fable, something in Paul's view is nonetheless sufficiently attractive to the philosophical mind to justify further inquiry. Indeed, at the end we are told: "But some joined him and believed, among them Dionysius the Areopagite and a woman named Damaris and others with them" (17:34). The Dionysius named here will lend his name to one of the most influential of negative or mystical theologians. Of Damaris we know nothing further, though it was by no means unheard of for women to be found among the philosophers.

This story, whether or not it captures events in Paul's own life, does seem to foreshadow what we know to have been true of some philosophical encounters with early Christianity (the case of Justin Martyr comes to mind). But it also may serve to suggest something of the method that I will employ here as I listen in on contemporary nonreligious philosophers dealing with Paul and with the issues with which Paul seems most concerned. Here the words of Spinoza may offer some encouragement: "None of the Apostles did more philosophizing than Paul" (144).

In reading this text in a fresh way it is still important to make sure that it is this text that one is reading. The guidelines for an appropriate interpretation of this text are still very much as indicated by Origen, who was the first to write a commentary on this letter. The parts of the letter should be understood in relation to the text as a whole. Taking a few favorite verses here and there, tearing them out of their context, and making them into pretexts for some or other point is simply bad reading. In my classes on Romans I encourage students to prepare a copy of Romans that first of all eliminates chapter and verse division to help focus on the overall flow of the argument. This is precisely the way we read Plato or Aristotle as well as Athanasius and Augustine. In my own rereading of Romans I will attempt to keep references to chapters and verses to a minimum, emphasizing instead the basic elements and movements of Paul's argument. Throughout this book the text from Romans is boldface (with occasional lightface insertions aiming at clarifying the translation or text) in order to help the reader identify the passages under discussion.

Moreover, if other texts are to be brought in to clarify this one, then it is important to first consider other texts written by Paul. If a text in Romans is to be understood, it should be understood first from Romans as a whole document. Then, since it is a text of Paul's, other letters of Paul must initially help us clarify what Paul is up to.

To this we may also add the warning that we will be reading a letter. That means that the text aims at particular readers and takes into account their presumed ways of understanding a text. This indicates something of the difficulty inherent in the reading of this or any other similar text. It is a bit like listening in on one side of a telephone conversation. Some of these difficulties will become evident as we go. They will never be completely soluble. In general it will mean that we will never have complete certainty about the meaning of certain phrases or arguments in the text. That is simply a part of what it means to read the text as the text that it is: written in a time and place, a culture and language, far removed from our own.

The inherent difficulties in reading Pauline texts is something already signaled toward the end of the first century in a text ascribed to the apostle Peter: "So also our beloved brother Paul wrote to you according to the wisdom given him, speaking of this as he does in all his letters. There are some things in them hard to understand, which the ignorant twist to their own destruction, as they do the other writings. You therefore, beloved, since you are forewarned, beware that you are not carried away with the error of the lawless" (2 Peter 3:15–17).

What is going on here? Note first that the writer knows several letters of Paul and that they are regarded as "writings," which is often a technical term for the Septuagint (LXX), the Greek version of the sacred writings of ancient Israel. Already the texts of Paul are regarded as difficult. And in part this difficulty may relate to the possibility that they may lead people into "lawlessness." Already at the end of the first century, then, Paul's writings were regarded as something like theological dynamite: handle with care. Much of subsequent reading may have attempted to render the text harmless.

A part of the difficulty is already anticipated in Paul's own description of his method of communication. This is how Paul explains his method:

For though I am free with respect to all, I have made myself a slave to all, so that I might win more of them. To the Judean I became as a Judean, in order to win Judeans. To those under the law I became as one under the law (though I myself

am not under the law) so that I might win those under the law. To those outside
the law I became as one outside the law (though I am not free from God's law
but am under Messiah's law), so that I might win those outside the law. To the
weak I became weak, so that I might win the weak. I have become all things to
all people, that I might by all means save some. I do it all for the sake of the gospel. (1 Corinthians 9:19–23)

We will have to keep this text in mind throughout our reading of Romans.
First, because it indicates something odd in Paul's relation to the law: free
of the law, but not of divine or messianic law. What can this possibly
mean? Already a certain fissure opens up in the idea of law, for divine
law seems to be contrasted with the law of Israel, the law of Moses let
us say, or the Torah. There is also the question of the weak, to which we
will return toward the end of Romans. But for our initial purposes what
is most important is the indication of the adaptability of Paul's manner
of speaking or writing. He maintains that he shapes what he is saying in
accordance with his understanding of the other person or group. And this
is not simply a matter of language or of idiom. It also holds for apparently
quite radically different religious perspectives. He speaks as a Judean to
Judeans. He speaks as a pagan to pagans.

Thus, an important part of the difficulty in reading Paul is that
he self-consciously shapes his argument in accordance with the worldview that he supposes to characterize his listeners or readers. Given the
paucity of our information about those readers' perspectives, we will be
at a considerable disadvantage in reading these texts. This is but one
reason for the necessity of multiple readings or interpretations of these
documents.

The test of any reading must be what sense it makes of the text it is
interpreting. If the reading I offer makes sense of what Paul has actually
written (that is, it is rooted clearly in the actual text), situates that text in
the social context of the first century, and at the same time helps us make
sense of recognizable realities we face in the world of the twenty-first century, then I will be content.

The title of this reading may be briefly explained. The text deals with
justice, but a sort of justice that is, as Paul says, "apart from the law," or as
I have written, "Outlaw Justice." In explicating this theme, I will depend
on some of the insights garnered from Jacques Derrida and other thinkers

of the political at the turn of this century. The way in which justice is to be conceived has to do with the messianic event that redirects human history and society, hence "messianic politics." Here some of the reflections of Giorgio Agamben are especially helpful in getting at what Paul is up to. The notion of a "theo-political reading of Romans" stems first of all from the beginning of the Enlightenment reading of Paul in Spinoza's *Theological-Political Treatise*, a theme picked up by Jacob Taubes, the great Jewish intellectual who was professor of hermeneutics at the University of Berlin, in his book *The Political Theology of Paul*, which is in conversation with Nietzsche, Freud, Benjamin, and Carl Schmitt.

The body of the letter begins and ends with Paul's explanation of his impending visit to Rome as well as the reasons for his delay in coming. The beginning of chapter 1 and the end of chapter 15 deal with this theme. All that comes in between may be understood as directed toward his arrival in Rome to provide some assistance to the messianic group there and to seek their assistance for his own messianic mission.

The argument then turns to a discussion of human social or political injustice as represented by what from his perspective are the two major political organizations of humanity: the pagan social order centered in Rome (1:18–2:11) and the Judean social order rooted in Moses (2:17–3:20). The possibility of this critique of injustice is related to the divine impartiality (2:12–16).

To this comprehensive indictment of injustice Paul contrasts the claim of a messianic justice founded not in law (as are the Roman and Judean systems) but in faithfulness with respect to the divine gratuity or unconditional generosity. This is presented first with respect to Abraham (as the father of Judean and pagan) and then, more radically, in relation to Adam—thus, the messianic is the transformation of the Adamic or of humanity as such.

The contrast between a legal social order and one that seeks justice by other means provokes a series of questions regarding the new social order and whether it is not simply an abolition of the claim of justice. To respond, Paul undertakes a series of contrasts (life or death, instruments and slaves of justice or injustice, married women or widows) to suggest what it means to be liberated from the rule of law, which then leads to the most fundamental contrast: between death and the law (7:7–25) or life and spirit (8:1–17). This spirited liveliness is then expressed in terms of a spirited solidarity that reaches out to extend to creation and that aims at unshakeable confidence in the divine solidarity with humanity and all creation (8:18–39).

This then provides the basis for Paul to address the question of the reliability of the divine promise in history, a subject anticipated all along in his argument. He shows how the divine promise works itself out in history through a series of unanticipated improvisations that respond to, yet overcome, human resistance (chapters 9–11), which then returns him to the assurance that all will be included in the triumph of messianic justice.

But what does this justice look like concretely now, in the emergence of the new messianic social groupings brought into being in the midst of actually existing social injustice? What sort of vanguard social reality can give persuasive evidence of the coming messianic transformation? Paul then comes to what may be the heart and culmination of his argument in addressing the improvisation of justice in these messianic societies (chapters 12–15). Of course, justice must have an improvisational character if it is not to fall back into the sort of legal structure that, in spite of its intentions, can only result in the perpetuation of injustice.

Paul's argument, then, is a complex attempt to persuade his readers, a small group of messiah followers living in the capital of the empire that had executed that messiah, that he can assist them in understanding and living out the extralegal response to the divine claim of justice in the midst of a world whose injustice is all too evident, not least in the execution of the messiah of God.

First Part of Romans

1. Making Connections (1:1–17)

We are going to read a letter written nearly two thousand years ago, from someone of whom we know very little, to people of whom we know even less. It is not addressed to us. We are, in a sense, accidental readers. Jacques Derrida has pointed out, in his work *The Postcard*, ways in which texts generally have this character, one that he identifies as a certain *destinerrance*, that is, a certain straying (*errance*) from its (intended?) destination. Like a postcard, it permits itself to be read by those to whom it was not sent and thus escapes from its presumed author's control or intention, from the direction in which it had been sent. The straying of this particular postcard from author and (intended) reader is largely the history of Christianity itself. The writer knew nothing of us and our circumstances, our culture, our language. He wrote to people of whom he presumably knew something, but we don't know much of what he knew. Like any letter writer, he could suppose that they knew some of the same things and had certain common perceptions of their world and of the ways that world was changing. Despite the often fruitful labors of scholars, we know far less than we would like to know about the emergence of early Christianity in the complex Greco-Roman cultural, religious, and political world within which Paul was writing. We have very little in common either with the writer or the readers. We are not only reading someone else's mail; we are almost unimaginably far from a shared culture or worldview, let alone community. Any interpretation, therefore, is going to be severely limited. Readers of biblical texts routinely forget how little we know or can know. This paucity of knowledge will prevent any reading, including this one, from being definitive, from putting an end to the possibilities of reading. Nevertheless, we will forge ahead in an attempt to glean what we can from this ancient document that has been so important to the shaping of the history of Western Christianity and culture.

It is a letter. It has a sender and an addressee, and the writer is seeking to convey something to the readers that bears upon their situation. It is not a treatise that can be divorced from its particular occasion or circumstance. Still less is it a summary of Paul's theology. But it does have a certain coherence, an argumentative "flow" that will require that we see the parts in relation to the whole rather than treat the parts as stand-alone reflections on particular themes.

As we shall see, the basic themes of the text as a whole are prefigured in the way the writer introduces himself and his intentions to the readers at the very beginning. In his *Time That Remains*, the radical political thinker Giorgio Agamben attempted to clarify the letter by focusing attention upon its first ten words. While such a procedure may be somewhat exaggerated (and Agamben himself deals with far more of this text and of Pauline texts generally than such a restriction might suggest), it is basically correct in sensing that much of what is essential to the text as a whole is already prefigured at the beginning. Accordingly, we will have to linger over the first few words—the introductory section—if we are to make sense of the letter as a connected argument.

Paul, slave of messiah Joshua

Already, before we begin, we are thrown into hidden perplexities. Who is Paul? Why does he call himself a slave? What sort of messianic liberator could even have slaves? What sort of slave could be attached to a messiah? What is happening here?

First, the name "Paul." Since the writing of the Acts of the Apostles some decades after Paul's death, everyone knows that the writer who calls himself Paul had also been known as Saul. (This information is not, however, found in the writings ascribed to Paul.) What does it mean that one who had been called Saul calls himself Paul? Some have suggested that this is a name change that reflects the conversion of one who had been a Jew (Saul) to one who has now become a Christian. Others suggest that he had had both a Jewish name (Saul) and a gentile or Roman name (Paul), for he was not only a Jew (and indeed a Pharisee, as he himself claims in Philippians 3:5) but also a citizen of Rome (as Acts suggests). In addressing gentile Romans, he would naturally use his Roman name.

Agamben points to another possibility that actually makes more sense of the messianic politics that we will be exploring: the name Paul means "small" "or insignificant." It thus corresponds to the self-designation of Paul as a slave, here and in other letters as well. Agamben writes: "The substitution of *sigma* by *pi* signifies no less than the passage from the regal to the insignificant, from grandeur to smallness—*paulus* in Latin means "small, of little significance," and in 1 Corinthians Paul defines himself as "the least [*elachistos*] of the apostles" (Agamben, *Time* 9).

The notion that the writer would call himself insignificant seems to be in considerable tension with his apparent assertiveness, especially in such texts as the letters to the Corinthians and Galatians where he seems to make much of his own authority. Since Nietzsche, it has been commonplace to notice the sometimes irritating self-assertion of this writer. Indeed, Nietzsche could say of Paul that "his lust was for power; Paul is the priest striving for power—he only had use for ideas, teaching, and symbols with which to tyrannize over the masses and to organize mobs" (*Antichrist* § 42). But is this view justified by the texts themselves?

We may recall that Saul is a noble name, the name of the first king of Israel, the kingly name of Saul's own tribe of Benjamin. If the writer has exchanged a noble and even kingly name for one that emphasizes insignificance and even slavehood, what would this mean?

It would mean that he is, in this at least, profoundly consistent with what he himself describes as the pattern of a certain messianic politics. In Philippians, writing to a community that he seems to have known well and with which he was on very good terms, he encourages them to adopt a policy, a common perspective, and approach to one another that Paul attributes to the messiah: "Have this perspective that also characterized the messiah Joshua, who though he was in the form of God, did not count equality with God a thing to be grasped but emptied himself, taking the form of a slave" (Philippians 2:6–7a).

Notice that this messianic policy is one that renounces privilege and power and goes so far as to take the form of a slave. Why slave? There is nothing in what we know of Jesus/Joshua that suggests that he had the legal status of a slave. The nearest that he approaches the status of a slave is in his being executed by means of crucifixion at the hands of the military government of the empire, for this was a form of execution often imposed upon rebellious slaves. It is perhaps no accident, then, that Paul mentions both slave and cross together in speaking of the messianic policy he enjoins upon his readers in Philippi in the passage just quoted. In that letter also, he had introduced himself as "slave of the messiah."

Has the writer, in taking to himself the name or nickname of Paul taken to heart this messianic polity and politics? This seems to be the likeliest explanation. The messianic policy that Paul had recommended in Philippians and that he seems to have adopted for himself is one that is otherwise attested in the later depictions of the policy of the one called the messiah in the narrative that came to be called Gospels. For there he is recalled as saying that those who would be the greatest should make themselves to be the servant or slave of the others (Mark 10:43–44). And certainly the messianic aspirations included a reversal of worldly status as suggested by Luke's version of the words of Mary: "He has brought low the high and has exalted the low" (1:52).

That "Saul" should become low also accords with Paul's own account of himself as having inherited and embodied a certain religious privilege: an Israelite, of the tribe of Benjamin, a Pharisee (Philippians 3:5). But all of this he views as of no account compared to what he has discovered in the messianic mission into which he has been summoned. Thus, he may describe himself, as Agamben has noticed, as "the least" of the apostles (1 Corinthians 15:9). In so doing he is simply imitating once again what he describes as God's policy in the world: "God chose what is foolish in the world to shame the wise, God chose what is weak in the world to shame the strong, God chose what is low and despised in the world, even things that are not, to bring to nothing things that are" (1 Corinthians 1:27–28).

Accordingly "Paul," the one of no account, is the name he has chosen for himself to signify his being incorporated into this messianic politics. It is therefore not surprising that he calls himself a slave, even if this is a slave of the messiah. But we should also pause here to recall that "slave" designated a social-economic and political reality within the Roman Empire generally and also within Rome itself. The empire was constituted as an economy and polity based on slavery. Its economic, political, and military power depended upon slavery. The majority of the population of Rome would have been slaves. This was true of all urban areas and of the great plantations upon which the privilege of the Roman ruling class depended. A principal means of acquiring slaves was war—the defeated who were not killed were enslaved.

A slave was one who had lost all personal identity, whose existence was completely determined by the whim of the master. It is quite possible that the majority of those to whom Paul addressed himself were in fact slaves. But Paul was not one. He ascribes to himself this lowly status as a gesture of solidarity with the dregs of the social order. Like his messiah, he identifies with the abjected masses of the Roman Empire.

Yet this downward social mobility, this identification with the lowest, is not situated within a static social stratification but within a force field so far identified with the word *messiah*. This name points to the uprising of the oppressed, enslaved, and impoverished and to the bringing down of the high and mighty, the powerful and the privileged. This reversal distinguishes a "messiah" from a king or emperor.

To say that one is a slave of the messiah is already to rupture language from within. It is to say that which ordinary language will not allow. It is to give voice to a mind-bending paradox of explosive social potential. We will see that this resort to paradox as provocation to thinking differently or otherwise is something characteristic of this letter.

Called apostle having been separated for the glad announcement [*euangelion*] **of God (which** [God] **promised before through his prophets in holy writings)**

The messianic slave is called apostle. Paul's "identity" is entirely determined by the vocation into which he is summoned. Here it seems that Krister Stendhal is correct to say that this calling rather than what has been termed Paul's conversion is entirely determinative (7–23). In certain respects Paul remains who he has always been (a Pharisee, an Israelite, and so on), but he is called to represent the divine message or announcement. Paul does not leave off being a Judean any more than he asks gentiles to leave off being gentiles. He is the Israelite (or as he himself says in Philippians 3:5, "Hebrew of Hebrews") who is called to represent the astonishing announcement of the God of Israel, an announcement that is directed to those who are not of Israel.

All that may be getting ahead of ourselves at the moment, for the paradox here lies in the juxtaposition of the being separated (a term that refers to that which is put aside for sacrifice) with the public mission of representing a public announcement. Thus, Paul is set apart or reserved for the divine reality that is itself extended outward to include all the nations.

Euangelion here is itself a political term. It refers to an announcement by the authorities that is put forward as good news for the populace in general. Examples might include the declaration of victory in war, a tax cut, or an especially good harvest. It is the announcement of something that would cause general rejoicing among the public. As such, the proclamation has a sort of performative force in that it brings about what it says: a tax holiday or a proclamation of peace, for example. Thus, as glad announcement it also makes glad; it brings about or aims to bring about the rejoicing that marks it as "good" news.

Here, however, this happy proclamation comes not from some government official but from God. It concerns something that this God, the God of Israel, had promised long before. That it is precisely the God of Israel whose proclamation is at stake is evident in that it is something promised in the prophets of Israel and contained in the holy writings of that people.

Thus, Paul is that Israelite, that Pharisee, who now is set apart in order to represent the public announcement of Israel's God. What is the content of this public announcement, and why should it occasion general or universal rejoicing?

About his son, from the seed of David according to the flesh, but designated son of God in power according to a spirit of holiness through a resurrection from the dead

The phrase is a bit elliptical, but I believe we can make sense of it by filling in a few blanks that will restore a certain parallelism. The divine son was designated or claimed to be of the seed of David in accordance with the "flesh." For Paul, flesh generally designates either opposition to God (and hence to spirit) or weakness (and so, lack of power). We shall see later that these apparently divergent meanings are in fact closely related. The opposition of spirit and flesh is a theme that Paul will strongly emphasize in this text. He will say that "**the mind that is set on the flesh is hostile to God**" (8:7). And he will contrast this to spirit "**that raised Joshua from the dead**" (8:11).

It therefore seems reasonable to suppose that the designation of the son as seed of David in accordance with the flesh comes from hostility to God, a hostility exposed through a resurrection from the dead. What is missing here is something that Paul has elsewhere indicated is the whole content of his message. Writing to those in Corinth, he had maintained, "I decided to know nothing among you but Joshua messiah, the crucified" (1 Corinthians 2:2).

Thus, the designation of the messiah as son of David does not refer to some supposed genealogical information (in the narratives written much later, in which we find genealogies, care is taken not to make him into a biological son of David). It can only refer to the cross itself—to the designation of this Joshua as a (pretended) king of the Judeans and as one in rebellion against the empire.

This verdict of the empire, executed through the crucifixion of a messianic pretender who threatened the "peace," is, however, overturned through the power of life-giving spirit through the return to life of the executed. The resurrection of the dead is first and foremost the return of the executed (as is also clear in the book of Daniel). The rule of the empire, and indeed the efficacy of any regime of law, depends upon the death penalty. Jacques Derrida, reading Walter Benjamin's "Critique of Violence" and citing Immanuel Kant, emphasizes the dependence of the rule of law on the penalty of death: "When one tackles the death penalty, one does not dispute one penalty among others but law itself in its origin, in its very order" ("Force of Law" 276). The point is that law and death are inextricably bound together. Death is the "or else" of law, without which law does not have the force of law.

But what happens when the efficacy of the death penalty is abolished through a resurrection to life of one of those who had been executed? The violence essential to the existence of the state, of any state, may be robbed of its power to intimidate, to exact obedience. Already here we may glimpse something of the radicality of Paul's messianic politics, a radicality whose power may be pertinent even today. We shall return to this. But Paul is writing about a particular state power, a particular legal order, that of the Roman Empire, which depended upon the efficacy of military execution by means of the cross to ensure the obedience of the peoples caught up in its embrace. If the instrument of imperial coercion is rendered inoperative through a resurrection of the executed, can the empire still stand?

Now we can guess why Paul has used such an elliptical phrase. He is handling dynamite. For he is, after all, writing to those in Rome, in the very citadel and capital of the empire that had executed the would-be messiah of Israel. Perhaps there is good reason to be careful here, for this letter is a sort of postcard (Derrida) that can easily fall into the "wrong hands," even after it has been received by its intended readers.

We also do not have here a precursor to a "two natures Christology," which would later be established in the ecumenical councils. The messiah is designated divine son through the resurrection (not, for example, from birth). It is a kind of adoption through resurrection.

Jacob Taubes emphasized the political nature of Paul's argument: "I want to stress that this is a political declaration of war" (16). It is in this sense that he argues that "the epistle to the Romans is a political theology, a *political* declaration of war on the Caesar" (16). Much subsequent interpretation will seek to make it safe for Caesar's eyes.

Joshua messiah, our leader, on whose account we have received favor and apostleship

The overfamiliarity of "Jesus Christ" as the subject of Pauline proclamation would be reason enough to alter the translation to "Joshua messiah." But there is more: Jesus or Yeshua is simply the transposition into Greek of the name Joshua. The conventional rendering of this name as Jesus may lead us to ignore its resonance in the history of Israel. It is the name of the war leader Joshua who led the people of Israel into the promised land, a land already occupied by, among others, the Canaanites. It is this history that the name of this messiah both recalls and transforms. While this new Joshua may have a fundamentally different way of guiding his people into a new sociality based upon promise, he nevertheless leads his people into the creation of a new society amid the ruins of the old order designated here by the name of Rome. Moreover, the conventional rendering of the name as Jesus may encourage forgetfulness of the Jewishness of this name, its embeddedness in the life and the memory of a particular people. By returning this name to its Jewish origin and its liberatory resonance, I hope to recover something of the way it may have been heard or read by the earliest adherents to the messiah.

Joshua is designated messiah, that is, the one hoped for by Israel who would liberate the people of Israel from imperial domination. At least for Paul, what had been conceived of as a "regional" messiahship (limited to the liberation of a territory or a people) will be regarded instead as universal in scope and radical in depth.

Our texts say lord (*kyrios*), but by itself this seems misleading. The point seems to be not the "sovereignty" of the one so designated but rather the designation of one to whom we are loyal. To anticipate this connection to loyalty, I have used "leader" instead of lord. It is on account, or for the sake, of this leader, the executed and raised messiah named Joshua, that Paul has received the gift and the task of being a representative, a delegate, an emissary (all ways of clarifying what the term *apostolos* signifies).

The glad-making proclamation then concerns the one who was executed by those hostile to God but who was returned to life by the power of divine spirit. To whom and to what effect is this proclamation directed?

In order to provoke the adherence of loyalty on account of his name among all the nations

Above all it is necessary to emphasize that what is generally rendered as "faith," and too often understood as belief or even "trust," should instead be rendered as "faithfulness." Only in this way is it possible to make sense of the conjoining here and elsewhere in Paul of *pistis* and *hupakoan* (hearkening or obeying). Standard post-Reformation perspectives set obedience against faith in ways that correspond to an imagined opposition between "faith" and "works" (i.e., obedience). But such an opposition has no place in Paul. Faith as faithfulness or loyalty is what is at stake, and this commonsensically entails something like a form of behavior that corresponds to the one to whom one is loyal or faithful. Indeed, in the Greco-Roman world, *pistis* was regularly associated with a set of mutual obligations that linked together patrons and their clients. It was demonstrated through specific patterns of action that gave concreteness to the loyalty that bound people together (Horsley 88–125).

As Agamben has rightly noted, Pauline *pistis* designates a faithfulness that binds together persons in patterns of mutually beneficial action. In this connection he refers to Emile Benveniste, who carefully investigated Indo-European linguistics and whose work is critical for many European reflections on political institutions. Agamben writes that one of Benveniste's greatest achievements "entailed using purely linguistic data to reconstruct the originary features of this most ancient Indo-European institution, which the Greeks called *pistis* and the Latin *fides*, and which he defined as *fidelité personnelle*, personal loyalty" (*Time* 114). It is this character that he attributes to Paul's use of the term. Jean Luc Nancy, the French philosopher with whose name the term "deconstruction of Christianity" is linked, notes that "faith is faithfulness and further that this faithfulness must be rigorously distinguished from any religious notion of belief" (*Noli me tangere* 83). Indeed, the recognition that Paul is concerned not with beliefs but with loyalty or faithfulness has come rather more easily to philosophers than to theologians. Already at the beginning of the twentieth century, Josiah Royce understood Paul in this way in *The Problem of Christianity*: "Paul's doctrine is that salvation comes through loyalty" (119). Royce took the object of this loyalty to be what was termed the "beloved community," which is not completely incompatible with the designation that I would prefer of the messianic project.

The announcement concerning the executed and risen son, then, aims at producing an unswerving loyalty to that messiah on the part of the hearers. They are to be taken up into this messianic project in their adherence to its aims and processes—to something that will later be termed "justice." But who is the intended recipient of this proclamation? Who are to be made to rejoice and to become loyal? "All the nations."

Jacob Taubes notices that one of the most basic terms in Paul's texts is "all" (26; cf. Agamben, *Time* 55). We will find it coming back again and again. The proclamation aims at a universal hearing, a hearing that will produce gladness among all and therefore loyalty to the messianic cause of true justice.

Including yourselves who are called to Joshua messiah

Paul was called; so are his readers. We might say that existence is vocation. Identity is determined not by some preexisting condition (ethnicity, gender, status as slave or free, etc.) but by a call or summons, a provocation that opens onto a vocation, a being set in motion that is brought to pass precisely within the context of the messianic vocation. The reader, like Paul, is taken up into that messianic mission. There may be a variety of ways in which this vocation may be given concrete expression. The readers have already been called by or toward this messiah, so are attached to this messianic reality. Their identity, like that of Paul, is subsumed into the messianic project.

The great Marxist and structuralist philosopher Louis Althusser (who was also friend and mentor of Jacques Derrida) wrote of calling as an "interpellation," whereby a subject is made to exist as a subject by being subjected to a call or summons. What he had in mind was the way in which ideological apparatuses of a state and a society (religion, school, culture) function so as to assign their members a definite place in the social order and a corresponding consciousness or awareness of self, as well as an obedience to roles and expectations assigned in and through such an interpellation or calling. But what Paul is concerned with is a calling that extracts one from the existing social and political order by subjecting one to an adherence to a radically disruptive existence and hence a new kind of subjectivity. His subjectivity, as well as that of his (intended) readers, is constituted by and through this disruptive interpellation, this messianic call. Although Althusser does make reference to Paul in discussing the idea of interpellation (116), he does not seem to notice the fundamentally disruptive character of the Pauline interpellation. This recognition will be the contribution of his successor, Alain Badiou, who will notice the disruptive character of the "event" of the resurrection of the crucified, adherence to which will constitute Paul and his readers as subjects. We shall return to this.

To all in Rome, beloved of God, called "holy"

This letter is not addressed "to whom it may concern." It has in view a particular group: those who are inhabitants of Rome, the center of the empire in whose name the one to whom they are loyal (Joshua messiah) was executed as an enemy of Rome and Roman rule. Jacob Taubes makes much of the fact, seldom given much weight in the commentaries, that Paul wrote "not to any old congregation, but to the congregation in Rome, the seat of world empire" (16). Indeed, "Roma" was even personified as a divine being, the center of a temple cult throughout the empire, soliciting the loyalty of her subjects. And as for those loyal to one who was crucified by those loyal to Rome—how might they be regarded in Rome itself?

The word *all* makes another appearance. This "all" does not seem to be present in other addresses to messianic cells in other cities, although it may be implied. Perhaps there is something about Rome that warrants the inclusion of this "all." How is it to be understood? Is this directed to all the inhabitants of Rome, or is the "beloved of God" a restriction to the small cell of messianists in Rome? I think it will be evident that both have a certain truth. The messianic message is not private: it is directed to all. All are to be called to loyalty to the messiah and his mission, or rather to God's mission through the messiah Joshua, who was executed by Rome. The aim is that all will be persuaded to change their loyalty from the empire to the messiah. Alain Badiou, perhaps the best known of the Marxist interpreters of Paul, notes the odd relation between a small band of messiah followers in a town or city and the entire region of which they are a part. He notes that "through their commensurability with a truth, anonymous individuals are transformed into a vector of humanity as a whole" (*Saint Paul* 20). How much more true would this be of those who are situated in the very capital of the empire! Here we have the first of a complex set of relationships that Paul deploys between whole and part. Here that part of the Roman populace loyal to the messiah Joshua is a kind of leading edge or vanguard that anticipates the whole of the city and indeed the empire. There will be many other metonymic substitutions or synecdochal representations of this sort in Paul's text.

But the members of the messianic cell (or cells) in Rome are the beginning, the first fruits of that mission, so they are holy. They are the ones who already hear and hearken to the word that they are beloved of God, but the rest are those for whom the public proclamation of the news concerning God's son is intended. And not only those who live in Rome itself. For Rome is the headquarters of a great empire embracing many nations or peoples who also must know that they are the intended recipients of that glad proclamation. That, as we might say, is a tall order. How is the population of Rome to be persuaded of such an audacious claim? That is precisely what Paul is going to help his readers with and with which they in turn will help him.

Generosity [*charis*] to you and peace from God our Father and [our] leader Joshua messiah

The ideology of empire, then and now, is that it confers peace. There is a certain plausibility in this. After all, the empire as empire seeks to abolish war within its bounds. It brings warring nations into the embrace of its laws and protection. This ideology had considerable prominence not only with Caesar Augustus but most especially under the youthful emperor Nero. Yet Agricola is cited in Tacitus concerning Rome: "The Romans rob, butcher, plunder and call it empire; and where they make a desolation, they call it peace" (Horsley 10). Paul has a different sort of peace in mind, although it, too, will embrace all the nations. It will be a peace not enforced by armies but spread through the proclamation concerning one the empire executed. And it will be enforced not by the death penalty but empowered by the spirit of life.

That spirit is the spirit of generosity (*charis*) by which the divine announcement seeks to include all in the gladness by which it comes to be called *euangelion*, good news. It is good news precisely because it has its origin in the unconditional or overabounding divine generosity that aims to welcome all into divine favor. (The term "grace," which is regularly used here, may make us forgetful of the abounding generosity and unrestricted welcome at the heart of the Pauline announcement.)

First I thank my God through Joshua messiah on account of all of you, because your faithfulness is being spoken about in all the world.

Again "all": all of you and all the world. That there is actually a cell, or collection of cells, of messianic loyalists in Rome itself is something that "all the world" is hearing about and speaking about. The sheer audacity of these adherents to the cause being present in the center and heart of the empire is something that occasions astonished praise of God, thanksgiving to God.

For my witness is the God whom I serve in my spirit in the good news of his son, that I always continually refer to you in my prayer. The longing of Paul (his prayer) is directed toward them somehow precisely because of the mission with which he has been entrusted (the good news concerning God's son). What is this yearning? **Asking that by God's will I may at last succeed in coming to you.** He yearns to see them and addresses this yearning to God. Here he will speak of his being prevented from coming and will further explain this at the end of the letter. But we should note that Paul's relation to the intended recipients of his letters is typically one of deep yearning to be present with them. Of course, it is only thanks to the frustration of this yearning that we have letters at all. It is the mutual absence of reader and writer that makes writing both necessary and possible. But the mark of Pauline letters as opposed to what are called "catholic epistles" is the yearning, the deep desire, to be present. It is in anticipation of the overcoming of absence that Paul writes of an impending visit.

What is most interesting at this point is the purpose of this visit: **For I long to see you so that I may impart some spirited favor to strengthen you.** What Paul has in mind is that there is some way in which he may be able to strengthen them in the very difficult circumstances in which they undoubtedly find themselves. I think it is fair to say that this letter is itself a down payment on that promised assistance. The letter itself will offer some spirited assistance to those in Rome who seek to be faithful to the messiah executed in the name of Rome.

I want you to know, comrades [*adelphoi*], that I have often intended to come to you but have been hindered until the present. Alain Badiou suggests, rightly in my view, that "brother" is simply "an archaic form of our 'comrades'" (*Saint Paul* 20). Paul does not yet say what obstacles have stood in the way of the fulfillment of (and perhaps increased) his longing to visit the community (or communities) in Rome. But his purpose in coming is **so that I may reap some harvest among you as indeed among the remaining nations.** Here again we are reminded that Paul's readers are among the gentiles. They are not Judeans but pagans.

I am under obligation to Greeks and barbarians, to the wise and also the foolish, so that as I am able I am eager to announce the good news also to you, to those in Rome. The obligation relates to the task of announcing the glad-making proclamation of God. This is simply what Paul as apostle must do; it is his task. But why in Rome? Because he says his call or summons places him in obligation to Greeks and barbarians, to wise and foolish. In a letter to those in Corinth he had used the wise-and-foolish dichotomy in a quite different way. Here he uses it in accordance with a certain Hellenistic propaganda. For the Greek-speaking part of the empire, Greek culture was the basis for anything that might be thought of as civilized. The rest were "barbarians," still to be brought into the orbit of Hellenistic culture. But Rome is the center of the empire that embraces both Greek and barbarian. Paul has spent his mission until now primarily in the Greek-speaking part of the empire, from Syria to Greece to the Anatolian peninsula to the Balkans. But he is obliged to announce God's good news not only in that part of the empire but also among the barbarians (which would include what we think of as France and Spain). Rome is the point of confluence of these different cultural streams. Thus, Rome is critical to Paul's practice of his apostolic vocation. Referring to Paul's itinerary, the Catholic philosopher (and friend of Louis Althusser) Stanislas Breton remarks that "his relation to the Gospel condemns him to the mobility of perpetual transit" (52).

Rome is also the point of greatest tension for the announcement of God's message concerning the "son" executed by Rome. This is both the importance and the difficulty of Rome, the challenge and the opportunity. **So I am eager to announce good news to you in Rome.** Of course, this cannot mean that Paul will be announcing the messianic good news for the first time to those in Rome; they have already responded with loyalty to this proclamation carried by others. Rather, it may mean that there is a dimension to this announcement that they may not yet have understood or received that will increase their gladness. What is this dimension of the announcement of the gospel that may still be news to this beleaguered messianic cell in Rome? It concerns justice.

For I am not ashamed of the glad announcement: it is divine power for salvation [wholeness] **for all the faithful, to the Judean first and the Greek. For in it divine justice is disclosed from faithfulness to faithfulness, for as it has been written: the just live through faithfulness.** This may be regarded as at least a preliminary statement of the thesis of Paul's argument in this text. By explicating this thesis, he will demonstrate the spirited gift that he hopes to share with his readers.

It is spirited first of all because it is audacious: Paul is not embarrassed about or ashamed of the message, not dubious or fainthearted about it, not ambivalent or reticent. Rather, he has the boldness that will enable others also to be bold in the face of ridicule, opposition, and persecution. In his last public lectures at the Collège de France, Michel Foucault engaged in an extended examination of the significance of this frank or bold speaking in antiquity dealing with the virtue or practice of *parrhesia*, which he defines as "the courage of truth." It is a form of truth telling that places one in a situation of danger since what one says runs counter to the interests or opinions of those who exercise a certain power. In this sense it is a political virtue, perhaps we might say *the* political virtue, insofar as its theme is justice. By using the example of Socrates, Foucault asks whether it is really possible to tell the truth boldly in the political space of democracy (78–79), just as the example of Plato in Syracuse will have served as a caution about truth telling in the space of tyranny (62). Paul insists on boldly speaking the truth within the democratic space of the messianic society that exists under the shadow of the political space of the tyranny of the Roman rule (1 Thessalonians 2:2). But he also seeks to engender this capacity among his readers.

However it may appear to others, Paul insists, the divine proclamation is power. In 1 Corinthians he had recognized that this proclamation (as the proclamation of a crucified messiah) must appear to others as weakness and folly yet, as he also insists here, is truly wisdom and power. What sort of power? It is the quintessentially political power, the power to save, to overcome and prevent harm, the power to give, sustain, and protect life, the life of the whole of human society. One difficulty here is that it is forgotten that salvation is basically a political concept. It has to do with establishing the common good, defending the common good from the predations of enemies or of overcoming the sort of civil strife that threatens the existence of society. For this reason the emperor could be called *soter*, savior.

This wholeness is connected to faithfulness or loyalty. Through loyalty to the divine announcement the world is protected from danger and human well-being is established. This faithfulness or loyalty that corresponds to the divine announcement and act, and leads to wholeness for all, is found first with the Judeans and then with the Greeks (and perhaps subsequently the barbarians). The message, after all, comes first to the people of Judea and spreads from there. For the God whose news it is, is first of all the God of Israel. Only as rooted in Israel among the Judeans does it then extend outward to the Greeks and beyond. This will be a recurring motif in this argument, and its full meaning will become evident only in chapters 9–11.

What loyalty engenders is justice. In antiquity the theme of justice is indissolubly linked to the space of the political. When Plato turns to a discussion of the *polis* in *The Republic*, he does so as a discussion precisely of justice. This is not a completely new theme to him. Indeed, in his dialogues he returned again and again to this theme of justice as the principal way of understanding the common life of human beings.

Something quite similar happens with Aristotle. He asserts, "Justice is the bond of men in states, for the administration of justice, which is the determination of what is just, is the principle of order in political society" (*Politics* 1253a.37–39). He will affirm that justice is the greatest good and the question of justice is that of the good that is common (1282b.17–18). He maintains that justice is a social virtue and it implies all the others (1283a.39–40). It is easy to see that justice is a fundamentally social concept that concerns how life in society with other persons is to be shaped.

This close correlation between justice and the political ordering of the social is carried forward by Cicero, who, unlike the Stoics and Epicureans of Paul's day, had not forgotten that justice relates to the ordering of interhuman relations in society. For example, in recounting the dream of Scipio, Cicero writes of the "communities of people linked together by justice that are called states" (*Republic* 6.13). Earlier Cicero had asked, "What is a state other than an equal partnership in justice?" (1.49).

Justice is the only possible basis for social well-being, for the well-being of the city or the body politic. Yet it is said that the just live through faithfulness; indeed, justice comes into being only as faithfulness or loyalty to what God is doing in the world. The reference to the LXX of Habakkuk 2:4 provides a graphic reminder that centuries earlier, in the writings of Israel, the essential themes that Paul undertakes to explicate are already announced. As one lives out faithfulness, one is or becomes just. But before this can be clearly shown, it will be necessary to undertake a demonstration of the injustice of existing ways of constituting social orders.

First Phase

THE UNJUST SOCIAL ORDER (1:18–3:20)

Since Paul is concerned with justice, with the claim of divine justice, he turns first to indicate how the quest for a just social order has failed. The most serious indictment of social injustice is directed against the Greco-Roman world (1:18–2:6), whose center is the city of Rome, where his readers constitute a messianic cell or vanguard. But he will also claim that a Judean polity based upon the Mosaic constitution is not the solution, for it, too, produces injustice rather than justice (2:17–3:20). The impartiality of this indictment is based upon the divine impartiality (2:6–16), which seeks and welcomes justice wherever it is found and rejects and opposes injustice wherever it is encountered. This will seem to lead to a sort of dead-end or aporia in the apparent impossibility of the justice that is nevertheless necessary. This aporia will set the stage for a consideration of justice that is not based upon law so is outside the law: outlaw justice.

2. The Critique of Pagan Injustice (1:18–2:5)

Paul has indicated that his concern is with justice, divine justice, and with the way this justice or the coming of this justice is the good news of God, the proclamation that makes glad a world that somehow may be represented as yearning for the actualization or realization of justice. He has also indicated that this incoming of justice is connected with the news concerning the messiah who has been brought back from ignominious death. The character of such a proclamation is that it be performative, that it somehow accomplish or begin to accomplish what it proclaims, as in a proclamation of war, a proclamation of peace, a proclamation of a tax holiday, a proclamation of marriage. Here the proclamation produces, or aims at producing, joy.

That the justice of God is, in important respects, yet to come means that the mechanisms for bringing justice and maintaining it have failed. It is the burden of the next several paragraphs of Paul's argument to show that justice had not been achieved. In this discussion he will first turn to an indictment of gentile justice, the justice enacted and administered by Roman law. He will then turn to an indictment of Israelite or Judean justice, which prides itself upon a superior polity or law but which nonetheless has not achieved or been capable of achieving justice.

Paul's basic presupposition throughout is that God requires justice—indeed, the name of God and the name of justice are virtually interchangeable, so much so that to turn away from the divine is to fall into injustice. Moreover, Paul will insist that justice is a political concept in that it applies to whole societies, not simply to individuals. The indictment, I argue, does not apply to individuals but to social realities named as Greek or pagan, on the one hand, and as Judean, on the other. We will see that even if individuals in either of these social realities may be regarded as just when considered as persons, they are viewed as embedded in deeply unjust social orders and to that extent are subsumed under the indictment that will be unfolded.

But why should an indictment of these social realities, these societies or polities, be called for? I believe that this stems from the fact that the messiah of God was rejected by the responsible representatives of Israel and was executed by the responsible representatives of gentile society—the Roman imperial order. At stake will be a collision between polities that extol the law and the divine or, as Derrida says, undeconstructible claim and call of justice. This collision had come to expression in the death of the messiah, a death by law, that exposed an ineradicable opposition to justice that has come to expression through the execution of the law. As Nietzsche had recognized, it is the law that executed the messiah, so it was a choice between the messiah and the law: "Up to that time that ignominious death had seemed to him to be the principal argument against the 'Messiahship' proclaimed by the followers of the new doctrine: but what if it were necessary for doing away with the Law . . . henceforth the Law is dead" (*Daybreak* § 68). Leaving aside Nietzsche's rather fanciful notions of resentment that make Paul out to be a pure Lutheran, I think the basic sense of a collision here is absolutely correct. In this sense at least I can agree with Derrida's suggestion about Nietzsche's "lucidity about Paul" ("Silkworm" 325). Jacob Taubes echoes this appraisal of Nietzsche concerning Paul at greater length (80–85).

This looking ahead at the orientation of the basic argument is necessary if we are not to get lost in the details of Paul's indictment. We turn then to the initial indictment of Greco-Roman civilization. This indictment has a triple structure that near the beginning of the third century Origen already regarded as being basically parallel, that is, three ways of depicting the same situation.

The general terms of the indictment are as follows:

From heaven divine wrath is disclosed against all human impiety and injustice that unjustly imprisons the truth.

The indictment will aim at demonstrating that those who pretend to judge— those who pretend, that is, to administer justice in the name of the law— are themselves under condemnation. It is the suppression of the truth, the willful imprisonment of or silencing of the truth that is the concrete expression of impiety and injustice. "Impiety" and "injustice" are Roman political terms and overlap considerably. Impiety has to do with both a neglect of the gods and a violation of ancient, universal custom or human decency. In general, it is that which insults the divine. For Paul's argument to work, he must operate on pagan terrain; his indictment of pagan society must make sense on pagan terms. Thus, pagans are not unjust or impious because they are pagans but because they do not do what pagans know would comport with true piety or true justice. The answer will not be for pagans to leave off their own paganism (or humanism) in order to become Jews, nor will it be for Judeans to leave off being Jews in order to become good pagans, nor even will it be to invent something new to be called Christianity as an alternative religion. This will bear some close attention.

In the meantime, it is important to note that Paul is using terms that are perfectly recognizable in Roman political discourse. For example, Tacitus can speak of the "melancholy and continuous destruction of our citizens who are being slandered when just and driven to suicide: Such was the wrath of heaven against the Roman state" (16.16). That is, the Pauline indictment agrees with that of Tacitus. This extends not only to the content of the indictment (slandering the just and driving them to suicide) but to the way in which social madness is itself the demonstration of the wrath of God, as well as, presumably, its cause.

For what of God can be known is manifest to them, for God has made it manifest to them; for even the most inaccessible of divinity is made evident through the world of things made: God's everlasting power and divinity.

Although for understandable reasons in the social chaos of the Nazi nightmare, Barth and others made a point of rejecting what was called natural theology, philosophers of the Enlightenment like the great Jewish philosopher Baruch Spinoza are right to see in Paul one who shares their confidence that the most fundamental theological knowledge is available in and through all cultures in their knowledge of the world of things, of existents. Spinoza writes in his *Theological-Political Treatise* of 1670: "Here [Paul] quite clearly indicates that by the natural light of reason, all can clearly understand the power and divinity of God, from which we can know and infer what they should seek and what they should avoid" (57). What is known precisely is divine power as evident in the existence of a world of existents. That things are at all and that they are in such a way as to present themselves as a "world" give evidence of divinity, of mysterious and efficacious power.

What is at stake here is not some or other metaphysics or ontology but what metaphysics and ontology try to think. Whether there is something rather than nothing, that things somehow just are, or that things are in some sort of relation to one another and to us, the ground zero of experience is an experience of multiple existents somehow there before us in relation to one another and to us. This is the basic ontological wonder that Paul articulates as indicative of divine efficacy. Here Paul is pointing to what reflective persons in the Greco-Roman world would already recognize. Recognizing this divine power at work in the constitution of the world is not dependent upon any particular religion nor restricted to particular cultures.

Moreover, since the basic point will have to do with the claim of justice, it is worth recalling that the most basic formulation of elementary justice seems to be the common property of all cultures: dealing with others as one expects or desires to be dealt with. Paul will come back to this later in his argument.

So they are without excuse, for although knowing divinity, they did not honor the divine as divine or give thanks, but became empty in their speculations and became willful and blinded in their thinking.

Perhaps the most important phrase here is "give thanks," that is, feeling and expressing gratitude in face of the sheer mystery of being. The importance of this is clear from the contrast: between thankfulness and the self-delusion that begins as willfulness (Paul says having an undiscerning heart; but heart in Greek refers not to sentiment but to will). It is when wonder gives way to willfulness, when gratitude gives way to a greediness that instrumentalizes all things, that the door to chaos opens. For now instead of a desire to understand based in wonder, there comes to be an expropriation of all things that makes them serve self-interest and a blind will to power. Instead of the science that marvels there arises the pseudoscience that manipulates. This is the dream and nightmare of Francis Bacon, who thought of science as an instrument for the human domination of nature. For every true scientist seeking to unravel the mystery of the atom, there is also the servant of power who would weaponize the mysteries of the universe; for every true scientist who seeks to unravel the wonder of the genetic code, there stands the corporation that would profit from a patent on a gene.

Their wisdom becomes idiocy, [their rationality irrational, their intelligence stupid. And] **they exchange the glory of incorruptible divinity for imitation images of perishing men or birds or quadrupeds or reptiles.**

Here one often speaks of idolatry, but Paul inveighs against things that the intelligent of the empire would also find to be just plain stupid. When Nero was young, Seneca mocked the divinization of Claudius, and before that, all Rome was horrified at the impiety of Caligula, who deified not only himself but also his sister and even his horse. The imperial eagle upon the standard of the legions represented the divinity of empire and of Rome. While some see an attack here upon Egyptian practices (deities represented as birds and hippos and crocodiles, for example), I would suppose that what is at stake is the capturing of the divine in corrupted images far closer to home.

In this, Paul is not dependent upon a specifically Jewish or even prophetic condemnation of idolatry. He is using the more or less common currency of Greco-Roman philosophical repudiation of superstitious practices. The point is that awe and wonder are transferred from the invisible to the all too visible, from what Jean Luc Marion, the Catholic philosopher and former student of Derrida, insightfully characterized as a turn from the icon to the idol (7–24). But here the idol is whatever instantiates or represents imperial power and excess. In our own time we may think of the ways in which the wonder at the intricacies of human interaction gives way to the idolatry of the market and to an astonishing faith (credulity) in virtual "wealth" that disappears in an instant when avarice runs over a cliff of its own making.

For God let them have the madness they had chosen so that they plunged themselves into every kind of filth and dishonoring of one another's bodies.

It has become difficult not to make of Paul some kind of prude since for us dishonor and "uncleanness" have somehow become focused on sex. But that is not likely the meaning for Paul or his readers. Rather, they refer to a descent into social madness in which human beings become their own worst enemies, arousing revulsion at the excesses of dishonor into which they fall. Instead of honoring one another's integrity (bodies), we dishonor one another and so also ourselves. This should not be too hard to understand: just as we know that racism or sexism dishonors not only its object (and its object's body) but also its agent, so too with all the ways in which humans dishonor one another. Moreover, this behavior, especially when exemplified at the top of the social order, tends toward a vicious cycle, a downward spiral of social decay and death.

In Greco-Roman thought of the time, the dishonorable passions would have been not so much "sexual" but social: such as unreasoning rage, anger, delight in cruelty, an insane need to accumulate or display wealth, a lifestyle given over to luxury. These are the "passions" decried by Stoics, Epicureans, and Cynics as dishonorable. This is also Paul's point.

To make this clear, I will go to the third and most detailed of Paul's tripartite indictment: **Since they did not see fit to acknowledge God** [note how this flows directly from what Paul has been talking about at the beginning of this indictment], **God gave them up to a debased mind and to things that should not be done: they were filled with every**

kind of injustice [this is the point, after all, and it summarizes all that follows—note that there is no punctuation in Greek; it must be supplied by translators], **evil, covetousness, malice.** [And then he expands on this basic list.] **Full of envy, murder, strife, deceit, craftiness; they are gossips, slanderers, God-haters, insolent, haughty, boastful, inventors of evil, rebellious to parents, foolish, faithless, heartless, ruthless.**

This is social madness. And it is almost exactly what Roman historians will also say about this period of Roman history, the period from Augustus's death (perhaps earlier) until the end of the century. It was a time of the rule of paranoid gangsters who sought to destroy any and all rivals: you got ahead by making up lies about your neighbors; informants and slanderers become wealthy and powerful. Anyone with a reputation for virtue had to be destroyed lest the populace seek that person to be dictator rather than the one who was in power or sought power. The first casualty was truth, but the result was social madness, a war of the powerful against one another as well as against the weak.

Tacitus, for example, writing around 120 CE, recalled that "the histories of Tiberius, Caius (Caligula) Claudius and Nero, while they were in power, were falsified through terror" (1.1). He remarks in his description of the reign of Tiberius what is true of the succeeding accounts as well: "I have to present in succession the merciless biddings of a tyrant, incessant prosecutions, faithless friendships, the ruin of innocence, the same causes issuing in the same results, and I am everywhere confronted by a wearisome monotony in my subject matter" (4.33). And as the historians will also say, the example of the rulers was often contagious.

They know the divine decree, that those who do these things deserve to die. Here it is not a question of specific legislation for which one can find capital punishment prescribed; rather, it is a question of a social madness or collective insanity that brings destruction upon itself. If there is a god, a divine power, then this kind of social chaos is itself a death penalty. Societies generally know this and will express it in different ways. In China, for example, one might say that the rulers have lost the mandate of heaven. But what can be discerned is that a social order that is really vicious is on the point of dissolution, of self-destruction. No one needs to look this up in a law book either in Rome or in Israel—or even in the contemporary world.

Yet they not only do these things; they actually praise and honor those who do them. This is one of the things of which the historians of this period, writing only a few decades later, really seem to despair—what everyone recognized to be vicious and outrageous conduct was nevertheless applauded in the Senate and on the street. One illustration: When Nero, after several attempts, finally succeeded in having his mother assassinated, he was welcomed into the city as if he had won a war. Suetonius reports that congratulations "poured in from the Army, the Senate and the people" (*Nero* § 34). This is the depth of social depravity.

The indictment that Paul has produced is one directed at the (rumored) behavior of the sociopolitical elites of Rome, the very elites responsible for the administration of what is called justice, yet their injustice is evident to any thinking person. This becomes evident in the histories of this period written by pagan Roman historians a few decades after Paul's writing. They themselves will claim that this sort of truth about the empire could not have been written at the time Paul is writing because of the reign of terror that was common from Tiberius and Caligula through Nero and beyond. Paul is thus treading in very dangerous territory here, for he is writing not during the dawn of a sort of Roman enlightenment a few decades later but in the midst of what Romans themselves claimed was a time of insane injustice.

Given this understanding of what Paul is saying here, we can return to the verses that constitute Paul's second indictment. Placing them in the context of the overall indictment will help overcome extraordinary misconceptions at how they are to be interpreted. I will attempt a more or less literal translation:

Therefore God handed them over to dishonorable passions; for even their females changed the natural [*phusikein*] use [*chreisin*] to that against nature [*para phusin*]; likewise, also the males leaving the natural [*phusikein*] use [*chreisin*] of the females burned in their desire for one another, males among males, working unseemliness [unfittingness] and receiving back the punishment that fit their error.

Because this text has been explained in terms of the extant Roman histories at greater length in the work of Neil Elliott (*Liberating Paul*) and in my own discussion of this passage in *Plato or Paul*, a brief discussion will suffice.

The term "dishonorable passions" certainly has no exclusive relationship to what we think of as sexuality, save insofar as this exhibits the traits of the social madness decried by Paul and by thinking Romans. The reference to "their females" directs our attention to the women at the apex of imperial rule. In later Roman histories we have a rather clear perspective on the behavior of the women most closely associated with the rulers of the empire. Whether what is said by Tacitus or Dio or Suetonius is in every detail historically reliable information about the persons named is not important. What is important is that it is suggestive of what was widely believed about the goings-on in Rome.

What might it mean to say that women of powerful men in Rome were acting against nature? Here it is important to recall that "against nature" tends to refer in Paul to what goes against the grain of civilized custom. He refers in 1 Corinthians, for example, to the custom of women wearing long hair and men wearing short hair as what accords with nature (11:14–15). He refers to men having long hair as not only against nature but also, or perhaps therefore, as being dishonorable. Obviously there is nothing biological going on here. We will have another example of his use of the notion of what is against nature later in this text, when God will act against nature (that is, custom) in the sense of horticultural practice (Romans 11:24).

What do their women do that outrages universal custom? They are rumored to seek to assassinate their husbands: Livia was rumored to have hastened the death of her husband Augustus (Dio 56.30.1) in order to secure the throne for her son Tiberius, with whom she sought to reign as co-emperor. Agrippina, the third wife of Claudius, was alleged to have murdered him (Tacitus 12.64–67). Many imperial women were famous for their adulteries, like the two Julias, one the wife of Augustus (before Livia), the other her daughter of the same name. Messalina, the second wife of Claudius, was said by Dio to be "the most lustful and abandoned of women" (60.14.3); he claims that she encouraged other Roman matrons to engage in adultery in the palace in front of their husbands, who were then favored with offices in the empire, and that she sat as a prostitute in the palace, again coercing or persuading other Roman matrons to do the same. The imperial mothers of Claudius and Nero even feigned incestuous relations with their sons to improve their own standing as powers behind the throne. They give away large parts of the empire to their illicit lovers. They reject the role of mother and matron for that of prostitute and assassin. This is all "against nature" by any Roman accounting. Again, we need not suppose that historians such as Suetonius, Dio, or Tacitus were correct about all the goings-on among imperial women in this period. It suffices that their texts are indicative of the sort of impression that would have been "common knowledge," informing both Paul and his readers in Rome.

Imagining that Paul is indicting lesbian relationships (something not attested in the ancient indictments of imperial women) seems to me to be sheerest fantasy. The "political" behavior of their women amply fits the description of impiety, injustice, or acting against nature.

Likewise, also the males leaving the natural [*phusikein*] use [*chreisin*] of the females burned in their desire for one another, males among males.

Likewise: the same class, the same kind of rapacious cruelty and viciousness. Again we will focus on what we may suppose people of common sense and decency and with some awareness of reputed goings-on in the imperial household might have recognized. Leaving aside the grotesque behavior of Nero or of Tiberius, we can simply summarize what was supposed to be the case about Caligula.

He was known for his delight in cruelty and torture and for threatening all who were close to him with his power to take their heads. He especially wanted those whom he killed to be killed slowly or with many cuts so they would know they were dying. His upbringing on Capri led him to astonishing levels of debauchery. He was the first to be publicly known as the lover and beloved of the same man—something shocking to Roman sensitivities. His sexual exploits, both active and passive, with a variety of people were widely rumored. But he was most given to rape, especially the rape of other men's brides. Indeed, apart from his incestuous relationship with his sister he seems to have sex with women primarily in situations of rape. If the "natural use of women" might be construed in terms of a Roman concern for something like "marriage and family values" (something about which Paul otherwise expresses considerable ambivalence), then leaving off this institution for incest and rape would certainly meet Paul's description. Caligula's rape of both young brides and their husbands served to demonstrate his absolute power over other men.

He met his end in a rather fitting way: assassination by a group of young knights, some whom he had raped, others whose wives he had raped. He was stabbed thirty times, "including sword thrusts through the genitals" (Suetonius, *Gaius* 58). It was the sort of death that Paul might well have described as **receiving in their own bodies the fitting recompense**.

There is no need to suppose that Paul has taken "time out" from his analysis of social-political madness to offer sentiments about conventional or unconventional sexual morality. If Paul inserted here a generic condemnation of same-sex erotic behavior, he would have fatally undermined his indictment. The point is to show the injustice of Roman society in terms that thinking Romans would agree with. But Romans had aversion not to same-sex erotic practices as such but to the very sort of excesses of rape and cruelty that the historians have ascribed to the powerful of his period. Again, it is not necessary to suppose that the ancient historians were in all cases accurately reporting what actually happened during this period; it is only necessary to suppose that they reflect what many or most people thought at the time about the behavior of the rulers of the Roman Empire, and, of course, of the city of Rome itself. It is for this reason that these accounts are so illuminating about the likely frame of reference for what Paul is writing to people in Rome about the Roman ethos.

The overall indictment of vicious cruelty that, in Paul's view, is itself the expression of divine wrath and is the result of a repudiation of the best insights of the Roman culture, may be summarized as injustice, the injustice of the social order that claimed to represent justice and prided itself on the administration of law. The point of this indictment is to delegitimize Roman law or the judgment based upon that law, a judgment that had resulted in the execution of the messiah. It will also open the way to a consideration of a different foundation for justice, one not tied to law, even Roman law.

Paul, who is **not embarrassed by the glad-making news of God concerning Joshua messiah** and who instead asserts that that news or proclamation is **the disclosure** [*apokalyptetai*] **of the justice of God from faithfulness to faithfulness**, has now shown what he means when he says that **the divine wrath** [*orgē*] **is revealed** [*apokalyptetai*] **from the skies against all impiety and injustice, against the human attempt to detain or imprison the truth in injustice**.

He has demonstrated this by showing in pagan terms that pagan society, the imperial social order, is not a just order but an order or disorder of injustice that has turned its back on its own insight about the nature and requirement of divine justice. It has become a society filled with all manner of injustice, that is, of the violation of one another in every way through every form of violence. In this indictment Paul has said what he supposes any sensible pagan would also recognize to be true of this society, especially those who live in Rome.

Therefore, he continues, **you have no defense, O human, whoever you are who pretend to judge**[, because in any process of] **judging another** [according to your "law,"] **you in fact condemn yourself.** Any judgment calls upon justice as its ground or basis; but if you in the name of justice, on behalf of this unjust social order, judge another, then you succeed only in awakening justice and so provoking condemnation against yourself. Judgment means holding another accountable to the requirements of some supposed justice and therefore entails that the one judging is also accountable to the claim of justice. This judgment recoils upon the one who intends to judge others.

Because you the judge [here it is not a case of someone acting in a private capacity but in a public capacity, that is, judging in the name of and as representative of the social order] **are acting in the very same way**, that is, in your official capacity—as representative of the society and its claim to be just, you are also the official representative of its actual injustice.

We know that the judgment of God rightly falls on those who practice such things. This refers us back to Paul's initial reference in his indictment to the divine wrath against injustice, to the concluding indictment of the social order (1:28–31) and the conclusion of the tripartite indictment: **They know the divine decree, that those who practice such things deserve to die.**

When you pretend to judge those who do such things, O human, do you imagine that you do not at the same time indict yourself? Note the repeated emphasis on judging (*krinein*), which is the application of some or other standard of justice. But if that in the name of which one "administers" justice (that is, judges) is itself unjust, then no possibility of judging remains. We should not forget that the basic question here has to do with the violence of the law, as it has already judged the messiah and so been judged itself. It is the violence of the law and of the enforcers or preservers of the law that sets it in contrast to justice as Derrida's reflections on Walter Benjamin's "Critique of Violence" attest ("Force of Law" 231–233).

At this point one might wonder whether the aim of an argument such as Paul's would be something like a reinstatement of the law, enforcing the law that has been violated with impunity by the elites, or a reformation of the law, the promulgation of better laws in accordance with a better "constitution"? Or is something far more radical at stake? It will become clear that a far more radical critique of the force of law is at stake here, one that will seek to give justice a different basis than that of law.

Note that here, for the second time, Paul addresses himself to the human: **O human.** First, **you have no excuse, O human**, and then **do you suppose, O human?** The human or *anthropos* is the one who judges and who does so in the name of the unjust social order, the order that pretends to administer justice. It is noteworthy that the one addressed is specifically not a member of the community of "saints." What Paul is doing is demonstrating to the community in Rome that he, Paul, knows how to address Romans outside this community or how to defend the community of messiah followers from the accusations of those who claim to speak in the name of law and justice. But the address to the human opens the way for an understanding of the impossibility of law-based judgment that goes beyond even the specific case of the Roman legal system. It aims at the question of legal judgment as such.

We are already seeing some space open up between the judgment of the social order and the judgment of God, the judgment that is in accord with true or divine justice. The judgment of the "human" will bring in its train the judgment of God, for justice is administered in the name of God or the gods. But if the divine requires justice yet is invoked by those who are themselves unjust or are representatives of an unjust social order, then those who judge bring judgment upon themselves. Much later in the argument, we will encounter Paul addressing the community about this matter as well. There he will claim that they also ought not to judge or condemn one another, even when such judgment might be justified on the part of those who may be innocent of the sort of indictment that Paul has leveled against the unjust social order of Rome.

We have heard that the sentence of death and destruction hands over an unjust social order to utter destruction. Such a social disorder cannot survive the disclosure of true justice; it has already sentenced itself to death and destruction. But that sentence has not yet been carried out. The society seems to prosper. It is victorious in war, unchallenged in military and economic power. It straddles the world like a colossus, the unrivaled hegemon, the envy of the known world.

Paul interprets this situation not as invalidating the sentence of death but as demonstrating the forbearance, the patience, even the kindness of God. He writes: **Or do you despise the wealth of God's kindness and forbearance and longsuffering?** This is how Paul interprets the fact that the divine judgment has not already overtaken this arrogant and violent social order: because God is patient. But why this patience? **Don't you realize that the kindness of God aims to lead you to repentance?** This patience has the goal of making space and time for **repentance**, that is, for turning away from injustice and toward justice. But if we are right here about the social context, then this would mean that an entire society should renounce its own injustice and turn instead toward justice.

Can we think of examples of whole societies or groups repenting of vicious behavior? Derrida has pointed out the extraordinary thing about our current geopolitical situation is that one does find societies actually confessing to and repudiating their crimes against humanity (*Negotiations* 382–383). North Korea admits to having kidnapped Japanese for the sole purpose of having them teach Japanese to would-be spies. And Japan in turn admitted to war crimes during its occupation of Korea from 1910 to 1945. This is happening with some frequency. Jacques Chirac as president of France admitted to French national responsibility for the crimes of the Vichy government; the Vatican says that the Inquisition is a cause for the examination of conscience; Southern Baptists make a sort of apology for having supported slavery even if they do not go so far as to support reparations; and a new US administration came under pressure (so far resisted) to condemn the war crimes of its immediate predecessor. Moreover, there is the remarkable phenomenon of "truth and reconciliation" processes beginning from South Africa and extending to certain parts of

Latin America. So even today, and perhaps as a distant echo of something that Paul is dealing with here, there is a series of public, national, societal self-accusations, confessions, and perhaps even repentances for crimes against humanity, even if the global hegemon still refuses to permit its own citizens to be accused of war crimes.

The despising of time and space for fundamental transformation toward justice is **a hardening of the will** [heart]. It is obduracy that plunges deeper and deeper into injustice, thereby making the sentence of death all the more devastating: **storing up wrath** [*orgēn*] **in a day of wrath and manifestation** [*apokalypseōs*] **of a just judgment of God**. The longer the day of reckoning is postponed without the desired effect, the greater the rage or fury that will befall those who arrogantly suppose that their time is a result of divine approval rather than a time of divine restraint.

Today there are also those who suppose that the success of the (American) empire demonstrates that God is on its side rather than permitting time for repentance, for a change of direction. And the more this time of turning is postponed the more severe may be the impending collapse.

Paul's reference to divine wrath again echoes the beginning of his indictment of Roman civilization and thus shows once again that the point of this indictment is an invalidation of Roman law, judgment, and so justice. But what then would count as human justice that would conform to divine justice?

3. Transition: The Impartiality of Divine Justice (2:6–16)

Perhaps in order to be clear that the foregoing indictment is not to be regarded as a partisan attack upon Rome, and to prepare therefore for an indictment also of Paul's own preferred polity, that of the Judeans, Paul will insist on the impartiality of divine justice, an impartiality that might be recognized by pagan and Judean as central to any understanding of justice. What would characterize a just or true judgment, one that could be called divine (of God)? Here Paul continues to speak in a way recognizable to a pagan, in a way that a pagan would certainly approve of and even would and did say as a matter of course:

For he will reward everyone according to works. To those who through enduring [holding fast] **work good, seeking glory and honor and incorruption, everlasting life; but to those who are self-seeking and disobeying truth and obeying injustice, wrath and fury. Anguish and affliction to every human soul that works evil** [*kakon*]**, the Judean first and the Greek; but glory and honor and peace to all working good** [*agathon*]**, to the Judean first and the Greek. For God is not a respecter of persons.**

That is, God doesn't play favorites when it comes to justice. How many Christians suppose that they get a "get out of jail free" card because they are in some sense Christians? At the end of the eighteenth century Kant had remarked upon the moral effects of an overreliance upon a sort of magical faith. Kant wrote: "Whatever, over and above good life-conduct, man fancies that he can do to become well pleasing to God is mere religious illusion and pseudo-service of God" (*Religion* 158). Emmanuel Levinas has pointed to the way in which the notion of a clemency without the demand for justice, supposedly based in Paul, is in reality an alibi that has permitted and licensed mind-numbing evil within a "Christian" Europe. With the horrifying perspective offered by two world wars and the Shoah, he writes: "The efficacy of the work is replaced by the magic of faith; the austere God appealing to a humanity capable of the Good is overlaid with an infinitely indulgent divinity that consequently locks man within his wickedness and lets loose this wicked but saved man on a disarmed humanity" (*Difficult Freedom* 104).

Although Paul again says **the Judean first and then the Greek**, he is using the opposite order, but he is signaling that he will be returning to the question of Judean justice and polity. He is also laying the foundation for the lengthy discussion of Israelite election in chapters 9–11. Throughout I will be using the term "Judean" to replace the more common "Jew" in reading and reflecting upon Paul's letter because the term "Judean" is closer to the Greek term it translates: *Ioudaios*. Also, as Shaye J. D. Cohen has shown (69–106), the term "Judean" corresponds more closely to the range of associations that the term comprised, all the more so when paired with the term *ethnoi* (nations or gentiles).

We must take into account that when he is speaking to pagans, Paul is using a pagan sense of how justice, including divine justice, works. Here the idea of justice is "to each his due," and the way the "due" is figured out is in accordance with works. That is, for Paul there is a decided starting point in salvation by or in accordance with works, a starting point consonant with Greek ideas about justice. Later we will see that this does not provide an accurate picture of divine justice, but it is a necessary starting point. We have to be careful. This isn't Paul's last word on how divine justice works. He will clarify as he goes along. But it is essential that there be a "point of contact" with pagan notions of justice. Key terms like "glory and honor," "lasting reputation," "everlasting fame," "immortality," and so on make clear this point of contact with pagan culture. These aren't "Jewish" terms. They are pagan terms, and Paul uses them in his address to pagans. Not only does Paul do this in Romans but we also have another fine example in Philippians 4:8: "Whatever is true, whatever is honorable, whatever is just, whatever is pure, whatever is pleasing, whatever is commendable, if there is any excellence, and if there is anything worthy of praise, take account of these things."

We should also notice that Paul is not one to speak too hastily of something like total depravity. His indictment of gentile or Roman society has been quite harsh and unrelenting. But this does not mean he supposes there are no "just persons." He knows perfectly well there are those in this and other societies who seek glory and honor and immortality by their endurance in doing good insofar as they understand the good.

How are we to put together Paul's awareness of the total corruption of a society, on the one hand, and the awareness that there are still those who seek to do good and so will receive "eternal life," on the other? The answer, I believe, lies in the pagan sense that there are men and women who persevere in trying to do what they know is right no matter what may be the case with respect to the social order that engulfs them.

If the letter were to end here, we might suppose that Paul is agreeing that we simply have to distinguish an unjust society from just persons. This was the solution that seems to have been proposed by certain forms of Stoicism. Here one can agree that the social order is hopelessly corrupt but suppose that it is still possible to find justice if we narrow our focus to the individual.

If we were to apply this to our own social order, we might say that we live in a society that perpetuates violence and avarice, that promotes insidious forms of white supremacy, and that teaches oblivion to the vulnerable. While this cannot be denied, we can at least recognize that there are relatively good people. They will have their reward. This more or less commonsense view is expressed in the title of Reinhold Niebuhr's book *Moral Man and Immoral Society.*

But such a solution will be too easy for Paul. He will help his readers find a more sophisticated solution—one that allows us to see that even the good are complicit in the evil of the social order and therefore without innocence. In our own social order, as a relatively privileged member of US society, I may deplore the impoverishment of millions through the machinations of the "market," yet my entire form of life is dependent upon practices of agribusiness, or sweatshops, or even the forced labor of those who harvest cacao. I am complicit through paying taxes in the practices that wind up killing civilians in Afghanistan or Yemen. The litany is in fact endless. So long as the social order in which I am immersed is unjust, I should not imagine that I have clean hands, even if, or perhaps especially if, I try to act in ways that mitigate or seek to mitigate the harm that is routinely done in and through this economic-social-political order. Because this is so, the "good" must yearn for the coming of a more comprehensive justice.

The indictment of the Roman polity began with the charge of imprisoning the truth in injustice. The indictment comes to a provisional conclusion with another way of framing the opposition between truth and injustice. One obeys one or the other. Thus, injustice is closely linked with deception while truth(fulness) and justice are identified. Truth here is no merely abstract idea but is brought into the sphere of the ethical and political. Simon Critchley, who has seriously engaged with the contemporary thinkers of the political who also inform my reading of Romans, has pointed to the connection made possible in English, between truth and "troth," where truthfulness has to do with loyalty so is inscribed in the sphere of the ethical (164–165). Truth, then, is no simple propositional matter but implicates one in loyalty to the other with whom one speaks. It is then a matter of justice. Jacques Derrida has shown how all speaking implies a promise to tell the truth, not to lie to, so not to mislead or betray, the one who hears or reads (*Of Spirit* 93–94, 134–135). Thus, truthfulness, faithfulness, and justice are bound together.

The catchphrase **Judean and Greek** brings us into a transitional phase of the argument. We begin to turn to a comparative situation. The key term that will link these discussions is "law."

All who have sinned without the law, without the law will perish; and as many who sinned in the law will be judged through the law.

Paul seems to be moving toward a Judean understanding of law as "Torah." Having spoken of divine impartiality in pagan terms, he now does so in Judean terms. Those who lack this law and who sin (let us say against justice) will perish not because any particular law condemns them but because they violate that to which the law points—justice. And those who have the law and are without justice will be condemned in the terms of the law. This will require considerable clarification as we move along with Paul through the course of his argument.

For it is not the case that those who have heard [or received] **the law are just before God, but those who do the law are those who will be made just.** This is common sense in a way but also shocking, even for us: it is those who do or act according to the law who will be made just or recognized as just. This could even be a Pharisaic perspective: Israel's relation to God depends not only on the possession of the law (of Moses) but on actually doing what the law requires (just as a Christian might say that what is important in God's eyes is not simply saying that Jesus is Lord but actually following him). Paul's argument will seem to take this back later, but does it really? We will have to be attentive to what sense it has to say that those who are justified are those who do what the law requires (and in what sense not). But in anticipation we can say that what the law requires, or aims at, or intends is justice, however much this aim or intent may come to be perverted. It is the doing of that which is aimed at by the law that will constitute justice. It is a good time to recall that the basis of justice has been said to be loyalty or faithfulness. We must await some further clarification from Paul.

Whenever nations [or gentiles, or pagans] **who don't have the law naturally** [*physei*] **do the things of the law, these who don't have law are a law to themselves—even if they don't have law.** This assertion seems to rely upon and expand what Paul had said earlier about the knowledge of God being available to all. Here it becomes clear that this knowledge includes the basic tendency of law. This will become the basis for speaking of a sort of "natural law" that will come to most sophisticated expression in Thomas Aquinas. But Paul seems to have something both more modest and more radical in mind: more modest because he does not develop a theory of natural law; more radical because he refers not to a natural law at all but to a customary (and in that sense, natural) doing that is independent of any particular law.

That one should not commit murder, for example, depends not on some or other law but, as Levinas suggests, on the simple encounter with the face of the other, any other (*Totality and Infinity* 199). Indeed, this is the very core of Levinas's attempt to think the ethical as such, and to think it as the most basic character of philosophy. What is complicated and "unnatural" is not the renunciation of murder but the torturous ways in which we have to persuade ourselves that murder is permitted (in war, or as a consequence of legal judgment, and so on).

Recalling that the things of God, including divine power, are disclosed to all (1:19–20), Spinoza and others take Paul here to be acting as a true philosopher who holds out for the rights of reason (Spinoza 144). This is not, I think, entirely wrong. Paul seems to want to maintain that the human is capable of doing the good, of behaving in accordance with justice. However much it will be necessary to complicate this picture, it is not something that needs to be abandoned to understand Paul's argument.

They **show the work of the law is written on their wills** (hearts). Recall that the law is to be written on the will (heart) according to Jeremiah 31:33. Paul is not repudiating the written law (the Torah, for example) but, in keeping with the prophetic tradition, is maintaining that what is fundamental is doing the justice at which the law aims. Thus, Spinoza claimed that the Word of God calls upon humanity "to obey God with all one's heart by practicing justice and charity" (6).

Their conscience testifies to them through conflicting thoughts that accuse or even excuse them. The conflict of thoughts of the conscientious person is something that we will return to later. How can one really have a clear conscience as a participant in an unjust social order? Should one even hope to have this? Is it perhaps the case, as Derrida suggests, that having a good conscience is precisely the sign that one has lost sight of the call and claim of justice? (*Gift* 67, 85). In every decision, for example, to be loyal to this or that person or principle, I necessarily betray or turn away from others who have a claim upon my loyalty and love. Derrida will maintain that the very structure of decision and responsibility, a structure that precipitates a choice between conflicting norms or principles, necessarily precludes a good conscience (Derrida and Roudinesco, *For What Tomorrow* 132). This might be especially true in view of the judgment of God, who exposes what is hidden from view—not only from others but perhaps even from myself. One need not think of unconscious intentions here but rather of the good or bad consequences of my acts.

On the day when according to my proclamation/gospel God, through messiah Joshua, will judge the secret thoughts of all. At this point in Paul's argument, the anticipation of divine judging may seem menacing. Even if we recall that the messiah is the norm and instrument of judgment, we might expect that this judgment would be "bad news" for the social orders and the world that had executed him. But Paul already anticipates a very different outcome for a judgment whose instrument is the messiah. Paul aligns this first with "good news," and he already anticipates the "all" that is the object of the divine action undertaken by means of the messiah. As will become apparent, the "all" is the object not of condemnation but of mercy, not of death but of life. But to arrive at that conclusion concerning messianic justice, Paul must first undertake several difficult and surprising maneuvers.

4. The Critique of the Polity of Israel (2:17–3:20)

Now Paul turns to the Judean, perhaps with the aim of being overheard by the gentile. After all, he has said that those to whom he writes in Rome are the nations, the gentiles or pagans. The indictment that follows is not an indictment of all Judeans or of what we might call Judaism as such. Nor am I sure that Stowers is right to suppose that Paul here simply constructs an imaginary Jewish interlocutor (144). The point is that even the legacy of the law and the prophets is not sufficient to produce a just people, a just society.

If you call yourself a Judean and depend on law [the possession of the law by which we as Judeans are distinguished among the nations] **and boast of God** [we have true knowledge of God, not like the heathen idolaters and polytheists]**, and you know the** [divine] **will and approve**

what is really excellent since you have been instructed from the law, and if you are sure that you are a guide to the blind, a light to those in darkness, a corrector of the foolish, a teacher of children [all of this may be the self-understanding of the Pharisee; that is, of one who knows that Judaism is not just for Jews but is also a light to the nations, and thus with a mission of instruction to those who are in darkness], **having in the law the form of knowledge and truth. You then who are a teacher of others: teach yourselves.**

Here follows an indictment: **While you preach against stealing, do you steal? You that forbid adultery, do you commit adultery? You that abhor idols, do you rob temples?** For this to make sense, it must be clear that what is indicted is not an individual who, for example, steals, commits adultery, breaks the law, and so forth. Rather, it is the people, the social order itself even under the better polity of Israel, the constitution founded on law in which justice itself comes to expression. Hence the proof comes from scripture (not the case for the indictment of the gentiles). It is a question of using Judean norms to test Judaism after using pagan norms to test paganism. We recall what Paul had said about speaking to Judeans as a Judean and to pagans as a pagan in 1 Corinthians 9:19–23. This opening movement of the letter to the Romans is exemplary of that policy.

The assertions about stealing, committing adultery, and robbing temples are rather odd here. I think we can make headway if we recall that adultery, for example, has to do with the assertion of the prophets that Israel sought security not from YHWH but from the nations, the empires. Something similar may be going on in the reference to robbing temples. What may be at stake is that those who abhor idols nevertheless acquire idols from other temples. How does this concretely happen in the history of Israel? It is well known that Israel acquired representations of other divinities that were then displayed in the (First) Temple, already beginning with Solomon (1 Kings 11:1–8) This was also a theme of prophetic denunciation (Ezekiel 16:1–63).

For ourselves, we may recall the furor concerning the display of the Ten Commandments in the United States at the beginning of the twenty-first century. Although the commandment forbids "graven images," this was certainly one graven image that people who thought of themselves as Christians were determined to display. One even cried, "They can't take away my God," as federal marshals tried to remove the graven image of the Decalogue. But we may also ask, How is a commandment to not covet other people's property to be honored by those who stole the land of the Native Americans? How is the commandment to not commit murder honored by those who committed genocide in the Middle Passage and against Native Americans? How is the commandment against theft to be understood when the oil of other nations is appropriated as if it were our own? How is the commandment against having other gods honored by the assertion "in God we trust" on our money, by the confusion of God and mammon? How is this honored by the confusion of God and patriotism enshrined in the "one nation, under God" of the pledge, or even more in the placement of national flags in our sanctuaries? There are multiple examples. For what is the history of the Christian West (and of the new center of the Christian West), if not a history of the systematic violation of the Decalogue?

The important thing here is to see the character of Paul's argument and, thus, its force. It comes to a head in this question: **You who boast in the law, do you dishonor God by breaking the law?** A citation of Isaiah 52:5 follows. The text may be read either as directing us to the history of Israel (according to the prophets) or as a piece of Pharisaic propaganda in mission to the diaspora. If we recall that Pharisees were a reform movement in the first century, active not only in Palestine but throughout the diaspora, then we may be able to combine these perspectives.

It is crucial to see that the critique of Judaism, including diaspora Judaism, is a feature of Pharisaic rhetoric. Paul is not proposing anything like a Christian critique of Israel but rather a Jewish (Pharisaic) critique. This is precisely on a par with his pagan critique of the pagan social order (or rather, Greek philosophical critique of the Greco-Roman order).

It is also possible that Paul is using accusations against the Judeans that were employed by gentile intellectuals against the Judeans. Paul is demonstrating to his readers in Rome a way of answering Judean opponents of the messianic cell, perhaps in anticipation of the return of Judeans to Rome after they had been presumably expelled under Claudius. As an insider with respect to Judean and Pharisaic rhetorical practices, he is in a good position to enable the gentile messiah followers in Rome to withstand opposition from his fellow Pharisees.

Now follows a reference to circumcision (verses 25–29), a topic Paul had dealt with rather heatedly in Galatians. But here the problem is not that certain Judean Christians seek to impose circumcision upon gentiles (as perhaps in Galatians) but of the nature of circumcision itself. Paul will be following a prophetic and perhaps Pharisaic form of argumentation.

The argument is one that, while it may offend some Judean sensibilities, is nonetheless built solidly on prophetic foundations. What is critical is what the law and the prophets call "circumcision of the heart." We know this tradition from Deuteronomy 10:16, Jeremiah 4:4 and 9:26, and Ezekiel 44:9. Derrida somehow supposes that Paul is ignorant of this tradition and is arguing from a specifically Christian perspective ("Silkworm" 344), but that seems to be mistaken. Instead, Paul is offering a fundamentally Jewish critique of Judaism in accordance with the law and the prophets.

Paul simply takes this view in a particular direction: **Circumcision is important, if you obey** [or hearken to] **the law. But it won't help if you do not hearken to** [or disobey] **the law.** Conversely, what if those who are not circumcised actually do what the law requires? (Paul doesn't say "obey it," for they don't know it literally; they are those we had already encountered in 2.12–14.) **They will be regarded as far as the promise of God is concerned as if they were circumcised, while those who are circumcised will be regarded as if not circumcised if they break the law. . . . The just uncircumcised will judge the unjust circumcised.** Here it does seem that Paul has gone beyond the view of the prophetic-Pharisaic perspective to offer the obverse of that argument. If circumcision by itself won't save you but a certain justice is required, he argues the justice alone without the circumcision should be enough to save. Indeed, this goes so far as to say that the gentiles who are just will judge the Judeans who are unjust.

Thus, **true circumcision is of the heart** [that is, the will] **and so is not physical but "spirited."** Any of his Pharisee compatriots would recognize the force of his argument. It is, after all, framed as a pastiche of phrases from prophets and from Deuteronomy. But for Paul gentiles as gentiles can be faithful to the messiah. It is here that his mission to the gentiles radically departs from what may have been his prior understanding of that mission as a Pharisee.

It is very helpful here to follow Barth's advice in appropriating this discussion to understand Paul's address to Judeans as if it were an address to the privileges of Christian religious affiliation: one could try to substitute baptism for example, or church membership, or some other way of being a "Christian" for the reference to circumcision. Thus transposed, the argument would run: It doesn't matter whether you are baptized; all that matters is whether you love your neighbor. The non-Christian who is just will judge the baptized person who is unjust. Moreover, there is no need to become in any way a Christian in order to be faithful to the messiah. Paraphrasing the argument in this way suggests at least the radicality of Paul's argument. It also serves to indicate how the reading of Pauline texts by contemporary intellectuals who have no interest in being "Christians" may have something important to offer. Jacques Lacan, the Freudian theorist who influenced many of the radical thinkers who have come to discuss Paul, had already maintained that one could read Paul with great profit without regard to belief. In encouraging his auditors to read Paul, he writes that analysts "do not have to believe in these religious truths in any way, given that such belief may extend as far as what is called faith, in order to be interested in what is articulated in its own terms in religious experience" (*Ethics of Psychoanalysis* 171). Alain Badiou, the great Marxist intellectual, could write in his remarkable study of Paul that "I care nothing for the Good News he declares, or the cult dedicated to him. But he is a subjective figure of primary importance" (*Saint Paul* 1). In Badiou's case the "primary importance" to be ascribed to Paul is that of a figure of a political militant that can offer an example of what it might mean today to undertake a revolution against the neoliberal economic order and thus to make the ever-elusive idea of communism a reality. The difference between Lacan and Badiou is that the latter, like many other thinkers to whom we have been referring, sees that what Paul is up to is a radical rethinking of the political. What I am suggesting is that such non-Christian readings may have more in common with Paul's point of view than readings that make him the founder of a religious institution or of that institution's doctrines.

What then is the value of being Judean? Or the value of circumcision? One might also ask what is the value of being a Christian, or being baptized, if the issue is really whether one is just or not? The question about the value of belonging to the Judean people follows directly from Paul's argument. Of course, Paul might have said that there is no advantage. Indeed, he seems to come perilously close to such a position in Galatians.

But that is most definitely not his position now, as he continues: **Much in every way. First because they were entrusted with the oracles of God.** (Paul doesn't say "you," but "they." The audience is still gentile.) What does this mean? The Judeans are the ones who bear the writings that point to or testify to the will, the promise, the aim of God. Even if those who had been claimed by God and God's promise and God's law as will to justice do not live up to this gift, it is still one that comes to them and comes to others through them.

What then? Will the unfaithfulness of some destroy the faithfulness of God? God forbid. Rather let God be true even if every human is a liar. The advantage of the Judean, then, is that God is faithful to God's word. This will be explored at greater length much later in Paul's argument, but it is crucial at this point because what is at stake throughout this argument is the faithfulness of God, the reliability of God's promise. For it is this that must serve as the basis for loyalty to the proclamation concerning the messiah.

Does the argument go too far in suggesting that the contrast between human faithlessness and the faithfulness of God only makes the latter stand out more clearly? Paul cites Psalm 51:4 to underscore his point. Perhaps here Paul looks ahead to where his argument is going and skips a step, for we immediately return to talk of injustice as the true meaning of faithlessness.

But if our injustice serves to show the justice of God, what then? Is God unjust to exhibit wrath? (I speak humanly.) Again, this piece of the argument is going to be picked up and developed quite emphatically in chapters 9–11. Here Paul does not really intend to answer the problem but to underscore it. **Absolutely not! For then how could God judge the world?** Paul had already maintained that the unjust empire could not judge, precisely because of its injustice—hence, the continued importance of the connection between justice and judgment when the subject is God. In Paul's thought, God does not get a sovereign exemption from the claim of justice.

But if through my falsehood God's truthfulness abounds to his glory, why am I still being judged as a sinner? The question repeats the first, save that this time truth substitutes for justice. We again see that for Paul these terms are closely linked. **And as we are blasphemed as saying: Why not do evil that good may come?** Has Paul's view been characterized in this way? By whom? In any case, he agrees that one should resist such views: **Their condemnation is just.**

These rhetorical questions serve to set a sort of agenda for Paul: issues that his subsequent argument will address. Although Stowers may be correct to liken this segment of Paul's argument to a diatribe with a Judean as his interlocutor (165–175), what may be missed by that approach is that Paul is setting up a number of issues that will in fact guide his argument all the way through to the end of the letter. The questions and preliminary responses seem to be meant to suggest that he knows full well the charges that are brought against the proclamation that he serves and he is therefore in a position to respond convincingly to these mischaracterizations of that proclamation. The pages that follow will pick up these issues and advance his argument as a response to these misrepresentations.

But first he will continue his indictment of Judean polity: **What then? Are we Judeans better off? Not at all. For I have already charged that Judeans and Gentiles are under** [the indictment of] **sin.** The phrase "better off" could also be understood as "worse off." The issue concerns whether one people is in fundamentally better or worse shape relative to the question of justice. Even though the Judeans have the advantage of possessing the oracles of God, these same oracles make clear that they have no advantage. Accordingly, Paul cites a sort of catena or chain of passages in which the people are accused (and accuse themselves) of being under sin. The passages come from the Psalms and Isaiah and seem appropriate for a collective admission of failure to do justice. They thus seem to stem from a liturgy of self-accusation such as might be appropriate for a Day of Atonement. In reflecting on Paul's "political theology" in Romans, Jacob Taubes is led to spend considerable time explaining the liturgy for Yom Kippur (28–38).

Since Paul has already used gentile or pagan arguments to establish gentile or pagan injustice, it is only fitting that he use biblical citations to demonstrate Judean injustice. In each case he makes use of a sort of internal critique to make his point about the injustice of these two forms of humanity, these two polities and peoples.

Now we know that whatever the law says it speaks to those who are under the law, so that every mouth may be stopped and the world held accountable to God.

Paul has in view Judean "law" as addressing Judean people, coming as it does at the end of citations from the Psalms. But his citations have not been from the law construed as Torah but from the Psalms. The indictment is not a narrowly legal one but rather involves a failure to instantiate the justice to which law (in the narrow sense) serves at best as a pointer. Paul's point is that all are claimed by the demand of justice, a demand that the law of the gentiles like the law of the Judeans claims to articulate, a demand that is not met, however, by either people or polity. Viewed in this way, the whole world (seen as made up of Judeans and pagan nations) is under divine judgment.

Before leaving this discussion, which has now accomplished the indictment of the polities that have been claimed to offer a legal order that seeks to bring justice, we should ask how this global indictment is to be understood relative to Paul's earlier admission that there are those, whether circumcised or not, who really can be characterized as doing what the law requires.

This can only be understood, I believe, if Paul is seen to be accusing social groups as such, rather than a collection of individuals abstracted from their social setting. Universal "sin" is the characterization not of individuals as individuals but of social totalities that are in basic ways "unjust." Individuals, whether Greek or Judean, seen simply as persons may, as Paul has said, do what is just and right. But when viewed as participants in unjust social orders, they are nonetheless judged as the social order is judged.

This is also the reason that it makes sense to indict whole peoples for the injustice of their leadership elites, who may be taken as the part that "represents" the people as a whole. This is something already clear from prophetic pronouncements of doom upon their own people: the injustice of the powerful and prosperous brings the whole society to ruin. And the same is true of the elites of pagan society. Paul's view is thus in harmony with that of those he is addressing, whether gentiles or Judeans. In our day, it is more often the case that we think in terms of isolated individuals. But even here we can see, even if with some difficulty, that social structures like racism, for example, so permeate ways of seeing one another and interacting with one another that none escape its stain, no matter how personally decent they might be.

The tendency to read Romans as having to do primarily with individuals rather than with social totalities is a great obstacle to understanding what Paul is up to. However, the "political reading" of Romans helps make sense of the basic structure and the continuing relevance of his argument.

Second Phase

We have heard that God requires justice and that without justice there is only judgment, death, and wrath. Yet no actually existing constitution of law has produced justice; moreover, it is impossible that any law can be just or produce justice—nothing can be made just through law, he will say. This appears to be a dead-end. In what follows, Paul will state this aporia starkly in order then to claim that the only way to break out of this impasse, to strike out from this absence of a way forward (the meaning of aporia), is through the seemingly impossible possibility of a justice outside the law, which I have termed "outlaw justice."

At this point Paul breaks with the ideas of classical political philosophy, for that political thinking had always proceeded by way of a close, indeed indissoluble link between justice and law. In the *Laws*, which is the longest, the last, and, I believe, the most tedious of Plato's dialogues, we have three people discussing what the laws should be in order for a society to be just and its people virtuous. In the beginning of their discussion they refer to the essential place in the history of the social-political order played by the great lawgivers: Minos for Crete, Solon for Athens, and Lycurgus for Sparta. They proceed to discuss these "constitutions" to get at what would be the ideal constitution or set of laws for a society.

In Aristotle's *Politics*, much of the discussion is devoted to contrasting constitutions or legal orders that may be viewed both as conducive to the common good and as ultimately destructive. This discussion closely parallels a discussion of possible constitutions in Plato's *Statesman* (*politikos*)—the wise legislator seeks to combine some of the best of each of the possible constitutions in a sort of mixed constitution that would provide for the good of the city.

But it is Cicero, writing in the century before Paul, who provides us with the most complete attempt to relate the question of the law to that of justice. In the *Republic*, Cicero is engaged in persuading his friends that they have a duty to engage in politics understood as legislating for the benefit of the social order. He insists: "For nothing is laid down by philosophers—nothing right and honorable at any rate—which has not been brought into being and established by those who have drawn up laws for states" (1.2). Here it would seem that the political has above all to do with establishing laws that will serve as the framework for the common life of the citizens. In this perspective it appears that laws have their origin in a reflection on justice (what is laid down by philosophers), which then becomes practical and concrete in the work of the legislator or maker of laws.

In the perspective of the greatest thinkers of the political, justice is made to coincide with law. It is through law that human societies, and thus human members of society, are made to be just. But Paul has come to the conclusion that law cannot produce justice, that there is an irreconcilable conflict between justice and law, that if there is to be justice, it must come apart from the law, as outlaw justice.

After first indicating that this is precisely what his proclamation entails, Paul grounds this first in the Abrahamic joining of gentile and Judean, for Abraham is "just" before the law comes into existence. He then uses the figure of Adam to make the case that this justice outside the law is a necessity for humanity as such, a necessity that becomes a reality through the messianic.

5. Justice Outside the Law (3:21–31)

Paul is by no means content to expose the injustice of gentiles and Judeans, even if by doing so he can show that these two laws that were deployed to condemn the one he regards as messiah and those who seek to be loyal to that messiah are themselves unjust. He has something far more audacious in mind: to suggest that law as such cannot produce justice, so another basis for justice must be sought. Moreover, he will claim that the true basis for justice, for just societies and a just world, is to be found in the messianic announcement to which he and his readers seek to be faithful.

We come now to a pivotal segment of Paul's argument, which, however difficult this may be, should not be separated from what has gone before. Almost from the beginning we have heard of justice, and this has come to be associated with a reflection on law and even circumcision. Paul already assured his readers that those who sinned without the law will perish and those who have the law and have sinned will "be judged by the law." In a certain sense this may be read as making the law, in the sense of positive legal system, irrelevant—what matters is whether or not one "sins." And this is said more or less explicitly concerning the nations: "**when they do what the law requires**," or later, "**not hearers but doers** [*poiaitia*] **of the law are** [made] **just.**" Paul returned to this in his discussion with his Judean interlocutor. There he speaks of obeying or "practicing" (*prassas*) and of keeping the law. Thus far, Paul may be seen to be in substantial agreement with the political thinking of his (or even our) time. But now we come to what seems a turning point.

Because all flesh [all absolutely] **will not be made just by works of the law** [*ergon nomou*]

The "all flesh" seems to indicate literally all mortals. Much later, Paul will indicate how flesh in the sense of human mortality and vulnerability is connected to flesh as hostility to God. But it is not the opposition or even the weakness that is most in view here. It is the "all." Having divided humanity into Judeans and gentiles, Paul gestures toward a radical universality. Alain Badiou, who seeks in Paul a paradigm for a new kind of militant figure to combat global neoliberal capital, maintains that this universality marks the distinctive contribution of Paul to a thinking of the political (*Saint Paul* 7, 11)

However, the "all flesh" points to an even wider universality than the one Badiou has indicated: it includes a reference both to all humanity and to all creatures. In the covenant with Noah, the phrase "all flesh" occurs insistently with reference to "every living creature that is with you, the birds, the cattle, and every beast of the earth with you" (Genesis 9:10). The promise not to unleash destruction again links "all flesh" with the earth itself (9:11); indeed, the covenant is termed one between God and "the earth" (9:13). In short, within ten verses that articulate this covenant the term "all flesh" is linked with the earth and with every living creature no fewer than eight times! We will have to see whether and in what way Paul will be able to make good on this hint that his concern with a universal justice is one that embraces not only all humanity but also "every living creature," and, indeed, the earth itself. What sort of polity or politics will be able to bring justice for the earth itself?

That it is the political that is in question here is made clear by the reference to justice. But we have come to an absolutely crucial point, for commentaries have generally opened the way to a depoliticizing of Paul's view by the manifold ways that being justified or justification is interpreted, interpretations that result in severing the connection between justification and justice. Thus, so-called forensic justification has God declaring people to be just who manifestly are not just, thereby vitiating the claim of justice itself. Something else is said to substitute for justice, whether this be some mere belief or some token participation in ecclesiastical institutions. By virtue of some or other substitute for justice, persons are said to be forgiven so that they may be regarded as just even if in fact they are not.

It would be difficult to imagine a more effective way to undercut Paul's whole concern and argument because Paul's issue is precisely that of justice, of how justice has become injustice and how justice is to be established. Paul's question then is how the "all" of "all flesh"—meaning first of all humanity as a whole or totality—is to be made just. The end result must not be lip service to justice (for this is already present in the polities that he has been critiquing) but real justice of the sort that averts the divine wrath directed against all injustice.

The question is, How is justice to come into being, to be brought into being, to be established? And the answer of political theory has been that this comes through the law and may entail securing better laws or securing more universal obedience to the law. But in any case, it comes through law, or what Paul here calls works (*erga*) of the law. That is the direction we have seen indicated by Plato, Aristotle, and Cicero. But Paul will claim that this approach does not and cannot work and that divine justice itself has brought forward a fundamentally new or different way of achieving the aim of divine justice. Thus, justification does not mean evading justice or offering a substitute for it. It means really becoming just, really embodying that justice that is the claim or demand of the divine, of God, if you will.

Becoming just with a justice that is outside the law seems to stand in complete opposition to what we had been reading earlier about complying with the law as something that must be done, whether or not one has the law or is under the law. Why is it that we now are directed to that which is apart from the law? For he had said that **the one doing the law is just rather than the one who hears the law**. How is this to be understood? How are we to hold both the one and the other set of propositions together? The theme of the next few sentences is that law does not and cannot produce justice—that works of the law (and how is this different from obeying, complying with, or practicing what the law requires?) do not make one just.

We may also consider the hypothesis that the emphasis here falls on the "all" and thus may be contrasted with "some." In that case, it would be true that in certain respects some or a few are "just" through the doing of the law. But doing the works of the law has proven incapable of producing a just totality or sociality. The efficacy of law in producing justice is severely limited: it produces only enough just persons as to demonstrate that humanity is without excuse relative to the demands of the law. If absolutely none were just, we could say that it's no use; it's impossible. So the presence of some, even very few, who are or seem to be just demonstrates the guilt of the totality, for the totality is not just, neither the Greco-Roman nor the Judean totality. On the contrary, these totalities are marked by their injustice.

What will complicate this picture of a few just individuals and an unjust totality is the way in which the just individual is contaminated by the injustice of the totality of which she or he is a part. When this is foregrounded, we will see that there are no just persons so long as there is no just totality or society. This may still be a long way, however, from the Augustinian and Calvinistic view of something like total depravity or of humanity as a "lump of damnation." The distinction between those who are (relatively) just and those who are not retains its force. Moreover, the goal, it would appear, is that not only a few here and there but rather "all flesh" may be made to be just.

Since through the law comes knowledge of sin. This will be what
he must explain later (7:7–12). For now it simply hangs here. (We therefore leave open the question of whether knowledge here means something
like understanding, or awareness, or if it means something more like the
Hebrew: intimate acquaintance.) We recall that in the writings of Israel
Paul has already discovered a knowledge of sin, an acknowledgment of sin,
particularly the sin of Israel itself.

But now, we return to the main thesis: **the justice of God has been
manifested.** We had heard at the beginning of the argument, in the form
of a thesis, **For in it** [the glad-making proclamation of God concerning
his son] **the justice of god or divine justice, is revealed** [*apokalyptetai*]
from loyalty to loyalty (1:17).

From that point, we have had the wrath of God revealed first with
respect to the nations and then with respect to the Israelites. That wrath
has as its basis an absence of justice. But now this divine justice is again
made manifest, and it is made manifest **apart from or outside the law**.
Yet it is not wholly unrelated to the law; as Paul says, **the law and the
prophets testify to it**. To what do the law and the prophets testify? To
a divine justice that is apart from or outside the law. Now we are in the
following position: The law testifies to (points to and affirms) a justice
that is outside or apart from the law. The law is not identical with justice
but points beyond itself toward justice. Here again we encounter the special privilege of Israel: it has the oracles of God, the very oracles (as law
and prophets) that point to this coming of a justice outside the law. The
law itself points beyond itself to that which exceeds so is ungraspable or
uncontainable by law, namely, justice.

Moreover, it is **a justice or divine justice** [testified to by] **the fidelity**
[or loyalty] **of Joshua messiah, to all who are loyal** [or faithful]. Paul's
thesis statement about the good news indicated a justice manifest from or
through loyalty to or for loyalty. Here this phrase specifies the agents of
loyalty: from or through the loyalty of Joshua (which testifies to or shows
divine justice) to or for the loyalty of all those who are also faithful or loyal.
That is, the faithfulness of the messiah brings about, or provokes, or intends
the faithfulness of others, those who are or become faithful in the same way.

Older translations always substitute faith *in* Joshua for faithfulness *of*
Joshua. Even apart from the implausibility of this construction of the Greek

grammar, this mistranslation undercuts the direction of Paul's argument in such a way as to eliminate the force of his concern with justice.

The reference to Joshua messiah further reminds us of why it is that this justice must be justice apart from or outside the law. For it was in accordance with the law, both Judean and gentile or Roman, that Joshua was made an outlaw and executed as an outlaw, whether as blasphemer from the standpoint of Judean law or rebel and subversive from the standpoint of Roman or gentile law. If he was just, then the justice involved is somehow outside the law. And perhaps it is precisely his loyalty to justice, or to God as justice, that places him outside the law and so fundamentally ruptures the connection between law and justice.

As for the claim that **there is no distinction**, we have already seen it with respect to the doing of what the law requires. But now it will change importantly: **Since all have sinned**, that is, every polity, whether gentile or Jew; all peoples have violated justice. Not each and every individual, perhaps, since we have heard that there are even gentiles who do what the law requires—as persons—even though the social reality named nations is under judgment, as is Israel. Paul is reminding the reader of the substance of the argument concerning pagan and Judean injustice. As a result, **they fall short of the divine radiance** (glory). Is this "glory" another name for justice? Is this the whole point of justice, that justice is itself the divine radiance, the divine shining forth, another name for God as such, or God as "present"? Justice is not then an afterthought to God but is God's very radiance or shining forth, God's "being." At several points in his reading of Derrida, Caputo wonders whether justice is another name for God or if God is another name for justice (68, 116, 338–339).

Since they fall short of this divine radiance, might the conclusion here be they are all condemned and so will perish? That is what we have been led to expect by the indictment that demonstrates why divine wrath or fury is manifest from the skies. But no: **They are made just as a gift** [freely, giftedly] **by his generosity through the redemption** [liberation from bondage] **in messiah Joshua, the messiah God set out as a propitiation through loyalty by his blood, as a demonstration of** [God's] **justice because of the forbearance of passing over previous sins in order to show** [God's] **justice in the now-time** [*nun kairou*]**; that God should be just and make just the one with the loyalty of Joshua.**

This is a very dense passage, and it is difficult not to get sidetracked. We begin with what is clear: We are concerned with justice, divine justice. We are pointed to loyalty or faithfulness, again the faithfulness of the messiah Joshua and that of those who become loyal in the same way or who participate in that faithfulness. The justice of God has to do with the divine kindness or forbearance that has withheld the wrath and fury and chosen another course, something related to what is called free gift, free favor, or sheer generosity ([*charis*]). Thus, it is not something compelled but freely given, as a new and astonishing reply, not one that could have been predicted or programmed—for that is what wrath and fury are, as has been amply demonstrated—but an event that overturns the expectation of destruction and turns fury into patience and wrath into generosity. It is this unconditional generosity that somehow lies at the basis of justice, a justice that is of course beyond the law—and that, moreover, not only is just but will actually produce justice.

We will return to the question of the togetherness or relation of gift and grace or gift and favor. At this point something is opening up, a contrast between gift and something else: law perhaps. Gift is outside the law. Which law? The law of exchange, of retribution and distribution.

What can deflect our attention here is reference to blood and propitiation. Whatever else is going on, we are being reminded of the cross, that is, of the price or cost of the messiah's loyalty to the divine justice. Thus, I have altered the normal translation, "to be received by faith," since the text has nothing corresponding to "to be received." Rather, the text connects loyalty to blood. And this is exactly what a reader of Paul might expect, since elsewhere Paul has said that the messiah had "become obedient to death, even death on a cross" (Philippians 2:8). Obedience and faithfulness are quite strongly connected in Paul, as we have already seen. Recall that Paul's goal in 1:5 is to bring about **the obedience of faithfulness**. Thus, the loyalty of the messiah is what leads to his death and so to his shed blood. But this is expressed at this point in quasi-religious terms (**propitiation**), that is, in a still-veiled or coded terminology. Paul seems to be wrapping political dynamite in a quasi-cultic covering. We will see if we need to take this coding more seriously on its own terms as we proceed.

This faithfulness to the death (blood) will produce redemption, that is, liberation of captives or prisoners or slaves. What happens in and through the messiah is to release them from that which is unjust and perhaps from the law considered as an instrument of injustice. But this would refer to the law that has actually condemned the messiah and has exacted his blood. This is the law as instrument of injustice, the law as fatally contaminated by injustice—the law that, in spite of aiming at or legitimating itself in the name of justice, has been exposed as unjust and (perhaps) not in this or that respect, but fundamentally in general, as such.

What God has done in or through or on account of the loyalty of Joshua is to demonstrate God's own justice, and God does this not only by being patient and withholding wrath (2:4) but also by providing for the construction of justice that does not depend on the violence of the law and that perhaps even exposes that violence and contrasts it with another way—that of loyalty.

Thus, **there is no boasting**, that is, no assertion of privilege relative to one another; no "I'm in and you're out"; "I'm favored and you're not." It is crucial to Paul's argument that at this point he is dealing with the boasting of peoples concerning their relative justice, their relative standing before God. It is with peoples (rather than a collection of individuals) that Paul is concerned, as the constant reference to pagan nations and Judeans makes quite obvious. Paul will develop this at some length in chapters 9–11.

How is this assertion of privilege that sneers at the unprivileged eliminated? **On account of which law? Not by a law of works but by a law** [principle] **of loyalty.** It is necessary to be wary: "Law" is being used in a number of senses. This is already a somewhat vertiginous situation. Law is being "deconstructed"—made to tremble, shaking what is supposed to be itself bedrock.

We seem to have two laws: one is a law of works, of compliance with the law, which is not incompatible with a certain boasting: we have the law and you don't; we do what the law requires and you don't. And the other is a "law of faithfulness" that precludes this boasting.

We all know that a certain function of law, or of compliance with a law, especially a "religious law," is that it is simply made for boasting: for example, I don't smoke or drink or dance, so I am different from those who are less observant of these rules, regulations, and commandments. On the geopolitical stage, we are becoming all too accustomed to a sort of boasting with respect to law. On the side of the Western democracies this takes the form of a boasting about human rights or separation of church and state or constitutional democracies. In the nations in which Islam prevails, there may be a certain boasting concerning the superiority of Sharia and its refusal of corruption, both moral and economic. There is a way in which law as law may lend itself to boasting, but not loyalty, according to Paul. Why not? Perhaps it has to do with gift.

We maintain that [the] human is made or caused to be just apart from works [*erga*] of law. Or is God the god of the Judeans only? Not also of the nations? Yes, of nations also. Since one God will make the circumcision just through loyalty and the uncircumcision through that [same] loyalty.

The opposition lines up in such a way that we are led to suppose that the phrase "works of law," unlike the doing of the law, for example, describes the peculiar relation to law of the Judeans: hence, not works of law but something called faithfulness for both Judeans and the nations or pagans.

This seems to place Paul's observations about doing the law as that which leads to justice on a new basis. The basis now is not doing the law but rather loyalty. Paul will still have to explain how it is that faithfulness leads not to "works" but to fulfilling the law (or the intention of the law). Those who are loyal, whether circumcised or not, are justified—made or caused to be just.

The oneness of God (perhaps an echo of Deuteronomy 6:4) is not a theoretical perspective but a practical one. It involves the relation of the divine to all nations, with the favor of God to all, and with the claim of justice upon all. This "oneness" is not a metaphysical category but more like an ethical category. Badiou writes, "The fundamental question is that of knowing precisely what it means for there to be a single God," and answers that Paul's "genuinely revolutionary conviction is that the sign of the One is the 'for all' of the universal" (*Saint Paul* 76).

Does this mean that the law is destroyed by this loyalty? Absolutely not. Indeed we establish the law.

In one sense it appears that law has been overthrown. In another, however, it is established, caused to stand. We are again in this vertiginous situation with respect to law. We are presented with a faithfulness that is outside law yet establishes law. Let us suppose that this means a justice outside the law (and in some ways even against the law), but still justice, and so that at which the law aims—that in the name of which the law stands—and so it is justice that is the true aim or content or goal of the law. Of course, this works only if what remains unshaken is precisely justice: God's, and thus also ours—justice that is heeded in and through loyalty.

This rather complex and vertiginous relation between law and justice is one that has preoccupied Derrida, even though he has not specifically traced it out in relation to Paul's argument. As I have attempted to show in *Reading Derrida / Thinking Paul,* Derrida broaches this relation in his reflections on Benjamin's "Critique of Violence" and develops it further in *Of Hospitality.* Derrida, whose name was associated with "deconstruction," had often been supposed to be a relativist or even a nihilist on account of his relentless questioning of apparent certainties or even the quest for certainty with respect to meaning. Instead of stable certainties rooted in the presence of some discoverable foundation or clear distinctions (literature or philosophy, performative or constative statements, presence or absence, and so on), Derrida pointed to the irreducible instability of concepts and categories received from the philosophical tradition. Attending to this instability is what comes to be called deconstruction. In a lecture in 1989 at the Cardozo School of Law, however, Derrida makes clear that from the very beginning his work had been animated by the question of justice. He writes that he is concerned "to show why and how what one currently calls deconstruction, while seeming not to 'address' the problem of justice, has done nothing else" ("Force of Law" 237). To make this clear, Derrida introduces a fundamental tension between justice and law, where law is always deconstructible but justice is not: "Deconstruction takes place in the interval that separates the undeconstructibility of justice from the deconstructibility of law. . . . Justice in itself, if such a thing exist, outside or beyond law, is not deconstructible" (243). Later, in 1996, in a text dealing with the question of hospitality, Derrida writes of a certain law or unconditional claim of hospitality (welcome to the stranger) that exceeds law and is even against the law—while still insisting on becoming effective as law (Derrida and Dufourmantelle 77–79).

Writing nearly two thousand years after Paul, and without invoking his name or his texts, Derrida appears to be noticing the very issue that Paul is wrestling with in writing to the Romans. It is the inexorable call or claim of justice that discloses an irreducible tension between that justice and any possible law or polity based upon law.

The reference to Derrida also reminds us that Paul is concerned precisely with the political question as the question of justice. The basic question of political philosophy has been, How is justice to be established for society as a whole? Thus, what is of importance here is not simply that Paul continues to insist that persons must be just (itself a considerable distance from certain Reformation perspectives) but also that societies must be so. His way of pointing to this dimension is the regular reference to Judeans and gentiles (nations).

The claim, then, will be something like this: It is through loyalty or faithfulness that societies are to be made just. We should also bear in mind that one way of referring to the injustice of the Roman world is the prevalence of "faithlessness." But how faithfulness produces justice Paul has not yet told us. We will have to continue to raise the question about this social or universal justice if we are to really read Paul as a thinker of the political.

6. The Justice of Abraham (4:1–25)

To this point in his argument Paul has spoken of two peoples: the nations (or pagans) and the Judeans. He has maintained that with respect to the basic question of justice, neither has a decisive advantage. Both kinds of people or societies are condemned by the just judgment of God: one through their own law and prophets; the other by the wrath made evident from the heavens against the unjust. Moreover, to both has been given a way of becoming truly just that does not discriminate between the circumcised and the uncircumcised. This way concerns a certain faithfulness that leads to a justice that is both outside the law and testified to by the law. This loyalty is somehow evident in Joshua messiah in such a way as to be contagious in producing a similar faithfulness on the part of both Judeans and gentiles.

It is important to note that for Paul there are only two kinds of people: Judeans and gentiles, or as he now says, circumcised and uncircumcised. Of course, only a Judean could divide up the human world in this way, just as only a Greek could maintain that the world is divided into Greeks and barbarians. (In certain forms of Eurocentric modernity, the world was similarly divided into whites and nonwhites.) The way Paul relies on this binary of Judean and gentile makes clear that he is thinking precisely as a Judean, but as one whose mission is directed toward non-Judeans. He doesn't cease being a Judean just because he is an apostle to the pagans. He has not converted into something else: everyman, for example—or a "Christian" for that matter. He is announcing that the God of Israel has done something in and through the "son," the messiah of Israel, that is of overwhelming importance for gentiles as gentiles (not as crypto- or pseudo-Judeans). This something relates to the divine project of calling for and making possible the establishment of justice.

Perhaps of even greater importance for understanding what Paul is up to in writing about Judeans and gentiles is his concern not with individuals but with societies. The condemnation anticipated in the wrath is one that does not aim at individuals in isolation from the social totalities of which they are a part but concerns them precisely as social beings, as part of and participants in those same social totalities: hence, the possibility of regarding the nations as represented by their corrupt leadership cadres and, following the prophets, of regarding Judeans in the same way. The question to which he and we will have to return is whether there will appear another way of "representing" these social totalities in such a way as to anticipate how all will become just in accordance with the divine intention.

In the meantime, Paul is approaching his theme through the binarism of Judean and pagan. He is employing and at the same time troubling this binarism, bringing it into question. This has already taken place with respect to the question of doing what the law requires, of falling under judgment, and of being offered a different way to become just—through faithfulness rather than "works of the law."

To explore more deeply, he turns to the figure of Abraham, which he had already employed in another of his letters. This has already been prefigured in his use of the binary circumcision/uncircumcision, for it is Abraham who receives the command to circumcise. Abraham is both the "father" (or ancestor) of the Judeans and one who is antecedent to the distinction between the circumcised and the uncircumcised. Paul will seek to think with this ambivalent status.

The argument that Paul deploys here is quite different from and even opposed to the one he develops in Galatians regarding Abraham. While elements of Galatians 3:6–9 are retained in Romans 4, the argument against the law of Galatians 3:10–14 and the purpose of the law as put forward in Galatians 3:19–4:7 is completely altered in this argument. The analogy of Sarah and Hagar (Galatians 4:21–5:1) also vanishes—it was apparently motivated by the particular context in Galatia, or Paul has thought better of it. In either case we must take into account the provisional rather than "final" character of any of Paul's arguments or positions. In Paul's letter to Corinth he suggests that "now we see in a glass darkly" (13:12), and this must be taken into account when reading Paul. Centuries of reading this text as "canonical" have obscured not only the contextual character of Paul's arguments and formulations but also what might be termed their "experimental" character. Rather than suppose that Paul has a ready-made system that is deployed in different circumstances, it may be more accurate or helpful to think about his letters as improvisations that uncover implications or potentialities in the messianic message that had been previously unnoticed or clumsily expressed.

One respect in which this may be seen is in his periodization of law relative to promise in Galatians, where the law comes several centuries after the promise to Abraham. But in Romans he does not exploit the centuries-long gap between Abraham and Moses. Instead, he places the beginning of law at the command to circumcise given to Abraham, thereby conflating circumcision with law, something that has already been anticipated by his argument to this point (3:27–31, 2:25–29).

What was found by Abraham, our patriarch according to the flesh? This "our" according to the flesh marks Paul as Judean, but later "our" will designate another corporate reality: those who, whether circumcised or not, share in Abraham's faithfulness or loyalty.

If Abraham was made or became just by means of works [of law], **he has something to boast about** [that is, to point to, as a way of competing with other people], **but not to point to as a claim on God. For what does the written say? Abraham relied on God and it was counted as justice.** (Genesis 15:6)

In Genesis, this follows the first word of Adonai to Abram, the word that calls him out of his home country (12:1ff.), a word that also had attached to it a promise and the indication that Abram heeded the word and set out. After a lengthy narrative, there is a strange encounter again with Adonai, in which he declares, "Look toward the heaven and count the stars if you can count them . . . so shall your descendants be," and it is said that "Abram relied on Adonai; and Adonai counted it as justice" (15:6). It is on this that Paul will hang the thread of his argument.

To get a sense of what is happening here, I have used "relied on" instead of either "believed" or "was faithful to." I do this in order to point to a mutual "crediting" that seems to be at work here. Abraham credits the divine promise, and God credits Abraham as being or becoming just. In both cases, we have a way of conjoining future with present, as suggested by the economic term "credit." To say that Abraham credits the divine promise is to say that he regards it as entailing a future accomplishment. A bank that gives credit to a firm advances a sum of money with the expectation that it will be repaid. "To believe" (in Latin, *credere*) in this case may have a similar structure. Abraham anticipates the faithfulness of God with respect to the divine promise. God anticipates the faithfulness of Abraham as leading to or as containing, in principle, justice. There is a certain mutual crediting or counting that seems to be at work. Perhaps it is a further instance of faithfulness producing faithfulness; here the faithfulness of God (as credited or given credence by Abraham) producing the faithfulness of Abraham (as credited, counted, or given credence with respect to justice by God). We will see if this works to clarify Paul's argument.

We now have another fateful division: **But to one who is working [*ergon*] the reward is not counted as a favor but as a debt** [what is owed]; **but to the one who isn't working, but relying on** [adhering to, loyal to] **the one who causes the impious to be or become just, his faithfulness is counted as** [or toward] **justice.** Here Paul opposes what may seem to be two sorts of economies: one of favor and one of debt. If Abraham is doing works of the law, then his being counted as just or credited with justice would not be a favor or generosity (*charis*) but the payment of a debt. That is, God would owe it to Abraham to count him as just. There would be no credit involved, no relying upon the other, no "grace." But Abraham is not yet complying with a divine command but with a divine promise—a promise here identified as one who is impious being made just, that is, one who exists outside (prior to) any particular law that would lay out a way to be "pious."

So also David speaks of the blessedness [*makarismon*] of the one to whom God credits justice without works. The citation from Psalm 32:1–2 indicates the happiness of one who is not accused of injustice. It appears as a counterpart to the citations from Psalm 3:10–18, which had the form of a series of accusations. It may therefore relate to something like an early synagogue Yom Kippur liturgy, as Taubes has also suggested (28–38).

In the citation from the Psalm we find the only occurrence in Pauline literature of the standard term for forgiveness, *aphethaisan*. This is quite remarkable, in that from the time of Luther it has been customary to suppose that forgiveness of sins is what Pauline theology is all about. This was no doubt influenced by the penitential piety of the Middle Ages, a piety that enters into a sort of crisis to the extent to which God is represented as angry, wrathful, and vengeful and thus as one from whom some shelter (in penance, for example) must be sought. In Luther's time, the supposition that God was filled with rage could seem self-evident. How else explain the descent of Luther's beloved church into arrogance and avarice? How else explain the wholesale and gruesome death that had swept over Europe as the plague? It is perhaps understandable that Luther, an assiduous reader of the Psalms, fixed upon this phrase that Paul cited from the Psalms as the key to understanding Romans.

Instead of forgiveness, the term that Paul characteristically uses is derivative of *charis* and is properly translated as having to do with a welcome extended to the other without preconditions. In what we have already read, this welcome without preconditions would be suggestive of the divine aim of making the impious become just. This theme will return, but first we must follow Paul's immediate line of thought, which is determined by the subversion of the binary of circumcised/uncircumcised.

Is this happiness for the circumcision or also the uncircumcision? We say that faithfulness was credited to Abraham as justice. How then was it counted? As being [of the] **circumcision or of the uncircumcision? Not in circumcision but in uncircumcision. And he received a sign, circumcision, as a seal of the justice of his faithfulness while in uncircumcision so that he**

would be the father of all the faithful in uncircumcision. And he is a father to the ones who are not only of the circumcision but who also follow the path of the uncircumcised faithfulness of our father Abraham.

Thus, Abraham, who first seemed to be the patriarch of the Judeans, is now the father of the non-Judeans, the gentiles or pagans—that is, of those nations outside the law whose faithfulness is (counted as or credited toward) their justice. The opposition circumcision/uncircumcision, which also stands in for the opposition Judean/gentile, is thus subverted in advance in the example of Abraham. At the same time Abraham is the father of the circumcised who imitate his uncircumcised faithfulness.

Nevertheless, I think it is going too far if certain formulations of Alain Badiou seem to make Paul the father of a type of universalism that simply ignores the distinction between Judean and gentile. Agamben is, I think, right in his critique when he writes: "No universal man, no Christian can be found in the depths of the Jew or the Greek" (*Time* 52). Indeed, Agamben can maintain that "it makes no sense to speak of universalism with regard to Paul, at least when the universal is thought of as a principle above cuts and divisions, and the individual as the ultimate limit of each division" (53). Rather, Paul is showing that this distinction is by no means absolute or finally determinative. It is not abrogated but rather, for certain purposes, suspended. Or, perhaps as Badiou intended, this and other identities (male/female, slave/free, etc.) become specific sites "capable of welcoming the truth that traverses them" (*Saint Paul* 106).

We should note that, for Paul, circumcision in the case of Abraham is not a substitute for faithfulness or a work that merits being found to be just; it is a sign or seal that follows the beginning of faithfulness that it signifies. In Christian terms we would say that baptism is not a cultic act that makes one right with God but is a sign of a preexisting, if imperfect, faithfulness. Thus, for example, Karl Barth was forced to conclude that baptism should be understood not as preceding faith(fulness), as in infant baptism, but as sealing an already exhibited faithfulness. It is this nonreligious faithfulness that Paul supposes counts toward or produces justice.

The promise to Abraham or his seed that they would inherit the world [kosmos] did not come through the law but through the justice of faithfulness.

This suggests that the promise is not a reward for compliance with certain obligations (being circumcised here, or obeying commandments generally) but is instead related to faithfulness as justice. Here we may be uncertain about how this works. Is the promise something that precedes human faithfulness or something that comes after? And if it comes after, how is it not a reward or payment? Or is it rather that the promise is predicated upon the faithfulness of the one who promises, which then engenders human faithfulness rooted in the credit extended to the one who promises? This will have to be clarified.

If those of the law are heirs [of the world], **then faithfulness has been emptied and the promise destroyed. For the law works wrath, and where there is no law neither is there violation.**

According to Paul, law does not produce loyalty but only works that earn a payment. Somehow only promise evokes faithfulness. And promise is so contrary to law or commandment that law destroys promise so leaves faith(fulness) without content. What is being established is a tight connection between promise and faithfulness that contrasts with law in its relation to works or violation.

The law may be correlated, then, with obeying (work) or disobeying (violation). And the penalty for violation (wrath) serves as the motive for obeying. In that sense obeying (working) or disobeying (violating) depends on wrath. Wrath is the hidden (or not so hidden) meaning of law. It is the "or else" that makes law to be law. As Kant recognized, a law without force is not law; it does not have the force of law (*Metaphysics of Morals* 6.231, 331–337). Derrida cites Kant's position in his discussion in "The Force of Law" as one of the factors that will distinguish law from justice (233). Derrida, who was a lifelong advocate for the abolition of the death penalty, suggests that the elimination of the death penalty means the elimination of the condition of possibility of criminal law (Derrida and Roudinesco 142).

Once again Paul is pointing to a different foundation for justice, one that does not have the "or else" character of law, one whose meaning is not wrath. It is **therefore of faithfulness in order to be of generosity, so that the promise shall be firm to all the seed, not to those of the law only but also those of the faithfulness of Abraham who is the father of all of us.** That which seems to contrast with wrath in this case is "generosity." If we had to line this argument up at this point, we would say that generosity takes the place of wrath as promise takes the place of law (and faithfulness will take the place of "working"). That is, generosity is that which "stands behind" or establishes promise, just as wrath stands behind or establishes law.

Perhaps now is the time to get a bit more clarity about the character of this generosity or favor: **before the God he credited: the one who enlivens the dead and calls the not being into being**. If there is a name for God here, that name would be "the impossible." The dead one does not have the possibility of life but rather represents the extinguishing of that possibility. The not being is not the possibility of being but its absence or impossibility. Yet the name of God is not an inert impossibility (death, non-being) but the overcoming of impossibility. It is an active or efficacious impossibility, or what Barth (and also Derrida) might call an impossible possibility.

Favor, therefore, has the character of that which overcomes its own impossibility. It is the same sort of thing that Derrida called the gift, or hospitality, or forgiveness. Thus, Derrida can say of the gift (as he will also say, "in the Christian sense") that "it is through the experience of the impossibility [of the gift as such] that its possibility is possible as impossible" (*God, the Gift, and Postmodernism* 60). This is extended to include the many themes of his philosophical concern—event, forgiveness, friendship, the promise, even death as "the possibility of the impossible, the impossibility of the possible" (*Negotiations* 359). Speaking of grace, Barth says that it is "the unobservable truth of men, it is their impossibility, which constitutes the very possibility of their acting or not acting (*Romans* 215). Similarly, he writes concerning spirit: "What is intangible and impossible . . . becomes concrete and possible" (274). While the formulations of Barth and Derrida are importantly different, the one maintaining a sort of transcendence, the other a sort of immanence, there is at the same time a remarkable affinity.

The character of faithfulness, the faithfulness that is related to justice, is that it is grounded in the groundlessness of impossibility. The concrete signifier of this relation of faithfulness to impossibility is precisely the impossible promise to Abraham (and Sarah): **Who beyond hope was faithful to hope**. It is one thing to hope when there is possibility (here we might speak of a more or less measured sort of optimism) but quite another to hope when there is no possibility, when what is hoped for is impossible (for example, the resurrection of the dead). The ambivalence of "hope" is what Paul is underlining here. On the one hand, it may designate a relation to that which is possible (whether likely or not); on the other hand, it may be used to designate a relation to that which is impossible, that which contravenes the way things are.

Paul calls the object of this hope promise, and in this case of Abraham this concretely means the promise **that he should become the father of many nations**. How is this impossible? **Not weakening in faith as he considered his own body, which was as good as dead because he was about one hundred years old or when he considered the death of the womb of Sarah.** Now this is certainly not without a bit of humor. Abraham's age-induced impotence (impossibility) and Sarah's procreative incapacity are fully taken into account yet do not debilitate Abraham's crediting of the promise. Moreover, in both cases the figure that Paul uses to name this impossibility is precisely "death": Abraham's dead body/ penis, Sarah's dead womb. Why death? Why life from death as the concrete meaning of fundamental impossibility? The impossibility that is the object of promise and so of a defiant hope that is at the root of faithfulness? We shall see.

He did not decide [or judge] **against the promise of God but was empowered by faithfulness, giving glory to God and being persuaded that God is able to do what God had promised.** Faithfulness here is the name of relying upon the reliability of the divine promise. It is a divine promise because it is, strictly speaking, impossible. The signature of the divine is the impossible. To put it another way: What is possible is immanent; what is impossible is transcendent. Thus, Abraham counts or takes into account not his own weakness but the promise of that which is immanently impossible. Relying empowers one to hold fast to the impossible; holding fast to the impossible is what names faithfulness. Already here we catch sight of how this relying on the impossible that is called faithfulness may be related to justice, for we recall that the origin of injustice was identified earlier as not glorifying God as God (Romans 1:21, 1:28).

That is why it was counted to him as justice, for relying upon and glorifying God is precisely the root of justice. We may note here that injustice may come to be "justified" through supposing that justice is "impossible." It is the (immanent) incapacity for justice rather than the promise of justice that "counts" or is counted. It is this accounting that makes it easy to excuse injustice or to acquiescence in injustice. Nobody is perfect, we say. Don't underestimate original sin, the Christian realist says. And this produces a politics of accommodation—to injustice. On the other hand, entrusting oneself to the promise of that which is or seems to be impossible (justice, for example) is what produces a becoming just.

But it was not only on his account [or for his sake] **that it was counted** [toward justice] **but for ours also.** This odd story of Abraham concerns those who are outside the law, those who are without the law: **It will be counted to us who are faithful to the one who raised Joshua our leader from the dead, who was delivered over though our violation and was raised with a view to making us just.** It was in order to make the tie to the resurrection of our dead leader that Paul had spoken of the dead bodies of Abraham and Sarah. It is the resurrection of the one who had been executed by imperial power that is the concrete impossibility that serves as the promise to which Paul supposes his readers are or seek to be faithful.

It is important that we note that being made just here is on the order of a resurrection from among the dead, or a coming into being of that which is not. Paul is not referring to a "nominal" justice any more than he is referring to an "imaginary" resurrection. That is, in the case of creation, or resurrection, or justification, what is at stake is a real, an efficacious, transformation. For our purposes what is important to underline is that Paul is not interested here in a merely "forensic" being made just, a mere empty pronouncement of innocence or anything of the kind. Just as he supposes that Isaac was really born of Abraham and Sarah, or that Joshua the leader was actually raised from the dead, so also he supposes that his readers become truly and not merely nominally just.

Moreover, for Paul there is something of a causal connection between the resurrection of the executed leader and our becoming just. The resurrection of Joshua is not a brute fact but something like a provocation to justice, a message that will produce justice as its intended effect. From what we have seen thus far this might mean that the message concerning the resurrection is on the order of a promise, adherence to which or faithfulness to which will produce justice. This will be clarified as the argument progresses.

Here we may ponder what it means to say that this leader was delivered over on account of "our violations." Whose violations, and violations of what "law"? Here I think we can make headway if we recall that for Paul, whether as Judeans or as gentiles (nations), we are said to be inextricably implicated in injustice. The unjust socialities that go by these names (Judeans, gentiles) are implicated in the violation of God, in the execution of God's own messiah. Joshua is put to death through our violence, the violence of the laws that govern our societies, whether Judean or gentile (and we recall that Paul is a Judean writing to gentiles).

The messianic event, then, is one that most fundamentally concerns the problem of unjust (and thus violent) social totalities and their (impossible) transformation into just socialities. Hence, injustice comes to a head in the putting to death of the messiah, while the resurrection of Joshua who had been (legally) executed is aimed at the establishment of justice, bringing justice into being, for us and for all. The resurrection of one who is put to death by the (or our) authorities is not a merely private or religious matter as we currently conceive these things. It is an inescapably political event, one that has everything to do with justice, a justice that is outside the law—a messianic justice.

7. Messianic Justice (4:25–5:11)

With the concluding statement of Romans 4, Paul turns away from the discussion of Abrahamic justice and toward the discussion of messianic justice. The discussion of Abraham has served several interconnected purposes. It has identified a point of contact between the circumcision and the uncircumcision, thereby further destabilizing the distinction between Judeans and gentiles, although without abrogating it. It has identified a point "before" the law for the discussion of justice, thereby pointing to the possibility of justice outside or apart from the law. It has tied together themes of faithfulness, promise, and generosity and set them in opposition to works, law, and wrath. And it has provided a bridge to the resurrection of the executed messiah through reformulating the promise to Abraham as life from a dead body (or actually two: both his and Sarah's). That is quite a lot of work to do in a page or so, so it should not be surprising that there are many questions left unanswered. Recall that the purpose of this letter is not to answer all questions and issues but to give those in Rome good reason to suppose that Paul could be of some service to them in defending their loyalty to the messiah within the heart of the society that had executed him. Although Paul will seek to clarify a number of issues related to this justice of God that he believes is the core meaning of the good news, we should not expect to find all issues resolved.

The last sentence of the previous section serves as a sort of heading for the discussion launched in chapter 5. Accordingly, we will reconnect the phrase to the new discussion: **To us who are loyal to him who raised our leader Joshua from among the dead, who was delivered** [to death] **through** [*dia*] **our crimes, and raised for** [*dia*] **our being made just.** We should note the double sense of the preposition *dia*. It indicates a certain causality; our crimes produce his being handed over, and his resurrection produces our becoming or being made just. But this causality reverses. We begin as the cause and end as the effect. "We" produce the effect of injustice, but his being raised produces the contrary effect: our being made just. Between our injustice and our being made just stands an event: the event of the resurrection of the executed.

In a certain sense we may say that this is the messianic event. The messianic event has in a certain way already taken place. In another sense it is still taking place (being made just) and will continue to take place. The strange co-implication of these tenses will be complicated in what Paul has to say. But this will above all have to do with his conception of the messianic. It is quite possible that as a Pharisee Paul had entertained a messianic hope. But this hope would probably have been entirely future oriented. In that case what would distinguish Paul's current perspective from an earlier one would be the supposition that in some way the messianic event has already taken place or has decisively begun to take place. The messiah is the one who is called here our leader Joshua. The event has already occurred. But Paul is not concerned with this event as an event of the past in and for itself. He is concerned with the way in which "we" (Paul and his readers) are caught up in this messianic event. The past event means the present and future. To put it differently, Paul is not interested in a past messianic event for its own sake, as an object of belief, for example, but with the messianic effects of that event: our becoming just or, even more, the advent of divine justice for the whole of creation (all flesh). The messianic event of the resurrection of the crucified has the character of a promise directed toward all that is mortal, to all flesh.

Therefore since through faithfulness we become just, we have peace with God through our leader Joshua [the] **messiah.** What is aimed at here is "peace" rather than enmity with God. This peace has justice, our becoming just, as its basis. And this justice in turn is based upon or derived from faithfulness or loyalty. And this faithfulness is provoked somehow by the message concerning Joshua messiah—our leader.

Through whom we have had access [by (his?) faithfulness] **to this generosity in which we stand and exult in hope of the shining forth of God.** On account of the messiah we have opened to us the divine favor that gives us a place to stand and to rejoice or exult in divine glory or radiance, or shining forth. The glory of God, wrote Irenaeus, is the human fully alive (*Against Heresies* 4.20.7). Here the glory or radiance or shining forth of God may be thought of as the creation fully permeated with justice and at peace with God. It is doubtful that the phrase "by faith," or as I would prefer, "by faithfulness," is germane here; it seems to be an addition. If I were to appropriate it, I would be inclined to emphasize the faithfulness of the messiah. The point is that access to divine favor comes through the messianic mission/event. It is through this mission/event that divine favor or generosity comes apart from the law.

The reference to "standing" makes possible a turn toward the present effects of the messianic mission, effects that Paul supposes may be readily recognizable to his readers. This present experience bears the marks of the messianic event of the resurrection of the executed.

And not only [exulting in the hope of the glory of God]**, but also exulting in afflictions, knowing that affliction produces patience** [endurance]**, and patience** [produces] **proof** [or character]**, and proof** [or character produces] **hope.**

In his early reflections on Paul in his seminar on the phenomenology of religious experience, Martin Heidegger, soon to be famous for his *Being and Time*, wrote of the "obstinate waiting" that characterized the Christian attitude or comportment as exhibited in Paul's letters to the Thessalonians and

Galatians (79). The obstinacy of the Christian comportment is on display here. The term "afflictions" is an apocalyptic (or messianic) term. It suggests the conflict of eons, of powers, as the new comes into opposition to the old. These afflictions may seem to contradict hope in its ersatz form of a more or less plausible optimism. But when viewed as the sign of the conflict brought about by the opposition of the old to the emergence of the radically new, these afflictions take on a different character. Indeed, by entering into the messianic, one necessarily enters into this distress so that faithfulness is itself an entering into affliction (67). As afflictions, they also become messianic signs pointing to the advent of the radically new. They become afflictions that produce endurance, a certain mental toughness that is not the same as a passive patience. What is in view here is a holding out in the face of terrible danger, a mental toughness that is not cowed by the forces arrayed against the advent of the messianic. In Latin America T-shirts and banners proclaim the saying attributed to Che Guevara: "One must harden oneself, but without ever losing tenderness." Something like that seems to be involved here. This endurance produces the "proof" of a steadfast character that does not waver, much as Abraham was said not to waver in his adherence to the promise in spite of its impossibility when measured against the weakness, the deadness, of his body and that of Sarah.

This unwavering mental and moral toughness, what Heidegger termed "obstinacy" or "obstinate waiting," is here said to produce (or be produced by) hope. A hope that is an evasion of this contradiction, this suffering, and this need for resolute endurance has nothing to do with the hope that is spoken of here. This hope is not a narcotic for the proletariat but is precisely that sort of undaunted determination that makes it possible to hold out against impossible odds.

The very existence of that fierce courage itself produces something like hope. This at least seems to have been the experience of those who called themselves Christians in the first three or four centuries. For it was the fearlessness of Christians in the face of the "afflictions" of persecution that served as the "proof" of the truth of the gospel and thus played an essential role in persuading others to align themselves with that movement of martyrs.

Now we must suppose that this is precisely what is meant by faithfulness. When in the Gospels Jesus/Joshua is recorded as saying, "Your faith has made you well," it is typically in response to a certain obstinacy, a tenacity, that refuses to let "realism" dictate action. Whether in the precipitous action of those who tear off the roof in order to break into Jesus's house for the sake of their paralyzed friend (Mark 2:4–5), or the woman who heedlessly pushes her blood-contaminated body through the crowd (5:34), or the centurion who recklessly seeks out a Jewish sorcerer to save his beloved youth (Matthew 8:10)—all have something of an obstinacy that is heedless of risk. Perhaps it is hope. Alain Badiou, who is committed to find a revolutionary alternative to late modern capitalism, remarks concerning Paul's talk of hope in this passage that it is "the subjectivity of a victorious fidelity, fidelity to fidelity, and not the representation of its future outcome." It is thus enduring fidelity (*Saint Paul* 95).

And hope does not shame us because divine love has been poured in our hearts through holy spirit given to us.

I am not ashamed, Paul had said earlier, **of the gospel**, and those who hold out in reliance upon the divine or messianic promise are also unashamed, undaunted in the face of the power arrayed against them, undaunted by the apparent foolishness of their hope. Somehow this lack of shame is related to the experience of love that comes as a spirited gift in such a way as to reorient the will (heart) of those who are captured by it, liberated by it. We know from other letters of Paul the importance of love in his thought. For the moment we can read this as the unwavering solidarity among the adherents that is itself a sign, even a proof, that their hope is not in vain, that is, their hope for the world in which justice dwells. There will be much more of this later in the letter. For now Paul offers the reader only a glimpse of where he is headed: the idea that somehow the justice that is coming arrives now in the form of love. We have already heard of at least two possible ways of attributing something like love to the divine: the divine patience that forestalls destruction, and the divine generosity that offers a way outside law to constitute justice.

Paul has gestured toward the experience of his readers as participants in the messianic polity, but now he will turn back from this experience shaped by the messianic to the eruption of the messianic itself, an eruption that will carry forward the sense of affliction and thus will serve as an antidote to a rejoicing unrelated to affliction.

Paul moves again to discuss that which grounds the experience to which he has just pointed. In doing so he will emphasize the death of the messiah as exhibiting that faithfulness that will in turn incite our faithfulness and lead to justice—for us and for all. Here we are concerned not with the resurrection of the executed but with the death of the one who will have been raised. The following passage is quite dense. Accordingly, I will first present it in its entirety before reorganizing it more or less thematically.

For while we were still weak, at the right time messiah died for the ungodly. Indeed, rarely will anyone die for a just person—though perhaps for a good person someone might actually dare to die. But God proves God's love for us in that while we still were sinners, messiah died on our account. Much more surely then, now that we have been made just in his blood, will we be saved through him from the wrath. For if while we were enemies, we were reconciled to God through the death of God's son, much more surely, having been reconciled, will we be saved in his life.

This, we said, has to do with us; we who are Paul's readers are implicated in it. Accordingly, the first set of parallels has to do with our condition before—a condition that serves as the ground or, better, groundlessness of the divine act.

When we were weak [6]; impious [6]; yet sinners [8]; while enemies [10]

These forms of incapacity, or we might even say anticapacity, serve to emphasize the utter gratuity of grace, the groundlessness of a "gift" that is thereby to be utterly distinguished from any sort of "reward," payment, or debt. The generosity or grace of God in the messiah is directed toward those who deserve nothing or, rather, who deserve death, toward those social totalities that merit destruction. Here it is not simply a question of resurrection in spite of death but of death (for another) in spite of the absence of whatever might possibly motivate such an act. That this is the direction of Paul's thought is made clear with the observation, **scarcely on behalf of a just man would anyone die; perhaps for a good man someone might dare to die**. If this is a parallel statement, then just and good are basically equivalent. Who would die in the place of a just man? It is rare. But it does sometimes happen.

Derrida, following Heidegger, has pointed out the impossibility of dying for another in the sense that one would substitute one's own death for that of the other in a permanent way. The most that one can do is to hasten one's own death and postpone that of the other. But everyone dies. Everyone dies his or her own death. No one can prevent my dying, not even by dying in my place. As Derrida writes, "I know on absolute grounds and in an absolutely certain manner that I will never deliver the other from his death, from the death that affects his whole being" (*Gift* 43). If this is so, what can be the meaning of the assertions regarding the death of the messiah?

Messiah died for the impious [ungodly]**; messiah dies for us.**

If this death is not to be viewed as a substitute for my own death, then in what way does it address me? How does it "speak" or testify? It may be that this death viewed in relation to the resurrection suggests a similar reversal for us in our existence, or in the existence of the world, or the society within which we live. Paul has said that it is on account of our sins that the messiah died, and I have ventured the interpretation that it is the injustice in which all humanity is implicated that has produced this death. But it seems this is not all Paul wants to say of this death. In some way or other it is also directed toward us as a way of doing or indicating something on our behalf. But what?

We can approach in a somewhat different way. If there is nothing on our side that could motivate the messianic act, Paul does say that there is something on God's part that does motivate a faithfulness or loyalty to the death on the part of the messiah. It is **God's love toward us**. This, and not (pace Anselm) the desire to save God's honor or justice, is the ultimate ground of this death—a death that, because it is outside the law and exposes the violence of the law, will deliver us from the law or, rather, from the condemnation of the law. We are therefore coming closer to understanding what it might mean to speak of a justice that is an "outlaw justice."

The effect of this action is expressed in several ways. First, **we are now made just by his blood**. We have previously heard that we are made just through faithfulness and that this faithfulness is somehow grounded in divine favor. We are now being told that this divine favor is somehow testified to or demonstrated in the death of the messiah. In addition, **we**

were reconciled to God by the death of his son. We should wonder at least about these tenses and what is implied. Reconciliation is what has already happened, and being made just is what is now happening as a consequence. Somehow the demonstration of divine love through the death of his son reconciles us to God. That is, we who were turned away from God are by this event turned toward God. Our bitterness (in Korean one speaks of *han*) toward God has been overcome. To be sure, this is the exact opposite of what we might have expected on the basis of some of what has been said before. We had earlier heard of the wrath of God, which would lead us to suppose that the problem is for God to be reconciled to us. And that is precisely the way classical theories of atonement, at least in the West, have operated. We are somehow delivered from an angry God. Paul will certainly point to deliverance from wrath. But when he speaks of reconciliation, he speaks not of God being reconciled to us but of our being reconciled to God. Thus, somehow the death of the son overcomes our hostility toward God by demonstrating the utter limitlessness of divine love. This reconciliation then serves to make possible our becoming just. If we are or have been reconciled to God, then we are already being made just. Presumably we are being made just because this reconciliation is awakening the faithfulness that is counted as or toward justice.

And this past reconciliation and present being made or becoming just is to be coordinated with effects that are yet to be anticipated: **Much more saved from the wrath.** Notice that Paul does not say "wrath of God," as the translators propose, but simply, absolutely, "wrath." I do not think that the nonattribution of wrath to God is accidental. Wrath has now become an impersonal force severed from God. How? Through the death of the messiah or, rather, on account of the love that now appears instead of wrath, as that which is truly "of God." This will be further clarified in chapter 8. For now we could speculate that wrath signifies utter destruction, a destruction that falls upon injustice. God has disowned this wrath in order to produce precisely that justice that will save from destruction. It will become clear that this salvation from the utter destruction that injustice brings upon itself is comprehensive in scope, applying not only to a few but to all.

Much more [as reconciled and made just] **will we be saved by his life.** It is life from death that opens up a comprehensive "salvation." Here it is the resurrection of the executed messiah that points toward life also for us. We shall soon learn just how comprehensive is such a promise or reality of salvation, of life and wholeness.

Not only so, but we also rejoice [exult] **in God through our leader Joshua messiah, through whom we have now received the reconciliation.** Thus, it appears that we have returned to where we set out in this discussion. We began with **"we have peace with God"** (5:1), **"we exult in hope"** (5:2), and **"we exult in tribulation"** (5:3). The direction of the argument has been to locate this exulting in the midst of tribulation and to somehow ground it in the death of the messiah. Paul has still not mentioned the term that seemed so central to his proclamation in 1 Corinthians: "the cross." It would seem that the necessity of avoiding the potentially incendiary political or military execution of the messiah when writing to those in the capital of the empire in whose name this had been done helps explain the odd circumlocutions that seem to be at work in Paul's rhetoric. Perhaps this is something he can take for granted that his readers (or the faithful among them) will have understood. Perhaps he supposes that in this situation it would be best to explain in person. But it does seem to me that the cross or the message concerning the crucified messiah is a sort of invisible sun around which the planets of his discourse turn.

Paul has spoken here of exulting or, as it is sometimes translated, rejoicing. He has in mind a certain irrational exuberance in the community rather than a grim "holding on." It is not only an obstinate waiting (as Heidegger thought) that characterizes the comportment of the messianic movement but precisely an exuberance that does not seem warranted by the facts of life in the situation of suffering or affliction. In Philippians Paul had even connected the prospect of his own suffering and death with rejoicing. He wrote: "I rejoice and rejoice together with you and in the same way also you rejoice and rejoice together with me" (2:17–18). Why then this exuberance, this exulting? We will have to wait a bit for Paul's explanation.

8. How Much More: The Adamic and the Messianic (5:12–21)

In Galatians, Paul had attempted to relate the messiah to Abraham as the fulfillment of the promise of seed. In Romans he has abandoned that strategy, settling for a partial analogy instead between our messianic faith and the faith of Abraham. But the emphasis on death and life moves the argument to a more fundamental level.

We saw that Abraham was anterior to the distinction between the Judean and the nations and is thus a comprehensive figure. But that really only applies to a particular issue (with which Paul is not yet finished): the relative advantage of Judean and gentile. We are now going to a much more basic dimension for which the name is Adam: earthling.

The name of Adam is used to name humanity as such. And it will be contrasted with another name, which also will be used to rename (or as Irenaeus will say, "re-head" or recapitulate) humanity as such. What is at stake is humanity from two contrasting perspectives, but it is still the "same" humanity. This humanity is what Marx, following Feuerbach, often termed "species being." Perhaps the most difficult concept, from a modern perspective, that Paul employs is precisely this notion of humanity as a unitary entity. Modern individualism finds it hard enough to conceive of sociohistorical totalities like Judean or pagan. Already here it is necessary to think of human beings as determined by their embeddedness in national and social totalities in such a way that each is infected by the corruption of the society of which they (or, rather, we) are a part. All the more difficult is the idea that humanity may be thought of as a single entity—but that is precisely what Paul invites us to think.

Paul had used this comparison and contrast before: "For since death came through a human being, the resurrection of the dead has also come through a human being; for as all die in Adam, so all will be made alive in messiah" (1 Corinthians 15:21–22). The insistence that "one" entails "all," whether for ill (death) or good (be made alive), is utterly critical for the perspective being expressed here. Viewed in this way, any individual is but a fragment of the totality named as Adamic or messianic. These fundamental ways of describing or naming the whole of humanity have fundamental political consequences. The consequences are political because they are determined by their relation to the quintessentially political question of justice.

In the previous segment of the argument Paul had emphasized the death of the messiah. Now it will become evident that this emphasis is related to the fate of Adamic humanity as determined by death.

Therefore, as sin entered the world through one human, and death through sin, so death spread to all humans, in as much as all sinned.

Paul does not give us anything like a doctrine of original sin but of universal sin. While death enters the world through one human, it is the case that all sin. In fact, the entry of sin is such that all sinned, and the effect is that all die. This may also be reversible: death or the fear of death makes us sin, makes us seek to preserve our life, at the expense of the other. Paul will return to this connection later, but it may be helpful to suggest how this might be understood in accordance with the Genesis mythos that Paul is using here as a tool to think with.

The immediate aftermath of the sin of the earthling is blame: shifting guilt, identifying someone else as worthy of condemnation and so of death, sacrificing the other for my own self-preservation. Hence Adam blames Eve, Eve blames the serpent, and indeed both implicitly blame God (who made Eve for Adam, or placed the serpent in the garden made for Adam and Eve).

God had warned Adam about death as the consequence of sin. Of course, neither Adam nor Eve actually dies as an immediate consequence of sin. Death may, however, be implicit already in the blame shifting that offers the other up to death in order to deflect blame (and death) from oneself. Actual death comes into the story, however, not as an act of God but as an all too human act. It is fratricide, the murder of Abel by Cain, a murder that is motivated by envy and enmity. Thus, death comes precisely as murder. Violence enters the sphere of history. It becomes universal. History is the history of violence and violation, of extermination and domination. And in whatever form, it is always fratricide.

Note that here death is not "biological" so much as it is "historical." Most death is historical still. Most people die because of the implicit violence of structures, whether political or economic. Here we may think of the millions who die every year of impoverishment. Death by neglect or as collateral damage of our avarice or indifference is still fratricide. (In legal terms it may be called negligent homicide.) The cycle of violence and counterviolence becomes so powerful that in the Noah tale, the divine finds the world filled with violence. So grave is the violence that God is said to repent of having made the earth. The earth then is to be unmade through a flood that cleanses earth of all life (except for the remnant preserved through Noah). This is followed by a further repentance in that God then promises not to unmake the world again.

This excursion into the mythos inscribed in Genesis (or the book of beginnings) may help us see how sin as violation and death as violence are connected in what Paul is dealing with here. For our purposes it may be that the myth has a somewhat different status than it did for Paul. It offers a way of thinking the universal. This was the function of myth for Plato (think of the myth of the cave, or of the transmigration of souls, among others). Paul does not exactly invent the myths he employs: they are "at hand" in the stories of his people. Paul does not simply repeat them as literal truths, however. His use of them is remarkably flexible after all. But he does use them to think with, to think the universal.

If we were to allow ourselves to be led by Paul in this direction, we would need to underscore the connection between sin and violence. For sin is not simply the violation of a statute; it is the violation of the other, and so is violence. Indeed, because this is so, Paul will be able to conclude that the law is fulfilled not by compliance with statutes but by love of the neighbor (which does no wrong to or does not violate the neighbor). This will be the content of a justice that is "outlaw justice" even if in important respects it consummates the law. But we have quite a way to go in the argument before this will become evident.

We may ask in what sense do "all sin"? Certainly not all are Cain. Nor do all do what it was that Adam did (as Paul is about to say). But recall that we are all part of social orders stained by blood, awash in the memory of blood that cries from the earth to the heavens. There is no social order, no nation-state that is not founded on "crimes against humanity" (Derrida, *Negotiations* 383). In this sense we are all the offspring not only of Adam but also of Cain.

Paul introduces a digression here, which seems to be misplaced save that it anticipates something that will be said later about sin and law: **Sin was in the world before the law, but where there is no law, sin is not measured.** This remark will be expanded later. For now we may say that violence or injustice is present in the world even without law. Law provides a way of measuring sin or, as he said earlier, of knowing it. Normally translations say that sin is "not counted," but this translation, while not incorrect in itself, may give the erroneous impression in English that Paul is saying that it doesn't count in the sense of not mattering. That is not his point at all. There is sin, but there is no standard against which it may be measured.

Yet death reigned from Adam to Moses, governing even those who did not sin comparably to Adam who was a type of the coming one. Paul has recognized that there are those who are, in important respects just, in compliance with the law, both those who adhere to the letter of Judean law (himself, for example) and also just gentiles. Thus, it is not the case that all are guilty of Adam's sin (as notions of original sin have typically maintained) but that all are implicated in the universal history of violation and of violence.

Adam to Moses may here indicate the entrance of the law, which measures sin. But violence and violation and death rule even before the law. And it is to put an end to this that there is law, or, if not an end, then at least a limit. This is the political theory of the state that Hobbes will formulate, in which he is followed by Kant. But does law work that way? Does it limit violence as philosophers of the political have regularly maintained? We shall see.

But not like the offense is the gift [*charisma*]. With this we are brought to the theme of the gift that has been lurking in the text. Already at the conclusion to the indictment demonstrating that all peoples are condemned by their own injustice—whether the nations by what they recognize as deserving of death, or the Judeans by their own divine law—Paul had signaled the direction in which he wanted his thought to move: **being made just freely** [*dorean*] **by his generosity** [*chariti*] **through the redemption in messiah Joshua** (3:24). Moreover, the nature of gift has been contrasted already with "wages": **to one who works the reward is not counted as gift** [*charin*] **but as debt** (4:5). And faith or faithfulness has been linked to gift (4:16). **That is why it depends on faithfulness so that gift may undergird the promise.** Thus, gift establishes the character of the promise that incites or awakens loyalty.

The discussion of Abraham had emphasized the relation of promise and loyalty. The discussion up to now in this section has shifted the ground somewhat to talk of death as the basis of what is promised and thus brings us back to gift as that which undergirds the promise. This again, like the shift to Adam and to life and death, shows that we are moving to a more basic consideration. A shorthand version is that Paul is beginning to show that gift is the basis of a justice that is outside the law. The discussion of trespass or violation has linked it to death; what is now to be seen is how the gift or unconditional generosity bears upon life or produces life (without forgetting that justice is necessary to life).

For if, by the offense [violation] **of one, the many died, much more the generosity** [*charis*] **of God and the gift** [*dorea*] **in favor of the one human Joshua messiah abounded to the many.**

Here and throughout this discussion, Paul brings together *charis* and *dorea*, favor or generosity and gift, as that which characterizes the advent of the messianic act of God in and through Joshua messiah. These terms are brought together in such a way as to seem virtually interchangeable. That gift should be related to the character of justice is something that Derrida has seen, as I have attempted to show in my *Thinking Derrida / Reading Paul*. In *Specters of Marx*, Derrida notes "the necessity and force of thinking justice on the basis of gift" (27). Although in this and related discussions Derrida does not make direct reference to Paul, his perspective almost exactly echoes the structure of Paul's argument. Moreover, Derrida recognizes that excess or superabundance is central to the idea of gift insofar as it must exceed the economy of exchange. The gift he says "is excessive in advance" (*Gift* 38). Thus, it may be no accident that the present passage in Romans is punctuated by "much more" (5:15, 17, 20) whenever Paul has the gift, grace, or divine generosity in view. I am inclined to understand *charis* as generosity, in part to overcome the narrowly religious notion that grace has become. But it is important to note the danger that generosity may be trivialized as a sort of "charity." For this reason the reflections of Derrida on gift as the "impossible" can be of so much help to us in reading Paul— the Paul for whom gift or generosity is linked to a hyperabounding marked here as "how much more." We should note that "the many" here designates those affected by sin as well as those affected by the gift of radical generosity. The "many" are in each case comprehensive. The difference between them is expressed in the "how much more" that refers to the gift and to those comprehended by this gratuitous generosity. There is no possibility, I think, of distinguishing the "many" of this phrase from the "all" that precedes and follows it. However inconvenient it may be for certain dogmatic purposes, Paul's thought here is unrelentingly "universal" in scope. At the end of the second century CE this was recognized, albeit in distinctive ways, by both Irenaeus and Origen. But in the fourth century it was Gregory of Nyssa who, influenced by Origen but without the latter's speculative flights, most persuasively maintained the universal scope of salvation, going so far as to maintain that divine redemption would also benefit "the adversary," a reference to Satan (chap. 26).

Paul is not maintaining that these two ways of characterizing the human are equally valid. The one on which he places the stress is the one based on gift or generosity. If violation, violence, and death are valid as comprehensive designations of the human, then divine generosity and gift are "much more" so.

The dissimilarity is emphasized: **the gift** [*doraima*] **isn't like** [that which happens] **through one sinning.** We are aiming at the "how much more," I think: for **the judgment from one is condemnation, but the free gift** [*charisma*] [in relation to many offenses leads to] **making just**. This passage seems rather dense, and many words have to be supplied. The disjunction is first that of condemnation, on the one hand, and making just, on the other. The alternative to condemnation is becoming or being made just. The ground of condemnation is the one sinning (Adam), the effects of which radiate out to encompass all or the many. The effect is "sin" or violence that carries condemnation (death). But if the ground of condemnation is violation, what is the ground of gift? Precisely what we have seen in the discussion of the death of messiah: sin. But now, not one but many. This is the (anti)ground, the groundless ground of the gift. The gift then is not because of, but in spite of, not *grund* but *abgrund*, the abyss (our helplessness, enmity, impiety, etc.). It is because the ground is the antiground of many, indeed, innumerable violations that the gift is precisely gift (and not payment, not what is owed).

But the result of the free gift or generosity, Paul insists, is justice; that is, the result of gift is that the human or humanity is made or enabled to be just. Thus, gift leads to justice and so is the basis of justice. It is as gift that this basis is outside the law. But as Paul will continue to insist, the goal remains justice. However, this justice has in the meantime become all-inclusive. It applies not to merely a few or some, not to this or that particular *polis* or nation, but to all. That is the point of the relation between the Adamic and the messianic.

For if by the offense of one death ruled through that one, how much more through the abundance of the generosity and of the gift of justice received will life rule through the one Joshua messiah. What rules over or governs Adamic humanity is precisely death. But even more certain than the fact that death rules all humanity considered as Adamic is the fact that the life that is the result of the justice produced through gift will rule over all, considered now as encompassed within the messianic. In his militant Marxist appropriation of Paul, Alain Badiou notes that "there is a fundamental link between universalism and charisma, between the One's universal power of address, and the absolute gratuitousness of militantism" (*Saint Paul* 77). This is connected to *dorean*, or gift, in which Badiou notes, "There is for Paul an essential link between the 'for all' of the universal and the 'without cause'" (77). Thus, Badiou notices that the groundlessness of grace, gratuity, or gift is indissolubly connected to a "for all"—a universality—that in his view is the necessary condition for the truth of any political proposal.

The structure of Paul's proposal appears to be as follows:

The offense > condemnation > death [for all]

[Excess] gift > justice > life [for all]

The reception of the gift appears to designate a process. As the gift is received (as gift), the resultant justice also spreads—so life spreads instead of death. Although Paul's phrasing is somewhat convoluted, the drift seems fairly clear. The gift is effective precisely insofar as it is received. There is no *ex opera operato* in the medieval sacramental sense. The gift must be recognized as gift. Reception is not a condition of the gift being given but rather of its efficacy. The gift itself has no prior condition and in this sense has no cause. It is groundless, as we have seen. For Paul this efficacy is unrestricted in principle. Indeed, if his claim is to be substantiated that this gift will produce justice for and in all, then he must suppose that all will receive the gift, will recognize it for what it is, and will respond accordingly. Perhaps this is the importance of messianic proclamation after all. For the proclamation has the burden of announcing the gift, so making possible its glad reception on the part of "the many."

Paul will return later to the relation between speaking and hearing as this relates to the in-breaking of justice, and thus of salvation, or wholeness, or flourishing.

Who is the many? **So therefore as through one offense** [or the offense of one there comes to be] **condemnation for all humans, so also through one just act to all humanity** [there comes to be] **justice making for life.** What is added first is the clarification that "many" means "all." But we are also moving toward identifying a just or faithful act that produces justice and therefore life for all. Just as by the disobedience of one human the many were constituted sinners, so through the obedience of the one the many will be constituted just. Again, with respect to Adamic humanity, the many really become unjust (sinners); with respect to messianic humanity, the many really become just. In both cases, this happens through one (Adam/messiah), and in both cases this happens through an act. Thus, if it makes sense to suppose that violation and violence spread in such a way that Adam is the name of humanity, so then justice spreads through many from one act of faithfulness. Justice or injustice has to do here not with being named but with being constituted. If the "before" is sin, the "after" is justice, not sin that remains in place and is merely *called* justice.

But the act of the second one is called **obedience**. And we recall that Paul has spoken of the obedience of faith (1:5) and of the faithfulness of the messiah (1:17, 3:22, 26). Obedience is that which corresponds to the divine will, promise, and claim. What is Paul thinking about here? What is the obedience of the messiah? Paul continues to be elusive, but it seems plausible to suppose that it has to do with what leads to the messiah's execution, because he is executed precisely for his loyalty, one that is outside and even against the law. The messiah is thus characterized by a faithfulness and a justice that is outside the law, a faithfulness that makes him an outlaw with respect to the law of the Judeans and of the Romans. There are certain forces that make Paul circumspect here. He elsewhere tells us that the content of his oral proclamation is the cross (1 Corinthians 1:23, 2:2; Galatians 3:1), but he never tells his readers what precisely he says about this. Most important here is that the cross may be understood in terms of a certain obedience. For instance, in Philippians he had written of being obedient even to the cross (2:8). This obedient (to

God) disobedience (to the law) is an act or comportment that corresponds to justice, as a loyalty or faithfulness beyond and against the law, and therefore as outlaw justice. And somehow this is the gift of the messianic, so the gift of God (always recalling that "God" may be understood as the impossible, as I earlier suggested).

Law came in order that the offense might abound; but where sin abounded, grace hyperabounded so that as sin ruled through death, so also grace might rule through justice to life everlasting through Joshua messiah our leader. Abounding versus hyperabounding. Excess is the mark of gift or grace again. The law somehow makes injustice abound (Paul will soon try to explain how this is so), but the gift or generosity makes justice abound—even hyperabound—an abundance that is or leads to undiminished, unlimited, overflowing life. Violence begets violence, propagates, and multiplies this death. But gift begets justice; it too propagates, multiplies, not as the law somehow aids the propagation of violence that it seeks to curtail but as hyperabounding, producing not more and more death but limitless life.

Is this plausible? Is it possible? Certainly where gift is understood as simply forgiving, or as a declaration of justice where none existed or was required, it has seemed to lead not to justice but to injustice, not to life but to death. Is it not the case that the assurance that we can be and are forgiven on the basis of something like belief serves as the very incitement of the hyperabounding of sin, of violation, of violence? How else explain the history of Christianity as the history of atrocity, of crusade and Inquisition, of hatred of the other, of enslavement and of the Holocaust, of colonialism and conquest, of death squads and torture chambers? Is Paul wrong? Or has he been terribly misunderstood? If the result of traditional interpretations of Paul is that injustice and death abound all the more on account of a certain gospel, or (mis)understanding of the gospel, then the work of reinterpretation is indeed urgent.

But whether in the end we agree with Paul, it is important to catch sight of the ambition of the project that is being indicated here. He is concerned with nothing less than the reign of life that overturns the reign or rule of death. And this means he is concerned with the advent of a universal justice. His claim is that universal justice comes not through the law, not through the imposition of a better or universal law, but from gift that produces faithfulness and justice. Justice is born not of the force of law but of a fathomless generosity, an unconditional welcome. Without justice thus engendered, humanity is fated to a death spiral that is total in its effects. Perhaps today we can glimpse at least the plausibility of the suicide of humanity in a cycle of violence. We may also have some perplexity about how that is to be reversed so that human and planetary flourishing may be hoped for. In that case we have an interest in considering the project that Paul is sketching in these pages.

Third Phase A

BEFORE AND AFTER (6:1–7:6)

We have raised the question of whether a certain Pauline theology (or perhaps misreading of Paul) has not produced the hoped-for justice but instead contributed to a death spiral of injustice, violence, and death. This question is not extraneous to Paul's own project. Already before he had turned to a discussion of the Abrahamic foundation for a justice outside the law and before his contrasting of Adamic and messianic humanity, Paul himself had raised the question, **And why not do evil that good may come?** (3:8). He notes that this is a (mis)characterization of the messianic message to which he seeks to give expression: **as some people slanderously charge us with saying**. And he had then replied, **Their condemnation is just.** Certainly one way of reading this would be that if indeed this had been Paul's position, then these (imaginary?) interlocutors would be right to condemn his position.

In the material that now lies before us, Paul will seek to answer this charge, or to make clear that any such notion requires a fatal misunderstanding of the messianic reality into which he and his readers are being incorporated. He begins this section with a reprise of the question that he had indicated was to be taken with utmost seriousness in chapter 3: **Then what should we say? Are we to continue in sin so that grace/favor may abound? Absolutely not** (6:1). And he will return to a version of the same question a bit later: **What then, are we to sin because we are not under the law but under grace? Absolutely not** (6:15).

By taking these questions (or this one question in several forms) with complete seriousness, Paul shows that the truth of the messianic message depends upon its awakening the effective capacity to be or become just. The transformation of Adamic humanity into a messianic humanity is not a nominal change, a change of names, nor does it designate a change in religious affiliation. This transformation depends on whether the messianic has in fact begun to occur or not. If justice is not the result, then the messianic has not really begun to happen or the readers have not yet entered into that reality.

To make this clear, Paul will propose a series of three (or four) partial analogies through which he seeks to make evident that we are being drawn into a messianic reality that effects a radical transformation in the comportment of those who are something like the vanguard of this new humanity. The analogies he offers point to fundamental changes in status: from death to life after death (6:2–11), a transitional analogy of tools or weapons (6:12–14), which prepares the way for the analogy of a transfer of ownership for slaves (6:16–22) and the freedom of becoming a widow (7:1–6). These analogies point to a radical disruption in the life of those who are being transferred from the Adamic to the messianic, a transfer so radical that it signals a break from the old order of injustice to the new order of justice (outside or beyond the law).

These partial analogies will point the way to his major analogy of the transition from death to life that occupies chapters 7 and 8.

9. Living After Dying (6:2–11)

The first analogy is dependent upon the language that has dominated the discussion of the contrast between the Adamic and the Messianic: the language of death and life. It is actually expressed in two different ways: as a reference to baptismal practice and (more essentially) as a reference to the death and resurrection of the messiah.

How can we who died to sin still live in it? Or don't you know that all we who have been baptized into messiah Joshua were baptized into his death? We were buried with him therefore by baptism into death, so that as [the] **messiah was raised from the dead for the sake of** [on account of] **the shining forth of the father, so also we might walk in newness of life.**

This passage is often read as underscoring the importance of baptism as a cultic or even sacramental act. This would indeed be strange for the same Paul who had argued that baptism was so unimportant for him in his own mission that he could not immediately recall whether he had baptized anyone (1 Corinthians 1:14–16). Here Paul's point has little to do with a cultic act and everything to do with a transformation in the comportment of those who are assimilated into the messianic event. It appears that messianists (much later to call themselves "Christians") did make use of baptism to signify entry into the messianic reality. Paul seizes upon this apparently rather common practice to invest it with ethical rather than cultic meaning. The point is that it should be impossible, unthinkable even, that those who have entered into this messianic reality should in any way continue in sin. Their form of life has been forever and radically changed. If the messianic event means that history has undergone a fundamental transformation, then this must apply as well to those who are incorporated into this event.

It may certainly be true that at least some of the plausibility of Paul's argument for his readers in Rome may have depended upon acquaintance with certain notions of incorporation into the fate of a dying and rising god derived from so-called mystery religions. But Paul's point is not that the believer will somehow be delivered from death but that the one so incorporated has already died so now must live as one who has died, as one for whom death lies not ahead but behind.

The analogy is complex. It requires that we see that if death is connected to sin, then the overcoming of death is at the same time the overcoming of sin, that is, injustice. For this to be plausible, we must recall that the law no longer has a grip on those who have died, for the law has force, the force of law, precisely as the threat of death; but if we have already died, then the law has no force for us, including that force of making sin abound. We are beyond the reach of the law if we have died, even if our death has been the sentence of death (just or otherwise) for sin or injustice. Our justice then will be "outlaw" justice.

Paul wants to tell us why we are definitively separated from a former (Adamic) life of sin and injustice so that any return is positively unthinkable. Having been in some way baptized "into" messiah Joshua, we are baptized into his death. The analogy may not be cultic at all since baptism with the messiah had the meaning of martyrdom in the Gospel of Mark and for some centuries thereafter. That is, baptism had the meaning of sharing the actual fate of the one who was condemned and executed by the legal officers of any and all law. This is certainly what Paul generally thinks about when he talks about sharing in or participating in the fate of the messiah, so his own suffering at the hands of opponents, especially legally constituted ones, whether Judeans or gentiles, is precisely this sharing or participating in the fate of the messiah. Later, what we think of as water baptism becomes a preparation for this blood baptism, which always serves as a fitting substitute for water baptism. But it is precisely this realistic sense, this historical sense, of identification with the death of the messiah that has to be effaced if we are to transmute this message into one that is politically safe rather than explosive.

For if we have been united [with him] **in the likeness of his death,** and here we must precisely ask, What is a death like his? Is it not, as the history of early Christianity attests, something on the order of what came to be called martyrdom? **We shall certainly be united** [with him] **in the resurrection.** The ground of this confidence has to do with sharing in the fate of the messiah, a fate that Paul always connects with suffering the actual opposition of the systems of injustice that also had inflicted suffering and death upon the messiah. He has already spoken of rejoicing in affliction, and we see that affliction here is the basis of confidence in sharing in "a resurrection like his."

I have modified the translation to reflect a certain ambiguity in what Paul is saying. The words in brackets are supplied by translators to specify that we are being united with the messiah. Although this makes a certain sense, we must also leave open the possibility that is left open in the Greek, which is that the being united has to do not with our being united one by one with the messiah but *with one another.* That is, the newness of our "walking" or comportment is precisely something like a common life, a shared life, a life in relation to one another. In 1 Thessalonians, Paul had spoken of the "work[!] of faithfulness, the labor of love, the endurance of hope" that characterized the common life, the *koinonia,* of the messianic sociality in which his readers shared (1:3). It is this form of common life within which justice will take hold.

We know that our old human[ity] was jointly crucified [with him] in order that the body of sin might be rendered inoperative [*katargathai*], so that we might no longer be enslaved to sin.

Here for the first time a word appears that has been oddly absent: **crucified**. But now this term is deployed not to designate the fate of the messiah but to suggest the execution of Adamic humanity.

We should notice that Paul regards the Adamic situation as one of having been enslaved. We have already been conquered by violence and made to serve violence. But the threat of death that held us captive has been overcome by the messiah's resurrection from the dead—a resurrection that anticipates and entails our own. It is this imagery that was to decisively influence the emergence of what has been called the ransom theory of atonement developed especially in the fourth century.

Although many translations suggest the death or destruction of the body dominated by sin, Paul indicates instead that it is rendered inoperative. Like the law, the body viewed as under the power of sin is also made to be inoperative (*katargathai*). This "inoperativity" is one of the most important features of Agamben's reflections on law and on the forms of the world, whether or not he is specifically thinking of Paul. To be rendered inoperative (whether the body as dominated by sin, the law, or the powers or structures of the world) does not mean to be simply annihilated but to be deactivated (Agamben, *Time* 97). Agamben will also maintain that "Messianic *katargesis* does not merely abolish; it preserves and brings to fulfillment" (99). If we were to apply this to the body as dominated by sin, we would have to say it is deactivated or rendered inoperative so that it might be fulfilled as a body of justice, or even as a body of glory or radiance.

For the one who has died has been made just from sin.

Recall that death is the penalty for "sin." If one has been put to death, by the force of law let us say, then the law has no further penalty to enact. Having been executed, one is outside the reach of the law, outside its power to accuse, to condemn, to punish. This is said not of the messiah alone but of all who have a share in his death. Thus, in dying with the messiah, we escape the power of the law to accuse or condemn. The death penalty no longer has force, so the law no longer has force—it is deactivated. The law of accusation and condemnation, we will learn in chapter 8, has been over-come. Of course, Paul's point is that this is an analogy. The one who has died is no longer accused, is out of the reach of the law that measures sin, accuses it, and punishes it. In this minimal and very preliminary sense, as not accused by the law, one becomes just.

But if we have died with messiah, we are confident that we shall also live with him.

The resurrection from the dead already overcomes death in the resurrec-tion of the messiah. If that is true for the messiah, then it also true for that humanity joined to the messiah. This messianic humanity is comprehen-sive in scope. The argument thus supposes that the resurrection of the messiah is the leading edge (Paul will have said "first fruits") of a resur-rection of all the dead, of all who are included in the fate of death or what Heidegger called a being-toward-death.

For we know that messiah, having been raised from the dead, no longer dies; death no longer rules over him.

That is, the resurrection is no mere resuscitation (as in the case of Lazarus, for example), in which the person still faces death ahead. For resurrection there is no further death. Death is not ahead but behind. It is deprived of its capacity to rule over life. And this rule is intimately connected to the rule of law.

Having died into sin, he died once and for all, but living, he lives to God.

The messiah died once. That is over and done with. Being alive through the resurrection, the messiah lives a life whose end is not death but God.

So you also must consider yourselves dead to sin and alive to God in mes-siah Joshua.

However undoubtedly perplexing Paul's language and metaphors are, the point he wishes to make is clear. Those who pass over into the messianic reality through identification with the messiah are those who must leave off the Adamic reality of sin and death. Living "after death" means for us as well that existence is no longer a "being-toward-death," just as it is no longer a living under the law but a living toward God. This is the messi-anic reality into which we are being incorporated.

This indicative is at the same time an imperative. Paul writes: **Do not let sin rule in your mortal body to submit yourself to its passions.** It is a question of sin as an overlord, as a ruler who makes the body serve its passion. This image of rule reminds us that we are in a political situation determined by the question of rule. The rule of the ruler is enforced by the threat of death so is a threat to the mortal body, the body that can die. Through this threat of death, the ruler makes the subject submit to the desire of the ruler. The ruler enforces rule by awakening fear. We are under attack, he might say, and our way of life, our freedom, and our civilization are at risk. If we are not swept up into this fear and the anger that it directs against the purported threat, then we are betraying the cause, the fatherland, the people, so are subjected to the penalty of death. I use these analogies because I am persuaded that the history of the interpretation of Pauline references to passions and flesh has so sexualized these terms that it has become extremely difficult to recognize that they have very different meanings for Paul: sociopolitical meanings. The passions to which we submit under the domination of sin are the passions of fear, anger, greed, resentment. These are all social or, rather, antisocial passions. They are the passions of the political, as any newspaper will testify.

10. Partial Analogies (6:12–7:6)

A transitional analogy that may be occasioned by the theme of rule is that of instruments or weapons. **Do not offer your members as instruments/weapons of injustice but offer yourselves to God as those who are alive from the dead and your members as instruments/weapons of justice.** When we are ruled by the (anti)social passions of fear and anger, we become tools of injustice, witting or unwitting accomplices in the rule of violence and death. In Paul's day, this might have meant that we become accomplices in the imperial project of domination. In our own, we become accomplices in the violent economic and military structures of our own imperium. In the recent history of the United States, for example, the vast majority of citizens seem to have been terrified into becoming willing accomplices in preemptive war, in torture policies, and, in general, in what can only be described as crimes against humanity. Manipulated by messages of fear, greed, and rage, otherwise decent people become tools of policies that they may come to abhor upon calmer reflection. Since we are as those who have been raised from among the dead, Paul says, we should now make of ourselves instruments of justice.

For sin shall not rule over you, since you are not under law but under generosity. Once again a connection between justice and favor is maintained. It is divine favor that raises us from among the dead, produces justice, and makes of us instruments of justice (even if it is a justice outside the law) rather than of injustice. **What then? Are we to sin because we are not under law but grace? Absolutely not!** We began with this issue, and it is clear that Paul has not yet dealt with it to his own satisfaction. Accordingly, he will venture additional analogies to press his case.

The first has to do with the analogy of a slave who is transferred from one owner to another. In exploring this analogy we must recall that Paul had introduced himself as a **slave of the messiah** and he will now explicate this designation as it might apply also to his readers. **Don't you know that if you offer yourself as obedient slaves, you are slaves of the one you obey?** Paul supposes that one might voluntarily choose to be a slave, even though the normal way of becoming a slave was to be captured in war or be kidnapped. It was perhaps not impossible to decide to become a slave in order to survive, to escape extreme poverty or, more likely, to escape the threat of extermination in war by surrendering even if it meant, as it normally would, being enslaved. The reason for the strange analogy is to pose an alternative that is rather stark: **either of sin toward death, or of the obedience that leads to justice.** One obedience leads to death, while the other leads to justice. Paul is not offering a speculative anthropology that suggests that one is in any case a slave; instead, he is seeking to pose the radical alternative between being determined or ruled by justice or by injustice. What is important for him is that leaving off the one (injustice), we enter wholly into the other (justice). Here there is no middle ground. We may also point out the suggestion that this **leads to justice** rather than itself being the same as justice. While there is a sort of inner necessity to this movement, it is nonetheless only a movement in the direction of justice. If it were simply automatic, there would be no need for exhortation.

But thanks to God you, slaves of sin, obeyed from the heart the form of teaching that was delivered to you. In the new situation the

obedience is **of the heart**, that is, willing obedience as opposed to the unwilling obedience to injustice (we will hear more of this at the end of chapter 7). The willingness corresponds to a kind of teaching that therefore relies upon understanding, informed consent. Patristic theologians will insist that God always acts through persuasion, never through coercion (for example, *Epistle to Diognetus* 7; Irenaeus 5.1.1). This is opposed to the bribery of the passions exploited by injustice. **And having been liberated from sin you have become slaves of justice. (I speak humanly because of the weakness of your flesh.)** The reference to speaking humanly here underlines the metaphorical character of what he is saying—most especially of the deliberately paradoxical phrase **slaves of justice**. (This perhaps also sheds further light on Paul's decision to introduce himself as a **slave of the messiah**.)

Just as you once yielded your members [we recall the members as weapons or instruments of the prior analogy] **to impurity and lawlessness** [the equivalent in the previous analogy to injustice], **so now offer your members to justice toward holiness.** Justice then leads toward holiness, toward becoming holy. Paul had already defined those to whom he is writing as those called to be holy, and here he makes clear that the basis for becoming holy is becoming just. That is, the way one belongs to the divine (holy) is through justice—a justice that comes not from the law or in accordance with the law but outside the law.

When you were slaves of sin, you were as though free from the claims of justice, but what did that get you except shame? The end of these things is death. Here it is good to recall the indictment of Roman civilization in the first chapter and, above all, the faithlessness and enmity that ruled the social order and whose end was said to be death and destruction. There also he had spoken of shame as well as death. Paul here seems to be addressing not only those already part of the messianic sociality but also those within reach of its testimony. But those who have heeded the messianic proclamation have begun to be separated from the shame and destruction that characterizes the old order of the world that is passing away.

But now you have been set free from sin and have become slaves of God; what you receive is sanctification and its completeness: life everlasting. If the one obedience leads to death, so the other leads to life. This life is everlasting since it has already passed through death, so has death not in its future but in its past. What we are being told is that obedience (of faithfulness we were once told) leads to justice, which leads to belonging to God (holiness), which leads to life without limits. This limitless life, this abundant flourishing of life, is the aim of the gift that comes to us through the messiah, through our adherence to the messiah and the messianic way.

For the wages of sin is death, but the generous gift of God is unending life in messiah Joshua our lord. What you get from obedience to sin is shame and death, and accordingly what you get from obedience to God is holiness and life. But here Paul wishes to correct a possible misunderstanding. What you get in the first case is a wage, what is owed. In the second case there is not a wage but a gift. The ground of the gift, we must remind ourselves, is the sheer grace, favor, or unconditional generosity of the divine.

The "either/or" character of the analogies so far developed (death, weapons, slaves) seems to have left behind the question of the law. They have emphasized the radical break with a past of sin, violence, injustice, and death and thus the entry into a new messianic reality of justice, holiness, and life. They have therefore emphasized that sin or injustice is no longer an option for those who are being incorporated into the messianic reality. Through the analogy of marriage Paul will now bring this discussion back more explicitly to the question of law.

Don't you know, comrades (for I speak to those who know the law) that the law rules over a person only as long as that person lives? This is the general principle, and it seems straightforward: legal obligations, for example, may be canceled at death. This returns us to the discussion of the sharing in the death of the messiah at the beginning of chapter 6. It also reminds us of the function of the law, like that of sin and death, as ruling or governing, and so keeps in play the sphere of the political.

For the married woman has been bound to the living male [*andros*] **by law. But if the male dies, she has been discharged from the law of the male** [*nomou tou andros*]**.** This is a daring analogy, first because it invites the reader (addressed just now as "brother") to think of himself as a wife, or a widow. This is, we might say, exceedingly queer.

And more than that, it speaks of the law of the male as governing marriage or, rather, of marriage as the woman being ruled by the law of the male. Of course, this is precisely true—marriage is, as Gayle Rubin has reminded us, based upon the male traffic in women. Women are the property, the first property, traded among men. And they are traded precisely as property, that is, as owned by the male, whose property rights must be protected by law, as the law of property rights. For the woman the only way out of this patriarchal (or andri-archal) law is the death of the male! (There is no specific term for "husband" as opposed to "male" in Paul's language.)

Therefore, while the male lives, she will be called an adulteress if she relates to a different male; but if the male dies, she is free from the law and is not an adulteress if another becomes her male. This indeed shows that the law of adultery is a male law. It is how the male assures himself of property rights. The woman is free from the law and able to choose another male if the first male dies. The male law no longer restrains her from doing as she pleases in choosing another.

Of course, this is "only" an analogy. We know that Paul does not think that the interests of the woman are best served by aligning herself to a new male. He is skeptical about marriage in general, as we know from 1 Corinthians. Moreover, this skeptical attitude toward marriage was one of the most attractive features of Christianity in the early centuries after Paul. Women (and men) found that being freed from the compulsion to marry was a great liberation from a social structure that apparently many (not only, but especially, women) found deeply oppressive. Paul's use of the "either this male or that male" alternative, however, keeps the analogy within the structure of a strict either/or—either sin or justice.

But now to apply this odd, actually queer, analogy:

Likewise, comrades [brothers], you have died to the law through the body of messiah, so that you may belong to another, to him who has been raised from the dead, so that we may bear fruit for God. While we were in the flesh, the passions of sins were working in our members to bear fruit for death, but now we are discharged from the law, dead to that which held us captive, so that we become slaves not in oldness of letter but in newness of spirit.

This appears rather convoluted. The analogy has perhaps become too queer and radical to pursue, and it was, after all, only an analogy. But from the wifely analogy we still have what appears to be something like getting pregnant (bearing fruit, bearing fruit either for death or for God). We are impregnated either by death, which excited our passions so that we might be thus impregnated, or by God or spirit so as to bear fruit of life or liveliness.

We are discharged from the law (this is like the male law for the woman) but now not through the death of the male but through our sharing in the death of the messiah. So Paul reins in the marriage analogy a bit in order to reconnect with the death of the messiah. But he got into this analogy (and perhaps a bit over his rhetorical head) in order to get to the question of law, whether as "male law" or as that from which we are "discharged," but now by our own death rather than that of the male.

In this discussion, what Paul has sought to emphasize is that the new life that follows from being incorporated into the death and resurrection of the messiah is to be above all a life of justice. It is thus radically distinguished from the life, or pseudolife, of what went before. Speaking of generosity or favor rather than of law is not a way of escaping the requirement of justice but of fulfilling that requirement in a way that is impossible for works of the law. Thus, the messianic humanity cannot go back into the Adamic humanity. Sin, like death, must lie behind us in a past that has no future, that is "dead and gone." It is precisely on account of this either/or that patristic Christianity was so perplexed about the possibility of "sin after baptism," which seemed to bring into question the radical transition suggested by Paul.

Third Phase B

Paul has been developing a number of analogies, all of which have the import that the messianic reality is to be radically distinguished from the Adamic reality. That distinction has to do with the question of the place of sin or violation in the new or messianic reality. His case is that sin has no place in the messianic and therefore that the new reality is one in which justice reigns in place of the injustice that had characterized the reign of law. He will be clarifying this same theme in the extended argument regarding law and spirit that he now undertakes.

11. Death and the Law (7:7–25)

The analogy concerning marriage has brought us back to the theme of the law that had appeared in the discussion of Abraham's faith, which produces a justice that is before or outside the law. Paul had said that the new justice has been disclosed **apart from the law** (3:21) but will not mean that the law is overthrown but upheld (3:30). He has hinted at a strange relation between sin and law: **but the law came in, with the result that the trespass multiplied** (5:20). He has further and more recently suggested that **while we were living in the flesh, our sinful passions, aroused by the law, were at work in our members to bear fruit for death** (7:5).

If the result of the law is that trespass multiplied or that our sinful passions (and we recall that these are "political passions") are thereby inflamed, it would seem that the law is somehow identified with sin. Paul has been at some pains to show that sin must now lie behind those who adhere to the messiah, and his analogies suggest that these messianists are somehow beyond the reach of the law (one meaning of "outlaw," surely). But many loose ends are still hanging, and some account must be taken of them. How is it that we do not abolish or overthrow the law? In what sense is it to be upheld?

Paul then begins with another question that is still outstanding: **Should we say that the law is sin? Absolutely not.** The subject of previous questions of this sort, with a similar answer, has been sin, but now it is law. We know that law and sin are closely related, yet they are not simply to be identified. How is this to be thought?

First, there is the connection between law and the knowledge of sin or violation or, as we heard before, the measuring of sin or crime. **Sin was indeed in the world before the law, but sin is not measured** [reckoned] **where there is no law** (5:13). Earlier he had said that **where there is no law, neither is there violation** (4:15). Paul has thus signaled before that this theme must be clarified or addressed. He now turns to that task. We can even see a progression in his thought. At 4:15 he simply said that where there is no law, there is no violation. But at 5:13 he clarified that there was indeed sin before the law, but it was not measured prior to the law.

What Paul now says is this: **If it had not been for the law, I would not have known** [about?] **sin. I would not have known what it is to covet if the law had not said, "You shall not covet."** Here we have a summation of the law already found in emergent Judaism in Paul's time (Käsemann, *Commentary on Romans* 194) as that concerning covetousness: the desire to have something that belongs to another as the very summary of all sin. This has a certain resonance with Stoic wisdom as well, in which the good life involves staying within the limits of what is one's own.

What are we to make of the introduction here of the first-person singular? Who is this "I" who is first "before the law" and then under the law, informed by the law, and so on? This is perhaps the most decisive issue in the interpretation of what lies before us. And here it seems clear that this "I" can only be what we encountered earlier as Adamic humanity (in contrast to messianic humanity). It is essential to recall that Adamic humanity is regarded in the argument of 5:12–21 as both before and (then) under the law. Indeed, the difference signaled between law and prelaw is that of knowledge and increase of sin. But what these aspects of Adamic humanity (before the law and under the law) have in common is precisely sin and death. The law does not solve but only clarifies and exacerbates (hyperbolizes) the basic problem.

What is at stake in the current discussion is precisely how, within Adamic humanity, the law winds up not eliminating sin (and producing justice) but actually making sin both more apparent and more virulent. This being said, it seems clear that the "I" is the Adamic humanity of sin and death, but it is also cognizant of law and even (as will be said later) loves law.

It is precisely by giving this "I" a different sense—by transferring it to the situation of the messianic human, that is, to one who is not under the law but under gift—that enormous damage has been done in the history of interpretation and in theology as a whole. Christianity then becomes an alibi for becoming "realistic" about the continuing power of sin and thus an alibi for continuing to live "under the law" in such a way that violation is simply forgiven rather than abolished.

The task then is to give full weight to Paul's messianic project. The character of the messianic is precisely that it must seem unrealistic when measured against what Alain Badiou calls the knowledge of the situation. Badiou writes, "A truth process is heterogeneous to the instituted knowledges of the situation" (*Ethics* 43). It is of the category of what Derrida calls "the impossible" so stands beyond or at the limit of knowledge. Derrida says of the gift: "The gift as such cannot be known, but it can be thought of. We can think what we cannot know" (*God, the Gift, and Postmodernism* 60).

A nonmessianic perspective has seemed plausible because of Paul's fundamentally sympathetic picture of one who is under the law, loves the law, yet is unable to do what the law requires. Paul does not take the worst case of one who is somehow obviously "depraved." His picture comports well with that of the just gentile who, in a certain sense, "does what the law requires." This will also be in accord with the just Jew who is "as to the law, blameless," as Paul had said of himself in Philippians. But Paul's basic argument is that in neither case do we have to do with the justice that comes "apart from the law." Messianic justice is one that is no longer corrupted by the admixture of sin, by the incapacity to do what is just, and so on. Instead, the messianic is empowered or spirited in such a way that it answers to the call and claim of justice, a claim based on divine gift or generosity (rather than the threat of wrath) and thus faithfulness rather than works. Accordingly, the correct way to understand this argument is to see it as another contrast like those we have thus far encountered. This discussion in chapter 7, beginning at verse 7, is again a "before," to which the early part of the following chapter (8:1–13) serves as a depiction of the "after."

But sin seizing an opportunity in the commandment produced in me all kinds of covetousness.

Here, it is said that precisely sin has somehow gained control of the law in order to turn it into a provocation to sin.

Apart from the law, sin lies dead. I was once alive apart from [before] **the law, but when the commandment came, sin revived and I died. The commandment that was** [supposed to be] **life for me became death. For sin finding opportunity in the commandment deceived me and by it killed me.**

For clarification of Paul's argument it may be helpful to turn to the reflections of Jacques Lacan, who, in his seminar of 1959–1960 on the ethics of psychoanalysis, introduces a paraphrase of Romans 7:7–11 as exhibiting the very dynamic that he had been trying to clarify in psychoanalytic terms (83). This becomes, in Lacanian psychoanalytic language, the tale of everyone, who begins life before the Law but then encounters the Law as the symbolic order, as the Law of the father, as the interdiction of desire, and so on. Instead of restraining what is prohibited, the Law only makes it more attractive or compelling. We thus have a dialectic of Law (as prohibition): the incitement of desire and thence transgression of the Law.

Since Lacan's reading of Paul on this point has a significant influence on later philosophical readers of this text (especially Badiou and Žižek), it is worthwhile giving it a bit more attention. In commenting upon this passage, Lacan writes: "The relation between the Thing and the Law could not be better defined than in these terms. . . . The dialectical relationship between desire and the Law causes our desire to flare up only in relation to the Law, through which it becomes the desire for death. It is only because of the Law that sin, *hamartia*—which in Greek means lack and non-participation in the Thing—takes on an excessive, hyperbolic character" (83–84). Later he suggests that "we are in fact led to the point where we accept the formula that without a transgression there is no access to jouissance, and to return to Saint Paul, that that is precisely the function of the Law. Transgression in the direction of jouissance only takes place if it is supported by the oppositional principle, by the forms of the Law" (177).

Slavoj Žižek, whose indebtedness to Lacan is evident in almost everything he writes, will suggest that Paul does not remain trapped within this dialectic of command, inflamed desire, and trespass but will offer an exit from this trap through the notion of love. He writes: "What if the Pauline agape, the move beyond the mutual implication of Law and sin, is not the step towards the full symbolic integration of the particularity of Sin into the universal domain of Law, but its exact opposite, the unheard-of gesture of leaving behind the domain of Law itself, of 'dying to the Law' as Saint Paul put it (Romans 7:5)?" (*Fragile Absolute* 96). He returns to this point in a later text, referring to Romans 7:7 (*Puppet* 135) and suggests Lacan's *Seminar XX* as following up this possibility psychoanalytically (114, 116). We shall see that Paul does indeed break out of this psychological (or political) deadlock.

While accepting that Lacan's reading of Paul makes good psychoanalytic sense, I propose that Paul is doing more than good psychology here. He is working on a far broader canvas, even if what he says is certainly relevant for understanding certain psychodynamics. To get at this broader canvas (and engage the political thinking that is at work here), let us attend to the way Paul's argument connects to the general case that he has been trying to make.

First we notice that life and death come into the picture again but in a very different way than in the previous discussion of the Adamic and the messianic. They are redeployed now with a rather different effect:

Before the law = I am alive; sin is dead.

Under the law = sin is alive; I am dead.

This contrasts with what was happening before in that there we were concerned with a different transition: from death to life, that is, we were focused on the transition from messiah (or messianic human) as dead, to being made alive. Now we are clarifying how it is that the human came to be "dead" or one who was ruled by death. This has to do (again) with the advent of law.

How are we to make sense of this before and under the law? We know that for Paul it is possible to say that even those "without the law" know enough of God to do the right or just thing; for that reason they are "without excuse." But who is this who was alive before the law and for whom sin was dead?

Paul doesn't say explicitly, thereby leaving open the door for a variety of suggestions. Among these suggestions is an autobiographical "confession" in the manner of Augustine or even more so of Luther (e.g., Breton 89). Indeed, Nietzsche's reading of Paul as conflicted about the law seems to read back into Paul precisely the torment of Luther: "Luther must have experienced similar feelings . . . an analogous feeling took possession of Paul" (*Daybreak* § 68). But this seems highly unlikely given Paul's assertion that he had been blameless with respect to the law. In this way I am in agreement with Krister Stendhal's view (78–96) that the "introspective conscience of the West" owes more to Augustine (and then Luther) than it owes to Paul.

We have already seen that Lacan can read this as the basic psychodynamics of "everyone." But if we try to stick with what we have in Paul's own argument, then we have two candidates: Adam and Abraham. Let us begin (appropriately) with Adam. He is alive; sin is dead. Or in this case sin is not yet in existence. The commandment says, Don't eat the fruit of that tree. This is already the prohibition of covetousness, that is, of desiring that which does not pertain to oneself. It is then "sin" that takes hold of the command and turns it against Adam to deceive. That is, after all, the way the story is constructed, that the human is deceived by that which turns the commandment into a provocation. Paul has said that sin came into the world through one human and that from it came death, which seems to be the very thing at stake here as well. Even though Adam doesn't die at once, he is under the dominion of death—which subsequently comes to expression, as we saw, as murder.

We may extend this analogy to another who has been said to be before the law, Abraham. The subsequent command to circumcise, in Paul's view, certainly becomes an incitement to suppose that there is a privilege in being circumcised, so one takes possession of this privilege as something that is one's own (as Christians may, for example, suppose that baptism—or even right belief—confers privilege before God). Paul has been at pains to demonstrate that this false sense of security leads to a certain laxness with respect to the law as such, or with respect to that at which the law aims, namely, justice. In either case, and there are multiple instances, we find this terrible irony: What seeks to offer us life comes to be the agent of death. It is overtaken by sin.

We might also deal with the broader question of covetousness and the law as the guardian of property, as that which divides mine from yours and "protects" the proper allotment of property. Breton has noted that "the mere fact of belonging to Christ seems to abolish all other forms of property and possession" (63). Thus, it seems to abolish even the desire for possession and in this sense strikes at the root of covetousness. The law, however, seeks to limit covetousness by distinguishing between mine and yours. But we all know that this comes to mean the defense of the rich (those who have) from the poor (those who have not). Adam Smith, the father of capitalist theory, lamented a similar meaning of the law, noting that when those who engage in commerce propose legislation, it is generally for the sake of duping the public.

So the law is holy and the commandment is holy, just, and good.

Here it should become clear that however much the law fails in producing justice, it nevertheless aims at or intends justice, and it is thus holy and good. What is at stake, then, is the tragedy of the law, or of commandment. It is this that Derrida has sought to make clear in his complex reflections on the relation of law and justice, in which law aims at and betrays justice so that justice, while inseparable or indissociable from the law, is nonetheless necessarily outside the law (Jennings, *Reading Derrida* 22–38). In one of his last essays, "Justices," Derrida makes use of a verb form of *justice* derived from the poet Gerard Manley Hopkins to phrase this relation quite vigorously: "Isn't this what gives us to think justice in its essential link to law, as well as its irreducibility to law, its resistance, its heterogeneity to law? Which would come down to seeing a suddenly looming justice break the surface, a justice that will always exceed law but which law, *by justicing*, would never begin to exhaust itself going after justice?" (714). Certainly for Paul the tragedy of the law comes to bleakest expression in the condemnation and execution of the one who turns out to be the messiah, and thus divine (God's son, as he said at the beginning).

In any case we have the law as that which is just (since it articulates the claim and call of justice, the necessity of justice) yet comes to be an instrument of injustice not only incidentally, in this or the other instance, but generally and necessarily. It is this that Paul is wrestling to explain, or at least to make apparent.

Did the good become death to me? Absolutely not! It was sin that, in order to be manifest as sin through what is good, worked my death.

Sin shows up as sin precisely as the agent of murder and, indeed, of my own murder, that is, of my own being subject to death. Paul could have said that the law, insofar as it has the force of law, condemns me to death, and in that sense what is good intends my death. But that isn't where he is going. Of course, he does not deny that the law itself condemns and in that way procures my death. What he says is that the good doesn't do this. The law is good in that it aims at life, so it does not aim at death. Rather, sin itself (personalized it would seem, almost like Satan) turns the law from being what gives life to what gives death. In this way we see how really awful sin is: it produces, procures death, and does so even through what is intended for life. Thus, **through the commandment sin becomes hyperbolically sinful.** It is, as it were, supercharged. Far from the law restraining sin, it becomes the fuel for the acceleration of sin. In the same way, the state that promises to restrain violence does so through giving itself a monopoly on violence and thus institutionalizes violence, thereby making violence not an individual act but the very foundation and articulation of the social order.

How can this be understood? How does this happen? The name we are going to hear is "flesh." Flesh is the weakness of the human *basar* (in Hebrew) or *sarx* (in Greek). It is the way we are vulnerable, exposed. Our life is subject to touch, that is, to what gives pleasure and pain, gives joy, and makes wounding possible. And it is somehow this very vulnerability that is going to be the explanation of how sin is able to overcome Adamic humanity, especially that Adamic humanity that is under the law.

How is it that an awareness of one's flesh—that is, one's vulnerability—becomes the incentive to turn from justice? We have too many examples of this on the geopolitical stage. We saw how the fear inflamed by the political manipulation of the vulnerabilities exposed by 9/11 served to arouse a willingness to engage in torture and indiscriminate war. And on the other side? The sense of cultural vulnerability to modern Western encroachment had more than a little to do with the launching of acts of desperate "terrorism." It would be all too easy to supply examples of the sense of weakness or vulnerability seizing control of that which intends life (let us suggest the traditions of Islam or Christianity or Enlightenment "freedom") to accelerate injustice, to hyperbolize violence and violation. Thus, flesh comes also to name hostility to justice or to God, the very hostility that crucified the messiah as son of David.

The law therefore is spirited, but I am fleshed. The opposite of flesh is not, however, impermeability but breath, liveliness, power. We met this contrast earlier where flesh named the death of the messiah, and spirit named that by virtue of which the messiah is raised as divine son. So far, we have seen that the law is spirited as that which aims at life, just as something like the resurrection of the messiah produces life. And chapter 5 contrasted messianic life and Adamic death. That is precisely where this argument is heading. Here the Adamic "I" is what is "sold" into sin, as a slave to sin and injustice, an instrument or weapon of injustice Paul has written. Wed to sin, he has also said. Owned by sin.

The bewilderment of Adamic humanity is now brought to expression. We recall from the indictment of gentile civilization that there are those, both Jews and gentiles, both with and without the law, who practice what the law intends. Paul is not concerned here with something like a doctrine of human depravity—far from it. He supposes that Adamic humanity does indeed want to do what is right but cannot, because it is caught in a web of sin and death. Here is the complaint:

I don't know what I am working [doing]**. For I don't practice what I aim at. But I do what I hate. I agree with the law that it is good. But now I no longer work it, but the sin dwelling** [at home] **in me** [works it]**; for I know that the good is not at home in me, in my flesh; for to aim at the good is present to me, but not to work the good. It isn't the good that I aim at but the evil I don't aim at; that is what I practice. But if I do what I don't aim at, then it is not "I" that works it, but sin that is at home in me** [works it]**.

Is this an alibi? Or is it the cry of one who has finally attained lucidity about the Adamic human situation? In any case, sin here is not something outside (like an owner or a husband) but something that has lodged deeply within, that has me at its mercy by having seized me at the most vulnerable place (flesh). The fact that it lodges in me yet still is not me is important to emphasize. As we shall see, this will also be true of spirit. Once again, it is not a question of autonomy but of subjection or, rather, subjugation. Here we can refer again to the idea of Louis Althusser that the ideological apparatuses of power (injustice in Paul's terms) interpellate the subject to "subject" him or her to conformity to the social, economic, and political world patrolled by those apparatuses. (Later Paul will exhort his readers to not be conformed to that world.) Here it is crucial that we are not dealing with the worst of human beings but the best, which distinguishes what is going on here from the indictment that started out Paul's letter. It is the problem of humanity that has the honor of Adam as well as the shame.

So I find it to be a law that when I intend good, evil is present. For I delight in divine law according to the inner human [what is most truly human in me delights in this law as something spirited]; **but there is a different law** [or rule] **in my members warring with the law of my mind and taking me captive by the law of sin that is in my members.**

What makes me human is the capacity to desire the good, to intend it. But something else is in my members, my way of engaging the world, of speaking and acting and walking, of interacting with my world, my fellow human. This is where sin is lodged, in my members, in my engagement with others. And I am captured as a prisoner of war, as a weapon of war, as a slave, as a captured woman sold into slavery or marriage. The aporia, or "no way out," is given desperate expression: **Wretched human I** [am]. **Who will redeem me from the body of this death?**

In both cases "I"—not someone else, not an alibi. The human, the would-be good and just human, is caught in a vise, incapacitated. In this at least Augustine was right. But not perhaps Luther. For this is not a description of the human who belongs to the messianic reality that has broken in: **Thanks be to God through Joshua messiah, our leader.** The exclamation is inserted following the lament, preceding the summary because "the answer" is what determines the diagnosis and the answer to the problem is what Paul supposes to be the glad-making proclamation, the one that incites gratitude, rejoicing. Thus, the problem is shaped by the "solution," by the message concerning the justice of God, which does not place one in an impasse but actually breaks one out of the "no way out." The aporia sets the stage for the eucatastrophe, that is, the catastrophic destruction of the world of sin and death that is at the same time glad tidings.

So then I myself, I serve the divine law with the mind, but with my flesh, the law of sin. All that Paul has been dealing with here is the before: the before of being a slave of sin. This applies not just to the worst, who perhaps gladly indenture themselves in this way, but also to the best, to those who want to be good, just, holy—who want what the law "wants" or intends. After all, for this reason there is law, even the law we pass in a democracy. It's not just evil persons or evil classes of persons who are to blame here (the rich and powerful, for example, who are sometimes very decent people and who sometimes really do want to do what is right). It is precisely when we intend or want or aim at doing what is good that we find ourselves brought up against the tragedy of law.

Here we may find some help in the reflections of Derrida in *Gift of Death*: "I cannot respond to the call, the request, the obligation, or even the love of another without sacrificing the other other, the other others. . . . As a result, the concepts of responsibility, of decision, or of duty, are condemned a priori to paradox, scandal and aporia" (68); "I can respond only to one (or to the One), that is, to the other, by sacrificing that one to the other. I am responsible to any one (that is to say to any other) only by failing in my responsibility, to all the others, to the ethical or political generality" (70). With an almost lyrical eloquence Derrida writes of uncountable others who are "sacrificed" in any attempt to do what is right or just, whose claims are ignored in order to respond to any one of them. Accordingly, Derrida can utterly reject any attempt at a "good conscience." That one aims at justice only makes clear one's immersion in injustice.

12. The Spirit and Life (8:1–17)

We have heard from Paul of the lament of Adamic humanity: the humanity under the dominion of sin that has taken possession of the fleshly vulnerability of the human and taken up residence in the members of this humanity. As a result, even when this humanity yearns for justice and delights in the law that aims at justice, it finds itself nonetheless trapped, subverted, mired in injustice. This humanity, we have seen, was sold out as a weapon of injustice, a slave of injustice, married to injustice.

But what is the other humanity, the messianic humanity, that is delivered from this past servitude? This humanity can scarcely restrain itself from the shout of gratitude for its deliverance: **Thanks be to God through Joshua messiah our leader.**

There is no condemnation to those in messiah Joshua. Once again we see a sense of solidarity with and belonging or adhering to the messianic, to that which has death behind it, so also law and condemnation.

No condemnation. The law is above all the law of condemnation, which propels the *orgai tou theou*, the rage of divine justice. And this comes to expression as the force of law, the death penalty that enforces the law. This very penalty has fallen upon the messiah and has been broken upon the body of the executed messianic leader. Somehow the execution of the messiah means that the power of condemnation has been broken. It has lost its power. There can no longer be condemnation for any who are taken up into the messianic event.

How is it clear that the condemnation that fell upon the messiah (from the law both of Israel and of the gentiles, so law always and everywhere) is broken, is made into past tense? By the resurrection, **the resurrection by the spirit of holiness**, the spirit or power of life that overcomes death and the threat of death that is the very force of law as instrument of death. Thus, we encounter this basic opposition that Paul had signaled at the very beginning of his letter—between flesh and spirit—the flesh as the weakness that overpowers us and the spirit as the force, energy, *dunamis* that empowers us:

For the law of the spirit of life in messiah Joshua freed you from the law of sin and death.

In both cases, there is a law, but they are quite different laws: the one of life, the other of death; the one that has become the servant of injustice, the other (as we shall hear) that makes us servants of justice. This conflict of law with law is echoed in reflections of Derrida on the claims of hospitality: "*The* law is above the laws. It is thus illegal, transgressive, outside the law, like a lawless law" (Derrida and Dufourmantelle

79). Paul has elsewhere made use of the idea, in a more compact form, of messianic law (Galatians 6:2; 1 Corinthians 9:21). The phrase and its function may bear echoes of Plato's suggestion in *The Statesman* that the best statesman would be one who governed without law (294a), although Plato makes clear that such a statesman would rule with or without consent and would still rule by violence if necessary (293d). Clearly this ideal statesman would not measure up to Paul's notion of the messianic law, since Paul has renounced the violence of law, not merely its rigidity as written law.

On account of the incapacity of law, its being weak through [having been overpowered by] **the flesh, God sending his son in the likeness of flesh of sin, condemned sin in the flesh, in order that the justice of the law may be fulfilled in us who walk not according to the flesh but according to the spirit.**

This is difficult but can be broken down. We know already that the law is overpowered by flesh, since **our sinful passions were aroused by the law at work to bear fruit for death . . . while we lived in the flesh**. The law had been overcome by our own resistance to our weakness as flesh, or our denial of our vulnerability. The law, as compensation for our weakness as flesh, cannot produce justice but tragically becomes an accelerant for injustice, injustice to the nth degree, hyperbolic sin. But now the divine action works outside the law. By coming as divine son (the one whom flesh/injustice acknowledged as son of David), the divine enters into the lump of humanity dominated by sin and death precisely in a likeness to sin, that is, as Adamic.

The messianic does not stand outside the Adamic but is precisely a part of this Adamic reality, the reality of "sinful flesh"—that is precisely where the messianic comes to be or takes place as an event. This is an extreme solidarity of the divine with the Adamic, such that the divine takes place precisely within the Adamic, within and as sinful humanity, "who becomes sin" (2 Corinthians 5:21), who is or becomes a curse or "accursed" (Galatians 3:13).

The result of the messianic taking place is that sin is condemned in the flesh. How is this true? It is true because the messiah is marked as a criminal and condemned to death. But his conviction by the law that condemns sinful humanity is itself overthrown (by a resurrection from the dead).

And this marks a dividing line within Adamic humanity, a before and after: the before of the Adamic, the after of the messianic. The "before" of walking according to the flesh, that is, in accordance with that very anxiety that makes us prisoner of the self-preservation that kills. The "after" of walking according to spirit, not according to lack but abundance, not fending off death but existing after death, so in "newness of life." Walking: a mode of living, an exercise of members, a manner of being in the world.

Of the spirited walk, of this liveliness of new life, it is said that through this mode of life the just requirement of the law is fulfilled. That is, the aim of this event is that what was impossible before now becomes actual—the doing of what the law intended, aimed at, sought: life and justice. (Paul will still need to clarify this toward the end of the letter since this is what his letter, his argument, aims at.) In this sense this walking is in accordance with the law, the spirited law, the life-giving rather than death-dealing law. That is the call and claim of justice.

We can put things slightly more schematically: Paul is here distinguishing the before and after. Let us first look at the before. To **walk according to flesh** or **live according to flesh** or have a **mind set on flesh**—to be determined by lack, vulnerability, weakness—**is death**. Moreover, **it is enmity against God**, that is, it is hostile to, resentful of, bitter toward God. Aware of the condemnation that is its due, it is resentful and filled with animosity, so **it doesn't submit to** [subject itself to] **the law of God** (the claim and call of justice). We have seen that **indeed it cannot**, even when it delights interiorly in the law of God, in justice, in the good, so it **cannot please God**. This is the trap that we have seen. I simply cannot do what God requires, so I am resentful of the claim and walk in enmity or hostility. It is in this condition, remember, that Paul had already said that the messiah died for us: while we were weak, (flesh) while we were sinners, while we were enemies. Moreover, the messiah was claimed to be "son of David" according to the flesh, by the testimony of those whose hostility to the messiah brought about his execution.

And now, the after: if we **walk according to spirit** (abundance, liveliness) and **live according to spirit** and have our **mind set on what pertains to spirit, to life to abundance**, then instead of experiencing death and enmity, we enjoy **life and peace**. We have heard of this peace before (5:1), a peace that comes from being made just and that is also called **reconciliation** instead of enmity. We are not talking about some distant future state. This is now: **You are not in the flesh; you are in the spirit.** This now is the now of belonging to the messiah, of being caught up into and by the messianic event.

We/you are in spirit, [are spirited, are flooded with this liveliness] **just as messianic spirit dwells in you** [recall what previously dwelled in you].

It is precisely the infusion of this messianic spirit that signals that one belongs to the messianic event. This is at least a partial answer to a question we have wondered about: How is the belonging to the messianic to be understood? Here it has to do with messianic spirit or liveliness.

Among **your spirit**, the **messianic spirit**, and the **divine spirit**, there is no absolute division. The messianic is flooded with liveliness. For spirit/*ruah*/*pneuma* is the breath by which we are animated, made alive and now lively. We still are not clear what this means, how this is manifest. Paul still has not explicated this liveliness, but he will soon. This liveliness will stand outside the law, but in such a way as to improvise approximations to justice.

There is another division: **If messiah is in you, even though your bodies are dead because of your sin, your spirits are alive because of justice.** Now our bodies are dead. For us as body, death still lies in the future, although not for us as spirit, where death lies in the past. Our body, our being in the world, is still dead "through sin," perhaps even now as we begin to walk, to live, to have the mind-set of life or spirit. But then that resurrection power that has already begun to invade us, to take possession of us, and will come fully into being in us so that **the one** [God/ Spirit] **who raised Joshua from the dead will give life to your mortal bodies, by that spirit which has now taken up residence in you.** Before, sin had taken up residence in us, but no longer. That was then; this is now. This energy or life force has taken up residence in us, so it must follow that the mortal bodies that we are will also be enlivened by the same life force that gave life to the dead messiah.

Note that the resurrection of the messiah portends our resurrection. He is, as 1 Corinthians says, "the first born . . . from the dead" (15:20). And in Romans Paul had said, **For if we have been united with him in a**

death like his, we will certainly be united with him in a resurrection like his (6:5). It is important to recall that this had been said of "all" (5:18): just as in one all died, how much more in one shall all be made alive.

So then comrades [brothers], we are debtors, not to the flesh to live according to the flesh. Note that the language of debt appears here with respect to flesh (and thus sin and the law taken possession of by sin through the flesh), but only to be canceled. For he will not say that we are debtors to the spirit, but before we were indebted to, sold to, or captured by this economy of sin, debt, and death. This is what walking in, or being indebted to, or bound by, the economy of death means: we die; we are condemned to death; death comes to all through Adamic fate. **For if you live according to the flesh, you will die; but if by the spirit the practices of the body you put to death, you will live.** Again this is rather difficult. The practices here that are being put to death are of course those that arise from anxiety in the face of death, those that make us like Cain, voluntarily or involuntarily. Putting to death is rather harsh. We have previously heard, **So you also must consider yourselves dead to sin** (6:11), or **We know that our old self was crucified with him** (6:6). But now we are no longer passive spectators but agents who affirm this death and in that way **put to death** the practices of the body. I think **putting to death the body practices of injustice** is better than the standard translation. The simplest explanation is that we put the activity of injustice behind us, turn away from it, and allow it to be what it really is: dead and buried. This is possible because now it is replaced by that which is far more, which is excessive, which corresponds to that "how much more" we heard about earlier and about which Paul is now to write far more extensively.

How has this to do with "politics"? The whole business of dying to the world, or of "putting to death" the ways of embodying injustice, has been connected by several contemporary thinkers with Paul's reflections in 1 Corinthians about living in the structures of the world "as if not." This "as if not" means treating these structures as if they no longer have the capacity to enforce themselves upon one, to define one's identity and "comportment." Slavoj Žižek can point to a certain "uncoupling" from these structures of social life. For example, Žižek writes that "uncoupling does actually involve a symbolic death—one that has to die for the Law that regulates our tradition, our social 'substance'" (*Fragile Absolute*

127). Moreover, love is "the hard and arduous work of repeated 'uncoupling' in which again and again, we have to disengage ourselves from the inertia that constrains us to identify with the particular order we were born into" (128–129). For Badiou this will mean that a particularity that seems to have a position of privilege is refigured in accordance with what he terms the "universal." Thus, the figure of Abraham "anticipates what could be called a universalism of the Jewish site" (*Saint Paul* 103). Or Paul can begin with what appears to be an endorsement of male privilege only to revoke that privilege in favor of an equalization of male and female (104). Thus, Badiou claims: "The necessity of traversing and testifying to the difference between the sexes *in order for it* to become indifferent in the universality of the declaration culminates in symmetrical, rather than unilateral, constraints within the contingent realm of customs" (105).

This unplugging does not mean an ascetic withdrawal from the world but a living in the world without being determined by it or its classifications and structures. Agamben writes, in this connection, about the Franciscan attempt "to create a space that escaped the grasp of power and its laws, without entering into conflict with them, yet rendering them inoperative" (*Time* 27). He sees this as a precise working out of the Pauline "as if not" that likewise renders inoperative given conditions without giving itself over to the task of abolishing them juridically (26). Nor is this simply a Stoic inner detachment that regards these things as of no importance compared with the cultivation of the self. What seems to be at stake here, as we shall see in Paul's development of this argument, is a corporate style of life in which we become more rather than less interconnected with one another and with the messianic reality that has dawned. Paul will speak of love, mutual care, and concern instead of detachment.

It is not wrong to speak of a certain nihilism here (Taubes 72), one that refuses to give authority to any of the structures of social, political, and economic life. But it is a nihilism that provokes a different form of sociality and thus of politics. All of this will be treated in more detail in the last stage of Paul's argument, when he describes the messianic sociality that is coming into being. At this point, what is critical is that Paul does have in mind a polity that is not determined by law but by what he calls spirit. The character of spirit is precisely its liveliness, its creativity.

Spirit has nothing to do with a rule book. Spirit improvises and does so surprisingly.

Paul has developed a series of before-and-after pictures of human being with an emphasis on how in the messianic reality the human comes to be just. What follows is a significant restatement of the after, the now-time, in the messianic reality. The passage that we are to read looks a lot like an argument that Paul has made in Galatians: "so that we might receive adoption as sons. And because you are sons, God has sent the spirit of his son into our hearts, crying *abba* father! So through God you are no longer a slave but a son, and if a son then an heir" (4:5b–7).

The combination of spirit, son, and heir come into play here in Romans, together with the connection to the cry of "*abba* father" and the opposition to the metaphor of slavery. What he now writes is this:

For all who are led by the spirit are sons [*uioi*] of God. For you did not receive the spirit of slavery to fall back into fear, but you have received the spirit of adoption [son-making] by which we cry out, *abba*! *Pater*! The spirit itself testifies together with our spirit that we are children [*tekna*] of God, and if children then heirs; heirs of God, joint heirs of messiah, since we suffer with him in order that we may shine forth with him.

Let us begin with the cry *abba/Pater*. It is often supposed that this cry of *abba* is peculiar to Jesus and designates a peculiar intimacy with God. This is implausible, because this terminology is by no means characteristic of Jesus. There is only one place in the Gospels—which in any case were written after the Pauline epistles—where Jesus calls God *abba*: in Mark's Gospel at the point of Jesus's desolation prior to death as he struggles in Gethsemane (14:36). In that narrative Jesus has no auditors. The disciples are left behind. In fact, not only does Jesus leave them behind but he immediately discovers that they are asleep. There are no ear-witnesses to Jesus's prayer. It is the reader alone who hears this—and the reader who hears this is precisely the reader who has heard from Paul that this is the sign of adoption. That is, Mark is concerned to show us that the adoption we experience is by no means an escape from the fate of Jesus/Joshua, who will be executed, who will face death. In this, Mark does not fundamentally depart from Paul.

The acclamation of God as *abba/Pater* then appears for the first time in Paul's letters, and it is here that we must discover its significance: an acclamation of God as father in two languages. Why two? Which two? The language of Judeans (Aramaic) and the language of gentiles (Greek). Paul has said "to the Judeans first and then the Greeks." It is Paul's concern, not only in this letter, to put together Judean and pagan believers. It is therefore both, in their own way, in their own tradition/culture, in their own tongue, who acclaim God as *abba/Pater.* Why? Perhaps because this is the appropriate response to discovering that one has been adopted.

Historians of the period present us with something like the following picture. A child is born to the wife or concubine of a Roman "father." Before the child can be taken into the family, the father must acknowledge the child. The child is placed on the floor before the father. If the father picks up the child, then it becomes a part of the family. If not, the child may be "exposed," left outside the walls for another to pick up, perhaps to use as a slave—or simply left to die. Early Christianity would be characterized by its complete opposition to the exposure of children; they would be adopted into the new family of faith(fulness).

Here the metaphor is even radicalized: The child is born a slave but is unexpectedly adopted, taken into the household, and made an heir. That is, the child is taken from the bondage of being another's slave and made now a son of one who gives life.

In Roman society, it is fathers who have the authority to adopt, the capacity to define the status of the child. For Paul, the "son" is both male and female, of course. It is the faithful one. But why then son rather than, as some translations suggest, child? Because what is at stake is not the becoming of an infant, a property, but an agent, an heir, one who is destined to receive and be responsible for that which is "proper" to the father. In our modern Western society there would be little problem in suggesting daughter as a translation of *uios,* but she would be a decidedly liberated daughter, one who has the same rights that previously belonged preeminently to the son.

That we have been adopted enables us to thus acclaim God as father, to know that we are not slaves (of sin or law) but adopted children. The slavery that Paul has employed rather dramatically before is here "deconstructed." Paul had introduced himself as a slave of the messiah, and in 6:16–17 there were two kinds of slavery. One was slave of one or the other. But not here— one is no longer a slave but a son. (Jesus will be said in the Gospel of John to have told his apprentices that they were no longer slaves but friends, a similar transformation.) That metaphor of slavery had a particular purpose, but we are now in a different situation, and the new is not really comparable to the old. Thus, we have not slaves of the old or slaves of the new but slaves of the old or sons (and daughters)—that is, heirs—of the new.

That we are heirs of the divine means that we are those who inherit divinity, or at least the reconciliation, the being at peace with God. In subsequent Eastern theology, we become those who inherit divinity, and this is not a bad reading of Paul; for that is what "sons of God" means. As heirs of God, we are also jointly heirs with another who is called son: the messiah. Being joint heirs will also have to do with being joined to one another in and through the messianic.

Badiou will claim that with Paul all are filiated as brothers rather than as slaves: "The resurrected Son filiates all of humanity" (*Saint Paul* 59). While Badiou may be inattentive to the continuing salience of the slave metaphor in Paul and perhaps be overinfluenced by a certain appropriation of a Freudian metaphor, nevertheless, it is true that here Paul wishes to insist on a new status: that of being sons (and so brothers) on account of the messianic.

13. Affliction and Solidarity (8:18–39)

This business of solidarity with and as sons (which is what makes us brothers, as Paul said in 8:12) is not without cost, as we are constantly being reminded: **since we suffer with him in order that we may be glorified with him**. The present still remains the time of the cross for us, the time of affliction (as we also heard in 5:2–5). Much of the following discourse is an elaboration and explanation of what had been touched on earlier. The term for "glory" was also there: the hope of the glory or radiance, or shining forth of God; and here, to be glorified or shine forth with the resurrected messiah. Before, we heard of having a death like his to share in a resurrection like his; here we hear of suffering with him leading to being made radiant or shining with him. As we said in discussing baptism, what is in view here is no virtual cultic death or virtual suffering but sharing in affliction that demonstrates or testifies to our solidarity with the executed messiah. Later Christians will call this testimony martyrdom.

For I consider that the sufferings of the present aren't worth comparing with the coming radiance that is to be manifest [*apokalyphthanai*] [in]**to us.** That which comes is an unheard-of light. All will be manifest. This is the language of apocalyptic hope. The sufferings, we may suppose, are those that have been indicated before: those of the opposition to the messianic that occurs within the world of sin and death, and the law that rules this reality. Before, Paul has used the "much more" to designate the new. Here he says that even with respect to the now-time of the in-breaking messianic reality characterized by suffering, what we hope for is truly incomparable and thus is incomparably "much more."

We have seen before how Paul shifts focus. We heard of the current polities divided between Israel and the nations, and we heard of Abraham, who stands before that division. Then we heard of the weakness of Adam, in whom is comprehended all humanity as such. Now the frame widens again, and we see the true dimensions of the apocalyptic horizon within which all of this is taking place. This horizon becomes visible precisely as the locus of a certain kind of suffering, moreover, of a certain solidarity in suffering and so in yearning.

This further extension of the Pauline frame of reference follows almost naturally from the designation of Adam as humanity. In Hebrew *adam* speaks of the earth, the earthling made of earth, of the solidarity of earth and earthling—hence we have the extension of the good news also with respect to creation and thus to all creatures. We recall that Paul had gestured in this direction when he spoke of "all flesh" as not being enabled to be just through law but through unconditional generosity. We will see this now played out in unexpected ways.

But we should also note that one way contemporary philosophy is "catching up" with Paul is in troubling the distinction, so fundamental to Western thought, between the animal and the human. Whether we think here of the reflections of Agamben in *The Open*, in which he interrogates Heidegger, or of the many essays of Derrida culminating in *The Animal That Therefore I Am*, we are the beneficiaries of a fundamental troubling of the self-evident distinction between the animal and the human. In this the patristic authors were more in tune with Paul when they thought of redemption as a redemption of the whole earth.

Creation itself is anxiously watching, eagerly expecting [on the lookout for], **the manifestation of the sons of God.** Like one who waits for the ship to appear over the horizon, pacing on the "widow's walk," alert for the first glimpse of what brings what one hopes for with bated breath, all creation is on tiptoe scanning the horizon for the appearing of what will turn its yearning to celebration. This yearning or longing is quite different from the "boredom" that Heidegger has attributed to the animal and for which he has been strongly criticized by Agamben and Derrida. Stanislas Breton writes: "By that *Eros* incorporated into their very essence, living and inorganic beings alike tend toward their supreme humanization in a revelation by which they are made to *participate* in the unheard-of dignity of the Sons of God" (117).

For the creation was subjected to futility. Here is the astonishing solidarity between the human and the creation, one that only Eastern theology was able to grasp and elucidate. In the modern West we have lost track of solidarity between the human and the rest of creation. And in theology it has sometimes been forgotten that biology, including evolutionary biology, has at least retained something of the sense of our bound-up-ness with creation. Most of our DNA, for example, is the same as that of the lowliest earthworm.

Here that creation of which we are a part suffers subjection to futility. **Not of its own will but by the will of him who subjected it in hope** is a phrase not all that astonishing today with our growing knowledge of how the planet groans under subjugation to the folly, greed, and rapaciousness of the human bound for death. Most translations relate the phrase "in hope" to this will to subject. But before going too hastily in that direction, we should recall that the one who had the vocation, according to Genesis, to subject the earth, was Adam, the one who became subsequently subjected to flesh, sin, the Law, injustice, and so on. In the first instance the one who has subjected the earth is the human. But we could also view this as a certain hope that the human would subject the earth to hope, hope for solidarity rather than enmity. But in this case the agent of hope (though not directly the one who had "subjected" creation) would be God. In any case, we are to see that humanity and creation share a common hope, as well as a common subjugation to "vanity." Stanislas Breton writes that "the human mastery of the *cosmos*, by its effect on the things themselves, affects the latter with its own historical fate, whether that fate be one of misery or of grandeur" (119).

But it will be set free from bondage to death and decay. The destiny of the earth depends on the destiny of humanity, a dependence that is one of hope, of yearning, of eagerly expecting. Our destiny is its destiny: **to obtain the radiant liberty of the children** [*teknōn*] **of God**. Just as it was subjected by our becoming subjected to death, so also it will obtain liberty as we do and become, as we do, the children of God. Thus, the evangel or proclamation of glad news concerns the earth itself and all creation. The bondage to death (which has to do with the entry of violation and violence into the world, accelerated by law) not only concerns the human but also the whole of creation. And the promise of liberation from this law of violence pertains not only to the human but also to the earth and its denizens. Such is the amplitude of Paul's message of the good news that stems from what the divine has done in and through the messianic event.

We know the whole creation has been groaning together in birth pangs until now. This suffering is really now to be understood as birth pangs, the groaning in agony of the great mother whose groaning is also our groaning, a groaning for redemption. **Who will deliver me from this body of death?** That is also the cry of the great mother who labors to bring forth a different kind of humanity than that which is subjected and has subjected her to death. And in this groaning all creatures, all creation, are "together." (We should pay attention to how often Paul makes use of the prefix *syn-* in Greek to indicate a togetherness: of suffering, of subjection, of hope, of care, and so on; it is one of his most characteristic word formations.)

Jacob Taubes notes that Paul's assertions regarding creation are reflected in Walter Benjamin's "Theological-Political Fragment" (70). Agamben will go further, claiming that Benjamin (in "Theses on the Philosophy of History") is able to give new expression to what is essential in the whole of Romans as one who lives in a homologous world crisis: "These two fundamental messianic texts of our tradition . . . both written in a situation of radical crisis, form a constellation whose time of legibility has finally come" (Agamben, *Time* 145). (One cannot help wondering whether this "finally come" might also be an index of Agamben's own messianism, his own messianic consciousness.)

And not only the creation but we ourselves, who have the first fruits of the spirit groan inwardly as we wait for adoption as sons, the redemption of our bodies. Our bodies as "the part of world that we ourselves are," as Käsemann rightly maintains (*New Testament Questions* 135), are destined for redemption *because* the earth is also destined for redemption. Adoption may be spoken of here both as already and as to come. For it is the redemption of body, so of creation itself, that is the horizon of hope. What we are or have is the first fruits, the springtime promise of more to come. But we have not ceased to groan. Our adoption is behind (so we cry *abba*); our adoption is yet to come (so we groan). Perhaps it is precisely the spiritedness that makes this groaning possible? Or even necessary? Breton notes: "From the highest point to the lowest on the ontological ladder, a single groaning, transmitted from one level to another, proclaims that the essence of the world is simply freedom" (117).

For in this hope we were saved.

We hope (now); we were saved (then). We should attend to the astonishing time out of joint, the hinge that is unhinged or that unhinges the grammatical tenses. The "were saved" occurs within the framework of hope. It is precisely in hope that we live. Like Abraham, who believed the promise and whose con*fid*ence in the promise was *fid*elity (faithfulness) and so reckoned up as, or credited toward, justice.

What has happened has happened in the key of hope: **Now hope that is seen is not hope; for who hopes for what he sees? But if we hope for what we do not see, we wait for it with patience, endurance.** Hope makes us capable of enduring—exactly when we don't see what we hope for. There is perhaps not yet a sail on the horizon, but we remain in hope; we endure because we hope, like the one who paces the widow's walk, who remains faithful to hope. And this, as we heard in the earlier discussion of the coming of the messianic, produces or is produced by a kind of obstinacy (Heidegger), a persevering in spite of appearances, a hope against hope (as Paul said of Abraham). In any case this is not optimism: it is yearning, groaning . . . in spite of appearances, in spite of what could be termed knowledge. It is the key of the messianic. What we have is the groaning, the yearning, and the resultant solidarity with all who yearn, so with creation as a whole. This is a solidarity that is itself the spirited solidarity that heralds a coming that cannot yet be seen, grasped, or possessed.

Likewise the spirit partakes of our weakness. The traditional translation, "helps us," is, I think, flat wrong—the spirit is a sharer, a partaker, in this very weakness of groaning, of yearning. **For we don't know how to pray as is fitting or appropriate.** How do we know how to say what we hope for or, yearn for, really, deeply, truly? We don't know the words that say or bring to speech that which has not yet ever been, that which is the deepest yearning of inanimate and animate nature. **The spirit itself intercedes on behalf** [of us, of creation, of God] **with unutterable groanings.** We/creation/spirit all groan, all yearn, all beyond speech, the earth-spirit groan. Before language. Before speech. Inarticulate. Somehow in this groaning and yearning, we glimpse the awaited solidarity of earth and humanity and spirit. The beginning of that solidarity for which we hope if we dared to speak its name is "already" present . . . as groaning. Paul elsewhere calls it God, all in all (1 *Corinthians* 15:28). Thus, the praying/yearning of spirit seems like weakness but is already the joining together of what has been separated, and thus is a strange kind of power: that which raises from the dead. In a later text, the Fourth Gospel, the resurrection of Lazarus will also be accompanied by a groaning, on the part of the messiah (John 11:38, 43).

And the one who scrutinizes the hearts knows what is the mind of spirit because in accordance with God spirit intercedes on behalf of the saints. This is a very enigmatic phrase. But it does indicate that the groaning of the spirit in and with us is in accordance with the will or intention of God. In this way, the spirit is the agent of power (precisely as weakness) of God in us, so in creation as a whole. The spirit intercedes precisely as groaning, as the yearning of the divine in and for us.

The material beginning at 8:28 amplifies what we found concerning exulting or rejoicing in 5:3–5. Thus, the intervening material serves to ground this more surely and in ways that will found this level of assurance.

And we know that to those who love God, all things are brought together by God toward the good according to the purpose that they have been called into being. The phrase **called into being** and similar phrases here have in view what will come in chapters 9–11. These are those who **love him**, that is, who adhere to him in joy and thanksgiving—those who are faithful adopted heirs, those for whom whatever happens turns into or is turned by God into good. That is, whatever happens is turned by God into the direction of God's redemptive purpose for all. There is, of course, nothing here of the pseudo-gospel of health and wealth. On the contrary, what is in view here, as in chapter 5 and later in this chapter, is precisely what might be regarded as terrible misfortune. But it will be turned into **good**, into redemption, and not only for "us" but for all, as the succeeding argument will show.

These who are summoned to faith are those who are **conformed to the likeness of the messianic son**, in order that he should be only the first and not the last, still less the only son, for all are to be incorporated into "sonship."

We now hear a drum roll of past tenses: **foreknew, predestined, called, justified, glorified**. In some ways, it is the future perfect. But the effect is to make even the future past and thus indubitable. The messianic time, which Paul sometimes calls the now-time, is a time unlike the time in which past-present-future seem to be unproblematically distinguished from one another. The foreshortening of the messianic time means that the verb tenses seem to get scrambled. What may seem future so invades the present, is so inaugurated in the past (perhaps as promise), that the tenses become interchangeable. Thus, it is necessarily unclear whether the messiah has come or is yet to appear (*parousia*); adoption can be spoken of as that which has occurred (so we shout *abba*) and as yet to occur (so we groan); being just may be both what is already true for those who are caught up in the messianic event and something that must be made true, must become true.

Giorgio Agamben writes of messianic time that "it is that part of secular time which undergoes an entirely transformative contraction" (*Time* 64). This contraction "implies an actual transformation of time that may even interrupt secular time here and now" (73). While he emphasizes the ways in which past and present pass into one another (the past becoming open with possibility, the present fulfilled or finished), it also seems that the future participates now in the fulfillment of the past. Messianic time is that contraction of time that renders discrimination between past, present, and future entirely precarious.

Paul is writing to a tiny, embattled, and almost overwhelmed group, yet he asks, **If God be for us, who is against us?** The whole of the empire, the whole of civilization, law, and religion are here reduced to naught in the apocalyptic horizon. Nothing whatever can stand in the way of the accomplishment of the divine promise and goal. The divine commitment to the project of which we are but the tiniest foretaste is absolute: the one **who did not spare his own son but on our behalf gave him up, won't he give everything to us?** This is not a theory of atonement but of free gift, of incalculable commitment/generosity. Having gone this far, will God pull back now?

Who will bring a charge against the ones chosen by God? It is God who makes just; who then can condemn? Earlier Paul had said **there is now therefore no condemnation for those included or sharing in the messiah**. Here we get again the idea of suspended condemnation. Will the one who was condemned and who is now the "judge" be the one who condemns? **It is messiah Joshua, who died, yes, who was raised from the dead, who is at the right hand of God, who indeed intercedes for us.** He will come to judge, but who is the judge? Will the one who was rejected by the law then judge or condemn? If it is God who has discovered a new way to produce justice at great cost, will God then go back to the old way? If the messiah is the one who advocates for us, how shall we be condemned? One can speak of forgiveness here to some limited extent, insofar as our embeddedness in the world of injustice will not count against us and our loyalty to this one and this way will be counted for us, as justice, as on the way to justice.

Then Paul "lets go" with an exultation, a rejoicing. For in a certain sense the proclamation is that **nothing can separate us from the love of messiah . . . from the love of God in messiah Joshua**. Accordingly, even in the midst of terrible sufferings—**affliction or distress or persecution, or famine or nakedness or peril or sword**—there is an exulting in irreversible victory: **we are more than conquerors**. For the rest, notice that it is precisely the situation of tribulation (as sheep for the slaughter) that shows our solidarity with the messiah and his with us. How then could what unites us with him (suffering) separate us from him?

For I have been persuaded that not death, not life, not angels, not rulers, not things present, not things to come, not powers, not

height, not depth, not any other creature—there is no need to belabor each word searching for special meaning (*height, depth,* etc.). Paul is on a roll, or perhaps we should say that he is writing a riff on his theme: **Nothing will be able to separate us from the love of God in messiah Joshua our leader.**

Fourth Phase

DIVINE PROMISE AND IMPROVISATION
(9:1–11:36)

The unshakeable assurance of Romans 8:31–39 must be tested. It has so far been grounded in the experience of the faithful in two ways: their own response to the glad-making proclamation in terms of the acclamation of God as *abba/Pater,* and the endurance of the community and its members in the face of affliction and persecution. Moreover, Paul has sought to ground this assurance in ways we might term "ontological" or "cosmological." This corresponds to and even exceeds the Adamic dimension that had been introduced in chapter 5. But Paul is by no means finished. From the very beginning he has signaled his interest in and concern for the way in which the action of God takes into account both Judeans and gentiles. At 1:16, he had announced that the gospel was directed "to the Judean first and also to the Greek." This formula is repeated in 2:9 with respect to tribulation and distress for those who do evil, and at 2:10 with respect to glory, honor, and peace for those who do good. We noted then that Paul's actual procedure in the opening argument seemed to reverse that priority, dealing first with gentiles and subsequently with Judeans. In the argument of the three chapters beginning at 9:1, Paul will now make good on the previously announced priority.

At the beginning of chapter 3 was a series of questions that seemed to be left hanging: **If some were unfaithful, does their faithlessness nullify the faithfulness of God?** (3:3). **If our wickedness serves to show the justice of God . . . is God unjust to inflict wrath on us?** (3:5). **If through my**

falsehood God's truthfulness abounds to his glory, why am I still condemned as a sinner? (3:7–8). The argument of the long discourse that we will track through the next three chapters serves as a reply to these questions. In the meantime, Paul has attempted to clarify the question of faithfulness outside the law and to argue that this faithfulness actually must produce justice rather than the perpetuation of injustice. He is now ready to take up questions earlier announced but left hanging. Thus, what follows is no mere appendix but has been aimed at from the very beginning of Paul's letter.

The basic issue—**Will their unfaithfulness nullify the faithfulness of God?** (3:3)—is now going to be addressed. But there is even more, for Paul had just maintained that those whom he foreknew he predestined and those he predestined he also called justified, glorified. Can this confidence be maintained in the face of the situation of the people of Israel who had rejected the messiah? Above all, they were foreknown, predestined, and called. Has that then been overthrown? If so, nothing can stand of this great hymnic riff of unshakeable assurance. If the promise of God has failed with respect to Israel, it cannot stand with respect to us. Who could then have confidence in the divine promise?

14. Has the Promise Failed? (9:1–29)

An issue must be resolved: How is it that God's promise to Abraham, a promise that has been the motor of Israel's history, can be utterly relied upon if Israel itself has turned away from the promise, has rejected the messiah? If human rejection can stop or stall the divine determination to save or redeem, how can we really have confidence? How can our assurance be other than hollow?

Of course, some maintain that this is all unnecessary. About a century later Marcion, believing himself to have the mind of Paul, will maintain simply that Israel's God is a different God and that the redemption that is in Christ is for the nations independently of the promise and the covenant with Israel. Thus, to read this argument, we must begin with the recognition that this is simply impossible for Paul. And we must ask why.

Before trying to answer this question, we must recognize that the history of the interpretation of Romans 9–11 has been semi-Marcionite. Christianity has often assumed it can do without a relation to the root of

Israel's history. The result has been the enablement of tacit or terrifyingly explicit anti-Judaism. The interpretation of the argument of this section of Romans is decisive in this regard, as Jacob Taubes dramatically confirmed in conversation with Carl Schmitt, who had given intellectual cover for many of the policies of Hitler's National Socialist Party. When Taubes read with Schmitt this passage from Paul, Schmitt reacted with surprise. Taubes remarks: "It is possible to read texts without noticing what their core point is," especially when this not noticing is protected by a "fifteen-hundred-year-old Christian history" of not attending to the point (51).

It is important to keep in mind two interrelated coordinates: history and Israel. History is crucial since God is involved in history, including some relationship to the history of the rejection and execution of the messiah. And God is bringing history to a consummation precisely through this act. Moreover, this act must be made sense of in terms of God's activity in history, above all, in history as the history of God's people. We are returning from the Adamic, which reached out to include all creation, to the Abrahamic as inclusive of Judean and gentile and thus of all humanity, considered as peoples in history.

Since the time of Augustine, the tendency has been to read Romans as if the basic argument had been determined by chapter 4; the chapter to which we are about to turn was read as entirely concerned with a question about something like predestination. The arguments about predestination, however, have ignored Paul's focus on political history generally and the history of Israel in particular. Accordingly, the talk of predestination has fallen into a non-Pauline (and nonbiblical) individualism. On these views, God predestines individuals to salvation or damnation. But that is not Paul's argument at all. Moreover, it ignores the fact that with Paul's emphasis on social or political history, the aim of the divine will is salvation for all rather than any sort of double predestination of either damnation or salvation. Karl Barth recognized that the doctrine of predestination as initiated by Augustine and then made rigorous in the early Middle Ages by Gottschalk (a view that becomes determinative for Wycliffe and Calvin) is both antibiblical and antievangelical, lacking relation to the proclamation of God's act in Christ (*Church Dogmatics* 3–34). Without endorsing (or contesting) Barth's particular way of resolving this issue, we will have to be attentive to this question in our reading of Paul's argument.

In Galatians, Paul had put forward a very different argument concerning the election of Israel, a view that certainly lends itself to the idea that Christianity supersedes Israel. But in the letter to the Romans, Paul will make a very different argument about the irrevocability of God's election of Israel. While specific factors concerning the audience addressed in each letter undoubtedly play a role in the fundamental shift in Paul's argument, his discussion in Romans seems to be far better thought out and at the same time more deeply connected to Paul's own commitments and concerns. The latter becomes evident from the very beginning.

I am speaking the truth in messiah—I am not lying; my conscience confirms it in holy spirit.

Recall that it is the spirit that has been spoken of as groaning with us—as yearning with us and all creation—for redemption. Precisely this spirit of solidarity and yearning is invoked here. That Paul speaks the truth in the messiah means that his words share in the yearning of the messiah for the messiah's own people, the people who have priority in the messianic purpose and passion.

I have great sorrow and unceasing anguish in my heart.

This is the very language of spirit, not in triumph but in sorrow and anguish. As earth groans for redemption of humanity, so Paul groans for the redemption of Israel: **For I could wish that I myself were accursed and cut off from messiah for the sake of my own people, my kindred according to the flesh.** Paul knows something about being accursed and cut off. This is his own experience with his own people. But his response is not to desire their destruction but to desire to substitute himself for them. In this case **kindred according to the flesh** refers to religiocultural identity rather than the spirited kinship that leads Paul to refer to fellow messianists as "brothers."

To what extent is the desire to be accursed for the sake of the other the mark of messianic desire? He is saying in essence, "I would rather that I be damned than that others be condemned." Is this not precisely what the messiah has done? Has he not become accursed for the sake of the deliverance of the others from the curse—even from the curse that they have brought upon themselves? The reference to the messianic here is so far double: Paul speaks in messiah, and this speaking in messiah is a desire to be cut off from the messiah so that others might be joined to the messiah. This is not simply an extreme expression. It is the very heart and substance of messianic faithfulness, of solidarity in the suffering of messiah.

They are Israelites and to them belong the adoption, the glory [radiance]**, the covenants, the giving of the law, the worship, the promises; to them belong the patriarchs, and from them according to the flesh comes the messiah. Blessed forever be God, who is over all, amen.**

Earlier he had said of the Israelite's advantages, **much in every way, for in the first place they were entrusted with the oracles of God** (3:2). Here this is expanded in the most extraordinary way. The reference to **oracles** has been expanded to **the covenants, the giving of the law, the worship**. Moreover, Paul adds, **adoption and radiance**. These are the very critical terms he has just been using regarding the messianic in the previous section. They designate the beginning (adoption) and the end (radiance) of the redemptive act. What he ascribes to those who are participants in the messianic reality belongs already to Israel! We shall see that this "belonging" is inalienable.

This will be true first of all because of the promises given to the patriarchs (Paul no longer makes use of the argument about two different seeds of Abraham that he had employed in Galatians). It is from the patriarchs that the messiah, hence the messiah of Israel, comes. The concluding "promise," then, is what connects all of this to where we began with Abraham and where we are headed, with messiah. Thus, the comprehensive promise comes to a head with the coming of the messiah, whose coming is good news "to the Judeans first, and then the Greeks."

The last clause (**Blessed forever be God**) should not be translated in such a way as to suggest a proto-Nicene-type creedal formulation of the divinity of Christ. The idea is that all of the "gifts" received by Israel are gifts that come from God and precisely the God whose sending of the messiah is the focal point of the divine action: from promise to ultimate radiance or shining forth, passing through covenants, law, worship, and so on. His assertion is not that the messiah is God "overall" but rather that it is God whose ordering of all is manifest in the coming of the messiah as the fulfillment of promise, and thus as the basis of adoption and consummation in the divine radiance.

It is not as though the word of God had failed. This is the nub of the problem that must be dealt with if the promise is to really be secure. The promise that has been expanded to include the nations and that extends from progeny to resurrection, so to the hope for cosmic transformation, must be secured at its core as a promise in the beginning to and for Israel.

Precisely because Paul is attempting to place "covenant, law, and worship" within this trajectory from promise to shining forth, the issue of God's having failed comes into view. If, as Paul believes, the coming of the messiah coheres with the promise that drives the history of Israel, then the rejection of that messiah by the official guardians of "covenant, law and worship" could be construed as the failure of the divine word. It is thus incumbent on Paul to show that the decisive features of Israel's covenant history may properly be understood as pointing to the shape of the divine "plan" or ordering of history toward the goal of the inclusion of the gentiles while affirming that every "setback" in this trajectory serves only to drive it toward its appointed goal.

Paul will now offer a number of arguments and analogies to establish this point, just as he had offered the sequence of arguments and analogies in chapter 6 to establish the before-and-after elements of his claim that sin is abolished through grace. It is important that these new analogies not be separated either from one another or from the series to which they belong and the point that they attempt to establish. This is all the more true since it is not Paul's intent to offer an "objective" survey of the history of Israel but to interpret key elements in accordance with what he now supposes the goal of that history to be. His survey hits upon key moments: the patriarchal history, the Exodus from Egypt (which includes the giving of the law), and especially, the perspectives of the prophets.

We begin therefore with the patriarchal sagas:

For not all Israelites truly belong to Israel.

Is this something that a Pharisee, rather than a Sadducee, might have said? This seems likely. It may also have been the basis for the work of John the Baptizer, since baptism may have served for the Pharisees and for John as an entry or reentry into the people of Israel. In any case, what will now follow is a way of maintaining that some serve in the place of all. Later, however, this will be reversed so that "some" leads to "all." Thus, the complex use of synecdoche enables Paul to move from representation as substitution to representation as vanguard.

The next sentences are concerned with the inheritors of the promise to Abraham. Significantly, he does not repeat the analogy he used in this regard in Galatians, where those who are in messiah are the exclusive children of the promise, while Israel is understood to be in the situation of Ishmael, children of the flesh. What is common to the two texts, however, is the emphasis on promise and who is the inheritor (son) of promise: Isaac, rather than Ishmael. **Not all the seed of Abraham are children of Abraham. But: "Through Isaac shall your descendants be named"** (referring to Genesis 21:12). Moreover, we see that the promise is set in some basic tension with "flesh." **This means it is not the children of the flesh who are children of God but the children of the promise are counted as seed.** We should note that here "children of God," a term applied by adoption to those who are incorporated into the messianic event, is also applied to those in the line of Isaac. To them also belongs, as Paul had said, the adoption. Adoption applies first to Israel and then subsequently to the recipients of the messianic proclamation and promise. There is no attempt to relegate Israel to the "flesh" instead of promise. On the contrary, the argument would lead one to suppose that flesh is somehow the bearer of promise, but always in a surprising way. One would even be led to say that the flesh of Sarah rather than that of Abraham is decisive here. **About this time I will return and Sarah shall have a son.** Thus, we have to do here not with the patriarch but the matriarch whose child is the fruit of the promise.

A second analogy comes from reference to Rebecca. Rebecca and Isaac are the parents of Jacob/Israel.

And not only so but when Rebecca had conceived children by one man, our forefather Isaac, though they were not yet born and had done neither good nor bad, in order that the purpose of God might abide according to [God's] choice, not because of works but because of the one who calls, it was said to her "the greater will serve the lesser," even as it has been written "Jacob I loved, but Esau I hated."

Neither Isaac nor Jacob is the elder son. In each case, we could say that the elder is "sacrificed" so that the younger might be the bearer of promise in opposition to the tendency of patriarchy. Thus, the promise of God is realized in such a way that it is utterly reliable yet completely unpredictable from human custom or expectation. Once again we notice that Paul has substituted matriarchal history for patriarchal history.

The reference to Esau and Jacob allows Paul to introduce another of his basic themes (not works but "call"). In this argument against works, however, the stress lies not on the faithfulness of the one called, as it had earlier, but simply on the origin of the call itself, that it is entirely the choice of God. The citation of Malachi 1:2–3 concerning loving Jacob and hating Esau does not refer to emotional states but to the decision that serves the interest of one rather than the other. The choice operates in such a way as to undermine the sense of entitlement of the "elder." The selection of one for favor occurs in advance of any merit, just as in the case of Abraham. Thus, the choice, the decision, the action, and promise of God are not as unreliable as our response but as reliable as is God's own word.

In this saga of Esau and Jacob, not only does the line of promise continue through Jacob rather than Esau in the absence of or in advance of any merit. Beyond that, it seems that if we were to calculate merit, we would have to go with Esau. He is not only the elder but he is also by far the more noble. Jacob is an utter scoundrel who robs his brother's inheritance (not without the collaboration of his scheming mother). In contrast, Esau's behavior in welcoming this scoundrel back without exacting the revenge that Jacob fully and reasonably expected is exemplary. But that is not Paul's point here. He is not really attempting to give an exegesis of the biblical story but to select one element from it to make the point that the fulfillment of God's promise does not depend on the "faithfulness" of the human actors.

Is there injustice on God's part? This would be an issue since Paul's whole argument depends on the call and claim of justice. The answer might seem unsatisfactory. **Absolutely not!** The point is that God acts precisely as God has said God will act. This echoes the question and answer already broached in 3:5.

Here he cites Moses (in the context of Law in Exodus 33:19) to establish his point: **"I will have mercy on whom I will have mercy, and I will have compassion on whom I will have compassion."** This citation stands in tension with the earlier **"Jacob I loved but Esau I hated."** What has changed is that Paul emphasizes mercy and compassion. Those who have used this text to support "double predestination" of some to heaven and others to hell have completely missed Paul's point. He is shaping or bending everything toward mercy rather than judgment, to compassion rather than condemnation. **So it depends not on human exertion or will but on God who shows mercy.** Paul is trying to keep this focused on mercy or generosity rather than on judgment. God's justice is precisely God's mercy now, not quite the wrath that we heard of earlier. But that will return in a new guise.

With the citation from Moses, we turn to the saga of liberation from Egypt and the example of Pharaoh. Of course, Pharaoh opposed the divine mercy that sought to deliver the Hebrew people from bondage, but in spite of his opposition he becomes an instrument of divine mercy. Now we enter the world-historical sphere: the arrogance of the powerful is precisely their hardness of heart, but this will nonetheless be bent to serve the purposes of mercy and compassion. We may apply this, for example, to Pontius Pilate or even the Sanhedrin. What they do may be opposed to divine justice and mercy but will in fact be made to serve that justice and mercy.

Thus, the rulers of this age owe their position and power to divine permission. But this permission has in view simply that they be made to be, in spite of themselves, the occasion for the "publicity" that their demise affords to the divine name. (We will recall this when we discuss the much controverted reference to "rulers" in chapter 13.) Their rule is ordered to their own destruction or frustration so that history may marvel at the faithfulness of God to those who are oppressed by these powers.

In the case of Pharaoh, we may read the story as the way that God (through Moses) seems only to make Pharaoh dig in his heels at the demand to let the people go. But this obstinacy only makes the eventual liberation more comprehensive (the Hebrew people don't simply go out to worship but go out to stay out) and more astonishing. **For the written says to Pharaoh: "I have raised you up for the very purpose of showing my power in you."** This is, of course, read as an anticipation of the way the rejection of the messiah by the powerful will only serve to make the "good news" more comprehensive (to the nations) and more astonishing (cross/resurrection). **So that my name may be proclaimed in all the earth.** This is indeed the very scope of Paul's own proclamation.

So then he has mercy on whom he wishes; he hardens whom he wishes. Although there are both hardening and mercy, the hardening serves only the aim of mercy, to make it all the more astonishing and comprehensive.

Why then does he still find fault? For who can resist him? If even opposition to God's intent can be bent to serve that intent, then why should God even care whether national leaders (for we must keep in mind that this is the level at which Paul's argument is proceeding) agree with the divine intent? Why does God condemn political and historical injustice? We recall that Paul had affirmed that God does indeed condemn that injustice in the first two chapters of Romans. Moreover, he had anticipated precisely this sort of question already in his discussion of the coming of messianic justice (3:5–7).

This question offers Paul the chance to move forward into the history of the prophets of Israel, the ones who most clearly articulate the action of God on the stage of world history. Here he offers a number of analogies drawn from the oracles of Israel's own prophets.

The response of Paul first sets the situation of the human as such who would contend with the divine. **O man**, as in chapter 2, has a universal referent but may also be understood as having the imperial authority in view (Pharaoh, for example).

Do you presume to argue with God? Surely what is molded will not say to the one who molded it: why did you make me like this? Or doesn't the potter have the right over the clay to make from the same lump either something honored or something dishonored?

The notion of the molded versus the molder goes back to a prophetic tradition and most closely resembles Isaiah 29:16: "You who turn things upside down! Shall the potter be regarded as the clay? Shall the thing made say of its maker, 'He did not make me,' or the thing formed say of the one who formed it, 'He has no understanding'?" As in that text, here also it is not the situation of the individual that is in view but that of the people and the nations. The analogy is brought forward with this contrast: from the same clay may be made something that has an honorable use and something that has a dishonorable use. From the same material may be made a bedpan or a wine goblet; either serves the intention of the maker.

What if God, desiring to show wrath and to make known his power, has endured with much patience the instruments of wrath made for destruction? This is an image again taken from prophetic tradition that refers to the great empires that serve the purposes of God in punishing Israel for its injustice. The ascendancy of these powers, which might seem to contravene the authority of God, winds up serving the divine purposes. They are temporary instruments of wrath, but they are themselves destined for destruction.

The purpose of these afflicting instruments is now further bent toward the overriding purpose of demonstrating the **riches of his radiance/shining forth for the instruments of mercy, which he has prepared beforehand for radiance** [shining forth]. The point is that the use of the afflicting power is temporary, but the use of the instrument of mercy is from forever and to forever, that is, it is everlasting. This is what the divine "plan" aims at: mercy rather than wrath. And this mercy is itself the divine shining forth or radiance in which what serves that goal also partakes or shares in that radiance.

Us, whom he called, not from the Judeans only but also from the nations [pagans]. Here we come into view, that is, Paul's readers or hearers who now are those who are molded to be instruments of divine mercy. It is important to note, however, that these are still merely instruments (*skeous*). They/we are not the goal of the divine action. We serve the purpose of the divine radiance so have a certain security as those in whom that radiance is to be manifest. But we are by no means its exclusive object. The object, as we have heard and will hear again, is "all." It is precisely this that is anticipated in the coming together of both Judean and pagan to be shaped as an instrument of mercy rather than of condemnation or wrath.

It is, alas, well known that the church has come to be as much an instrument of wrath as the empires or those who persecuted the community ever were. For the church often punishes, ostracizes, and afflicts, not only in the Inquisitions of old but also in its presumed authority to exclude those of another faith or no faith or those of disapproved "lifestyles." Thus, we cannot understand ourselves to be those who are here designated "instruments of mercy." Earlier we were called to be instruments or even weapons of justice. This justice is now increasingly clearly identified with compassion.

There now follow three citations from Hosea and Isaiah that have the purpose of exhibiting the unpredictable but reliable way in which the divine mercy comes to be demonstrated in the history of God's people.

The first, from Hosea (**Those who were not my people**) comes from the end of that book. What happens here is that the earlier rejection of Israel (transgendered as YHWH's unfaithful and promiscuous wife) is finally overturned and those who were divorced, abandoned, and rejected are now reclaimed (in contravention of the legal codes of Deuteronomy 22:21–22). This is an anticipation of the argument that Paul will make in chapter 11. The point now is that the rejection and punishment of the faithless Israel simply aim at restoration. The judgment of Israel aims at the redemption of Israel.

A similar point is made with a quotation from Isaiah, in which the notion of the remnant (to which Paul will return) is first deployed as an illustration of divine wrath (**only a remnant will survive**) and then as a demonstration of mercy: **without a remnant** [but here called **a seed** (*sperma*)] **we would have perished as completely as Sodom.** Thus, the threat begins to appear as promise or as serving the promise.

As an earlier generation of theologians learned from reading Karl Barth, the divine NO, however severe and unrelenting, has no other aim than that it serve the manifestation of the divine YES. These are not to be thought of as alternatives that are "side by side" but rather as subordinate and superordinant or as arranged in such a way that the judgment has no other meaning than that all be saved.

We come then to the (provisional) conclusion of this segment of the argument, a conclusion that brings us back to where we were in chapters 2–4: the question of the astonishing fact that it is the pagans who respond to the message of the messiah and thus who embody a certain justice. This consideration most immediately returns to the problem that Paul had set out at the beginning of this section of his argument. The problem was that many of those who seem to represent the people chosen by God to be the object of God's promise have rejected the one who is to bring that promise to fruition. And in an even more pointed fashion the problem remains (which is yet to be addressed) of the consummation of that promise for Israel as such or as a whole.

In this argument Paul has attempted to show the complete reliability of the divine word, promise, and election. This has been maintained in at least three ways.

First, Paul has demonstrated that God acts in accordance with what God has spoken. In accordance with the pronouncement of God to Moses "I will have mercy on whom I will have mercy," God had chosen Isaac rather than Ishmael, Jacob rather than Esau. In accordance with the word transmitted through the prophets, God has chosen pagan empires as instruments of punishment or of mercy. In accordance with the word of the prophets, only a remnant of Israel (so far) welcomes the messiah. That is, what has happened thus far with respect to the proclamation of the good news (that the nations are responding but much of Israel is not) conforms to rather than contravenes God's word.

Mixed in with this argument is another that aims to show that God's way of acting does not conform to human expectations but is based solely on the divine good pleasure. Thus, the divine choice does not depend on physical or social priority (not the firstborn Ishmael but Isaac), nor on works or apparent moral priority (not the noble Esau but the scheming Jacob). For this reason, God's act is not forced or constrained by presumed right or even by the better claim of being obedient.

Finally, Paul has shown that even that which opposes the divine promise and act is made to serve the divine intention. Thus, the opposition of Pharaoh or the actions of unjust empires were made to serve the divine purpose against their own intentions. This will set up Paul's argument that even the opposition of God's own people will come to serve the divine purpose of the coming of messianic justice for all people.

In consequence, God's word can be shown to be utterly reliable. But it is absolutely crucial to keep in mind that we have here not many words or decrees but basically one: the promise to save, the promise to take back all creation. That is the point at which Paul ended chapter 8. He will come back to this assertion of total victory of the gospel (of which we recall he is not ashamed) by the end of this argument, and we will gain new insight concerning the totality of the redemptive aim. It is critical to keep the idea of election in this passage connected to the idea of total redemption that we have heard in chapters 5 and 8. When the pieces get separated, theology runs off the rails and antievangelical doctrines (like that of double predestination) are generated. Even more ominously, some might look to this prophetic history of the use of the unjust empires to discipline Israel as a way of interpreting the horrors of the twentieth-century Shoah. But this would be quite impossible for Paul. It would suppose that we are still living in pre-messianic time—for in the now-time, the divine justice is fundamentally bent toward mercy, as the prophets Paul has been quoting also realize. Just as there can be no justification for the empire's injustice elaborated in chapter 1, injustice that executed the messiah, so also there can be no legitimation for the unspeakable rebellion against God perpetrated upon the people of the messiah in the Holocaust.

15. The History of Justice (9:30–10:4)

We have seen Paul argue for the reliability of the divine promise despite the vicissitudes of history. But this is only one side of what needs to be established. The reliability of God's promise must also be connected to the question of justice. What the promise, the mercy, the generous gift of God aims at is precisely justice, a just social order or polity. Some aspects of the previous argument might have led us to forget the insistence upon justice: the apparently arbitrary nature of the divine choices and perhaps especially the fact that these choices are not dependent upon whether anyone is just (as in the case of the preference of Jacob over Esau before either one had done good or bad). In the section that follows Paul turns from what has been the objective basis of confidence in the divine promise to something like the subjective basis. He will again show the relation between faith and works that had been set up in chapters 3–4.

What shall we say? **Nations that did not pursue justice arrived at** [or were found by] **justice, but a justice of loyalty** [or faithfulness]**; but Israel pursuing a just law did not arrive at that law.** We are seeing set up a distinction between justice of faithfulness and justice of law. Only faithfulness will actually arrive at justice. Despite the seeking and pursuing of justice through law, the justice at which law aims is not arrived at. But why? Because it did not pursue it through faith(fulness) but as if by works. The point is that Israel seeks to achieve justice through what it can control—its works or compliance with legal requirements—rather than by way of faithful adherence to the claim and call of God.

We are returned to the argument of 3:20–31. The apparently scrupulous yet also mechanical compliance with rules and regulations that the law specifies can lead one to lose sight of what the law fundamentally aims at: justice. The justice that comes to the nations who are bereft of the law in the Israelite sense is one provoked by gift and promise (or the gift of promise) and thus awakens faithfulness rather than scrupulous observance. Legal compliance cannot truly correspond with the call for justice. This can happen only through loyalty or faithfulness. Justice cannot be captured in a knowable legal system that one needs only to repeat and obey. Justice is an immeasurable claim that bends toward mercy and compassion. It is only love, as we shall hear, that can do what the law ultimately intends or requires: justice, whose other name we are beginning to learn, is mercy (or, as we have already heard, generosity or gift).

In our own time we find many who seek to comply with a law or legality that they believe represents the will of God. On this basis they think they are entitled to exclude or condemn those whose lifestyle, as they call it, seems to them to be condemned by "the law." Yet there are others who suppose that God is doing a new thing, that this is a "stone of stumbling," that what is called for is not mere inclusion but welcome, not condemnation but celebration.

They have stumbled over the stumbling stone as it is written (Isaiah 28:16, 8:14–15). How they have done so Paul will now clarify: it has to do with the now familiar question of loyalty or faithfulness, understood in contrast to seeking reward for work done or rules complied with. The image of the stumbling stone conflates Isaiah 8:14–15 with Isaiah 28:16. How does this conflation occur? Käsemann agrees that it is something of a mystery but the two may have already made up something of a messianic text (*Romans* 278), perhaps cited by the Pharisees. The point is that what God is doing will bring many to stumble. But not all will stumble, for some—those who rely on the promise or are faithful to it—will not be put to shame. Note here the return of the theme of shame that began the whole argument of Romans when Paul claimed that he was not ashamed of the gospel because it is the justice of God (1:17).

The heart of the passage is the reference to Isaiah 8, which has Israel stumble over a rock in its path, a rock that is God, God's will or judgment. Put differently, what causes the religiously privileged to stumble is God's own call and claim. It is common for Christian theologians to give this a Christological interpretation, but the justification is slender at best. The point is that God's unpredictable way of fulfilling God's promise is a cause of stumbling for those who think they can go on "automatic pilot"—who believe that they know how it is supposed to be or turn out and that they therefore can keep going in accordance with their own understanding or knowledge. They run into a rock over which they stumble, stagger, and fall. That rock is God, who, as we have seen, improvises in history to be faithful to the divine promise.

Paul returns to his yearning for the salvation, healing, and inclusion of those who have been the instruments of condemnation of the messiah and those who ally themselves with that messiah: **Comrades** [brothers], **my heart's desire for them, and my plea to God on their behalf is for** [their] **salvation.** This is, of course, quite different from what the church will subsequently think it can justify from Paul: an altogether too complacent and sometimes even vengeful or gleeful desire for their destruction, a destruction that has appeared all too clearly in history. If the reference to so many passages from the law and the prophets has caused us to lose track of what is going on here, Paul brings us back to his own passion. He had said, **I have great sorrow and anguish.** Paul yearns for salvation for his people. Recall the yearning of creation and how this yearning now connects to the historical reality of Israel. If we hear the echo of that earlier yearning, we will not be astonished at where this is headed in the conclusion to this penultimate phase of Paul's argument.

For I testify [or witness] **of** [or for or to] **them that they have zeal for God, but not according to knowledge.** Paul knows a thing or two about zeal and how this sincere zeal can run off the cliff. His own zeal (in Philippians 3:6 he had said that he was, prior to his messianic call, "as to zeal a persecutor of the church"), like that he is attributing to his fellow Israelites (Pharisees), is, however, one that does not correspond to its object. The proper object is the will of God or the call to true justice. Note that the problem is not hypocrisy (as in the Gospel of Matthew) but a certain fervent sincerity that has misplaced its object or true orientation. Indeed, as we learn every day in the newspapers, a misplaced sincere commitment often does enormous damage and produces horrifying injustice. The attacks on civilians by Al Qaeda and the "righteous" crusade against "terrorism" are made all the more ruthless through their manifest sincerity, their fervent zeal. Zeal may be a good thing, to be sure, but only when guided by understanding, in this case an understanding of justice (and mercy).

For not knowing the justice of God, and seeking to establish their own, they did not submit to the justice of God. They have sought to establish a different basis for justice, for divine justice, than the foundation to which the justice of God called them. The desire to be "right" with respect to the other or the outsider, or even in relation to God, leaves us in the situation of establishing for ourselves the rules of just behavior that prevent us from relying on what is the very call and claim of justice itself. It is all too easy to recognize this situation in what is called the church. Communities of Christians are only too glad to invent for themselves ways of being obedient to God and of requiring others to be obedient: don't drink, don't smoke, don't dance in some traditions; attend church, tithe, and so on in others or the same traditions; attend Mass, go to confession, and so on in others. Wherever one turns, one finds the zeal for God deflected into the proliferation of rules and regulations that have nothing whatever to do with justice and mercy. Indeed, the very meaning of the transformation in English of Paul's concern for justice into a concern for righteousness is the deflection into institutional petty moralizing of the call and claim of justice.

For messiah is the end [*telos*] of law so that justice may be based on loyalty.

The term *telos* signifies the end of the law both as fulfillment (because the end or goal is still justice) and as catastrophe of the law (because of the force or violence of the law). The messiah does not abolish the call and claim of justice but sets justice on a new "foundation," that of loyalty or faithfulness that comes outside the law and that the law had seemed to condemn or outlaw.

16. Speaking and Hearing: How Justice Comes (10:5–21)

The argument that follows serves as a counterpoint to the argument about how justice derives from faithfulness. If this is so, then how does faithfulness itself arise? Paul will seek to show that faithfulness is awakened or provoked through the hearing of the announcement of the gospel rather than through compliance with the (written) law. This hearing, and the speaking that awakens it, stands in contrast with what we might term the "distance and inaccessibility" of the law. This inaccessibility of the law is brought to expression in Kafka's parable "Before the Law," which receives a remarkable reading in an essay with the same title by Derrida, which will also link it to Paul's argument in Romans.

The first part of this argument at first looks like a further contrast between law and the justice that is aimed at through adherence to the law, on the one hand, and the faithfulness (and justice) that is enacted through the hearing and heeding of the word addressed, on the other. Paul will first notice that this contrast, or even opposition, is already found within the law itself.

Moses writes [*graphei*]: "The one who does the justice of the law will live in it" [Leviticus 10:5]. **But the justice** [that comes] **from faithfulness says: "Do not say in your heart, who will ascend into heaven (that is, to bring the messiah down) or who will descend into the abyss (to bring the messiah up from the dead)." But what does it say [*legei*]? "The word is near you, on your lips, in your heart [will]"** [Deuteronomy 30:11–14]. **This is the word of faithfulness that we announce.**

Paul first sets up a contrast between Leviticus and Deuteronomy. The former might well serve as a kind of proof text for compliance with the written law. It is introduced with the association of Moses and the written (*graphei*). But the modified citation from Deuteronomy is introduced with the assertion that the justice (that comes from) of faithfulness says (*legei*). The contrast between law and faithfulness is thus inscribed within the law itself.

The revision of Deuteronomy is quite audacious. Most obviously it introduces a substitution of the messianic for the law. The passage from Deuteronomy refers to the commandment (30:11) and even to "the commandments and statutes written in this book" (30:10). In place of this assertion regarding the "written commandments" Paul substitutes the messianic event: the coming of the messiah and the raising of the messiah from the dead.

Leaving aside the question about whether Paul has invented this messianic substitution or whether it is something already to hand in a messianic Judaism that he has appropriated, what seems to license this gloss in his mind concerns the question of the drawing near of the word: "the word is near you," in contrast to the distance to be associated with the law as legal edifice. He may have adopted this contrast from, for example, Jeremiah's contrast between a law written on stone or tablet and a law inscribed on the heart. It has to do with the will (heart) that acts not so much out of duty as out of desire. We might say that the justice of faithfulness is not heteronomous but springs from the wholehearted commitment of loyalty to another. Simon Critchley has pointed out that for Rousseau the basic issue had to do with how citizens of a democratic polity could be induced to love the law rather than simply fear or obey it (40–42). The answer Paul provides is not something like a civil religion (as Rousseau and Critchley seem to suggest is necessary) but rather the nearness of heart and lips, of loyalty to the messianic, which will issue in social solidarity.

Here what is near is the word that Paul announces and that provokes loyalty: **Because if you affirm with your mouth that Joshua is the leader and from your heart that God raised him from the dead, you will be saved.** We have, on the one hand, the depiction of an unreserved commitment (mouth, heart), and on the other, the object of that commitment, which is the impossible. We recall that this orientation to the impossible has already characterized the faithfulness of Abraham. He adheres unwaveringly to a promise whose content is the impossible. And we recall that Derrida had spoken of gift (and thus of justice) as not merely impossible but *the* impossible. Here the impossible has to do with the affirmation that the executed is the messiah and that the one executed through the law has been raised from among the dead. This affirmation (*homologetai*) is a basic "yes-saying," a vow or oath (Agamben, *Time* 113–118) that affirms the promise and thus the impossible, so confirms one's orientation toward the impossible as the origin of faithfulness and thus of justice. Concerning the relation between oath and faithfulness Agamben notes that in many Greek expressions "*pistis* is synonymous with *horkos*" and points to "binding ourselves in a relationship of loyalty" (*Sacrament of Language* 25). In reference to this passage in Romans, therefore, he suggests that the connection between lips and heart signals that "it is the performative experience of veridiction that [Paul] has in mind" (58).

The confession and faithfulness that Paul refers to are not something that substitutes for the claim of justice but is the way that claim becomes effective. The affirmation, or yes-saying, concerning the messiah is what sets one on the road to a comprehensive wholeness (salvation) through orienting one's life to this impossibility, to the event. Here we may recall Alain Badiou's suggestion that a "truth process," through which one becomes a subject, has precisely to do with the reorientation of one's existence on the basis of the event. But any such event is a rupture with what the world knows and thinks, so is, from the standpoint of a given situation, strictly impossible. The affirmation is a vowing of loyalty to the messianic, a swearing of allegiance that is therefore the ground of an unwavering loyalty or faithfulness. **For with the heart [will] one is faithful to justice and with the oath of loyalty is saved.** Again it is justice that produces wholeness or salvation, and this justice is produced through loyalty. Thus, anticipating what he will say in his reflections on the oath, Agamben notes that "the word of faith enacts its meaning through its utterance," so it is possible to think of "something like a performative efficacy of the word of faith realized in its very pronouncement" (*Time* 131).

In this respect Paul maintains once again that **there is no distinction between Judean and Greek; the same Lord of all is generous toward all who call on him.** This double reference to "all" (God as lord of all, as generous to all) recalls elements of Paul's argument in chapter 2 and 3:22. Here it is sandwiched between a citation of Isaiah and one of Joel, both of which also aim at a certain "all" (*none* put to shame; *everyone* who calls will be saved).

Thus far, Paul has sought to establish a connection between hearing and heeding the proclamation concerning the messiah, and the faithfulness that leads to justice and to "salvation." But now he turns to underscore the connection between that hearing and the proclamation itself.

But how are they to call on one to whom they are not faithful? And how are they to be loyal to one of whom they have not heard? And how are they to have heard without one announcing? And how are they to announce who have not been commissioned [*apostolousin*]**?**

Justice enters into human history, the human world, through an announcement and thus through the hearing of an announcement that awakens glad adherence or loyalty. This is to be contrasted to a dutiful compliance with a certain legality, a legality that even aims at justice or that operates in the name of justice but comes to substitute itself for the call and claim of justice.

In its place we have the announcement of that which exceeds every expectation and is therefore contrary to what might be expected. Only through such an announcement does hearing as an affirmation of the impossible come into being. The announcing itself, however, comes from a call, a commissioning, a being seized by the event and set in motion by it. It is how Paul described himself at the beginning of this letter, as one who had been set apart to announce the glad proclamation to all the nations, so to those in Rome.

That the mode of proclamation is affirmed by the written is verified by reference to Isaiah 52:7—but not without introducing the discordant note from Isaiah 53:1 concerning the "not all" of those who have not heeded what has been announced. This is setting up the issue to which Paul will turn soon. But first a summation:

So faithfulness has come through what is heard and what is heard comes through the messianic announcement.

In affirming the role of proclamation or announcement here, Paul is in accord with what he had already said in 1 Corinthians concerning the essential role of proclamation, which is the weak instrument adopted by God for the salvation of God's world (2:18). Whereas here Paul emphasizes the resurrection from the dead, in 1 Corinthians he emphasized the crucifixion of the messiah at the hands of those he called "the rulers of this age" (2:6, 8). For Paul these are two sides of the same event, the messianic event. We should, however, note that the messianic announcement does not begin either with Joshua messiah or with Paul's proclamation. Paul is asserting that it is always already somehow there: in the prophetic word (for example, of Isaiah) and in the word (of promise) to the patriarch Abraham.

Although Paul has developed a distinction between the written and the spoken that is already inscribed in the law itself, he will now refer to a (spoken) proclamation that is already written, this time in the prophets, that will appear to answer the question of how the proclamation has come to the Judeans. **Have they not heard? Certainly!** Instead of referring to apostles to the Judeans, he refers to the proclamation whose written trace is found in the Psalms. The citations that follow, however, make what might seem to be a contrary case: that the proclamation did not have the desired effect with respect to its intended recipients but instead "spilled over" into the wider sphere of the nations. This is verified with reference to the law (Deuteronomy 32:21) and the prophets (Isaiah 65:1–2).

These texts confirm the centrality of proclamation and at the same time open up a gap between announcing and hearing (and faithfulness and justice). This gap is Paul's chief concern, as it bears upon Israel. The texts cited by Paul already set up the basic form of the argument to follow: God did announce good news to Israel. Those who were not of Israel heard and heeded this proclamation, but only "some" of Israel did. The response of the gentiles or pagans will make Israel jealous. This jealousy will itself become the instrument for the salvation of Israel.

Before turning to that argument, however, we briefly note some issues raised by the foregoing interpretation of these texts. The first concerns the traditional tendency to overemphasize the Christological concentration in Paul's argument. I am persuaded that the attempt of standard exegesis to impose a specifically Christological focus on Paul's text is a mistake. The agent of promise and of salvation is God throughout. The object of faithfulness and of obedience throughout is God, not Christ—who is, rather, the exemplar of obedience and faithfulness. What is at stake in the resurrection of the messiah is the focalizing on the messianic proclamation of God that, for Paul, has been present in the word spoken (by God) to Abraham and the word spoken to Israel through the prophets.

The citation from the written, which is extraordinarily supple here, has the goal of demonstrating that what has happened in Israel conforms to Israel's own literature and history, to the oracles of which it is the trustee and legatee. The collection of texts appears to be the fruit of reflection on the unexpected reality that all Israel has not yet recognized the messiah of God. But the citation of these texts also seeks to vindicate God and to assert that God's word, God's promise, has not failed. In this context, they also serve to demonstrate to the gentile readers of Paul's text in Rome that Paul can be of some help to them in deploying Israel's texts in ways that will defend them against possible marginalization or exclusion on the part of the Judeans. Paul is (deliberately or not) brandishing his expertise as an interpreter of Israel's texts, of the law and the prophets, with the aim of validating the faithfulness of the gentiles.

Paul is able to do this precisely because he remains a Judean. He is not a convert to some non-Judean religion or faith. Rather, his commitment to the God of Israel remains unshaken, but his contention is that the God of Israel is the God of all, which is consistent with Israel's own self-understanding as this had come to expression in the prophets. That God is the God of all and is, moreover, benevolent to all and intends the salvation of all is what Paul articulates as the messianic announcement.

The basic issue, then, has to do with the relation between the messianic horizon of the "all" and the historical reality (so far at least) of the "not all" of Israel's response to the announcement of God's grace or gift. Upon this "all" depends the faithfulness, the reliability, of the divine promise that has in view justice for "all flesh" and thus the salvation of all creation. All that we have had thus far is prologue to Paul's decisive response to this question.

17. The Redemption of (All) Israel (11:1–12)

In chapter 9 we heard that the promise of God depends upon God alone and that God's work in history proceeds in spite of and even through rejection and opposition. By itself this would suggest that the response doesn't matter. Accordingly, Paul has argued in chapter 10 that the response to the act of God comes through the hearing of the proclamation and that responding does make a difference. But then we may be back to the problem of the reliability of the divine word and promise. If Israel has had the chance to hear and some at least have rejected, does this rejection mean that they are rejected in turn—in which case the promise, from Paul's point of view, would have failed, at least in regard to the "all"? Of course, there would be no problem if God did not intend that all would become just, or if becoming just (through hearing and faithfulness) didn't matter, or if the salvation of a few were enough for God. There are many ways to make this issue less daunting, and theologians have at one time or another chosen all of them. But Paul will not take any straightforward or easy way out of this aporia. He will not relinquish the universality of the promise, the seriousness of the claim of justice, or the responsibility of the hearer to be or become truly just.

Again the question: **Has God rejected his people? Absolutely not!** (11:1). Isaiah has been quoted as characterizing Israel as a "disobedient and contrary people." Obedience in the sense of hearing and heeding the proclamation is essential to faithfulness and so to justice and so to salvation. It would seem to follow that God would reject those who reject his word or promise, yet, **Absolutely not!**

We recall that what is at stake is the reliability of the divine promise, gift, election, as the reliability of the promise to the nations depends upon the reliability of the promise to Israel. This is not just a question of Israel; it is a question that bears upon the very possibility of relying upon the promise of God also for gentiles.

I myself am an Israelite, a descendant of Abraham, a member of the tribe of Benjamin. In Philippians 3:5–6 he had expanded this to include "a Pharisee, as to the law blameless, as to zeal a persecutor of the church." What is at stake here at first is the question of whether "some" have responded to the call and promise of God. It would not be out of place to recall that for Paul his own inclusion in those who have been called to be faithful to the promise is itself a matter of an extreme gratuity. By his own admission he had been an enemy of the gospel, a persecutor of the messiah and the messiah's people. He was one who had the zeal he spoke of earlier, but **not according to knowledge**. That an enemy of the gospel should be made its advocate is a demonstration of absolute gratuity: **While we were yet enemies.** Paul himself then is a demonstration: if even he could be chosen by sheer gift, then who not? But this is getting ahead of the story.

God has not rejected his people whom he foreknew. Paul has maintained that foreknowing and predestining refer to Israel. This means not this or that individual (still less, individual gentiles) but precisely a people in its extension through time as a history. In terms of Paul's argument the "foreknowledge" is that of promise, the promise to Abraham concerning his seed. (This sort of foreknowledge is quite different from, indeed opposed to, the sort of abstract and timeless foreknowledge that Augustine, in a Platonizing move, attributed to God in such a way as to make predestination an inevitable consequence of the unchanging foreknowledge of history attributed to the divine unchanging aseity.) This promise, which launches a new history, is not without effect, because some descendants of Abraham, Isaac, and Jacob have responded to it—for example, Paul of the tribe of Benjamin, a son of Jacob. Predestination and foreknowledge here do not have to do with some abstraction that can be made into an aspect of the doctrine of the nature of God but, rather, with the history of promise to Abraham. God's "pre"-knowledge is quite simply God's promise; the same is true of god's "pre"-destination. This has to do exclusively with the character of promise as promise.

Moreover, Paul is not alone either in being a descendant of Abraham or in being one who has heard and responded to the promise. Here he turns to another moment in Israel's history when it seemed that all had deserted the call and claim of God: **Do you not know what the written says of Elijah? . . . "I have kept for myself 7000."** This Paul applies to the current situation by saying, **So too at the present time there is a remnant.** The idea of a remnant has been anticipated earlier in chapter 9 where the sparing of a remnant prevented Israel from the total elimination that had characterized the fate of Sodom (9:27, 29). **So therefore also in the present time a remnant has come to be according to a selection of favor** [generosity].

Giorgio Agamben has shown that the idea of a remnant that arises in the prophetic literature of Israel has an eschatological or messianic character. A remnant is that which survives judgment but is also the bearer of salvation. In Pauline thought the remnant has to do with the now-time, which is for Paul the messianic time, the time in which time comes to its messianic end. Agamben notes, "The remnant is not so much the object of salvation as that which properly makes salvation possible" (*Time* 56). The idea of the remnant exists only in messianic time, the now-time.

The remnant in Paul's thought is a particularly loaded form of synecdoche, a rhetorical figure in which the whole and the part enter into substitutability. On the one hand, the remnant is only a part of the whole, for example, the part of Israel that survives the Babylonian captivity (Isaiah) or the part that is faithful to YHWH in the time of Elijah. Yet this part is also the whole as the bearer of the promise to the whole people. We may recall the bargaining of Abraham with YHWH about the fate of Sodom, in which a few just persons would substitute for the demand of justice and avert judgment from (all of) Sodom. Thus, the part tends to include the whole. In Paul's argument thus far, this has happened already in interesting ways. His condemnation of pagan social order, for example, is a condemnation of that part (the elite) that represents the whole. Or in another example, Paul can suppose that some, considered as not all, of the pagans may be just (that is, fulfill the requirements of the law so become a law to themselves). However, viewed more precisely as a part of the whole, they may be swallowed up in the judgment that overtakes the whole, and this will be said again soon both of Judeans and gentiles.

In the messianic time, the now-time, the remnant (not all) and the "all" will enter into a sort of interchangeability with one another. The remnant will serve as a testimony to the divine commitment to justice and to the reliability of the promise but will also serve as the anticipation of a whole or all that will overflow both the remnant and the whole itself (thus, the all of Israel will come to include as well all the nations). Agamben notes concerning Paul's view of Israel at this point: "It is therefore neither the all, nor a part of the all, but the impossibility for the part and the all to coincide with themselves or with each other" (*Time* 55). Agamben goes on to suggest certain parallels between this notion of the remnant as an all-inclusive part in Marx's reflections on the proletariat, which also assumes a certain messianic function. In Marx's view the proletariat is a certain part of society (an excluded part as it turns out). However, because its condition is the sum of all oppressions, its liberation as a class entails the abolition of classes as such, so the anticipation of the classless society (64–65), or as one might now say, the messianic society.

The remnant, Paul insists, is one that is selected altogether without its own merit but simply on account of unconditional generosity: **If it is by generosity, it is no longer from works; otherwise generosity would not be generosity.** Earlier Paul had insisted that **the promise rests on generosity** (gift) (4:16). And he had already pointed out that what is paid out as a wage is certainly not "generosity" but is instead a debt (4:4). In this way Paul transfers the meaning of remnant from that of judgment (all that is left after destruction) to that of gift, of a generosity that intends salvation or wholeness.

The passages Paul then cites pick up the problem of Israel not responding to the messianic proclamation that had been the subject of the previous chapter—as we might expect, a word from Isaiah (29:10) and from the Psalms (69:22–23). They are connected by the trope of unseeing eyes, and the latter passage is especially harsh, calling a curse upon those who persecute the just. These seem to articulate judgment, so Paul immediately corrects course: **So have they stumbled so as to fall? Absolutely not!** The stumbling metaphor reminds us that those who now persecute the faithful are those who have stumbled upon the strange, even if reliable—the strangely reliable and reliably strange— way in which God (or justice) acts in history. But as Paul makes haste to say, this stumbling opens up an unexpected way for justice, and the promise that is its actual basis, to take effect, again, unexpectedly: **Through their trespass salvation has come to the pagans in order to make Israel jealous.**

Israel's rejection of the messiah and the messianic event opens up the way to the announcement of the messianic event to (all) the nations. What does this concretely mean? We may surmise that for Paul the repudiation of the messiah (condemned according to the law by its official interpreters) places the messiah outside the people of Israel in such a way as to become the messiah of those outside, the nations or pagans. Joshua is turned over to the pagans (the Romans) by the leaders of Israel, and in this way the law is exposed as that which is an instrument of injustice opening the way for the coming of justice "outside the law." (I have attempted to offer a more extended explication of this in *Transforming Atonement*.)

We should note in addition that the trespass is said to be of the "whole" Israel even though it is of the part (though not the remnant), namely, certain elites or opponents. Here again we find a synecdoche: **The elect obtained it, but the rest were hardened.** But all this, Paul suggests, is going to make Israel jealous. Of what? Of the opening of the announcement of Israel's God to the outsiders. The notion of jealousy here is quite wonderful. Israel has, it supposes, a "monogamous" relation with his "husband," God. Even if Israel is not impeccably faithful, still Israel wants his husband to be so. Yet God woos another, the dreaded pagans. So Israel is jealous. This strange and wonderful soap opera will play out in surprising ways. (It is odd how seldom people notice that both Israel and God are putatively male characters in this improbable love story!) Note that in this love story, God acts with a close eye on Israel: the turn to the gentiles is supposed to have an effect on Israel. The gentiles, as we will see, are simply a tool to get Israel's attention.

The purpose of their stumbling over God, over the surprising way that God acts, is not that they might be rejected but that others might (also) be included. Thus, even the "hardening" of Israel means only that redemption is now immeasurably widened in scope. Israel is an instrument of justice and mercy, whether as elect or as hardened. **Now if their trespass means riches for the world, and if their failure means wealth for the nations, how much more their fullness?** The point is that if the reduction to a remnant is what makes for wealth (the gifts of God or the favors of God) for the world of the nations, then how much more wealth will the inclusion of all of Israel (not a remnant only) mean for the world? We should note that cosmos and nations name the two keys in which Paul has been developing his argument: cosmos as that which yearns for deliverance (Romans 8); nations as that which had been without hope of redemption. The redemption of Israel can only mean the ratification of this astonishing hope.

The logic here is that some means wealth and all means astonishing wealth. This is obviously not a zero-sum game in which wealth for one means impoverishment for the other. One of the most important characteristics of messianic politics is that it is not based upon a logic of scarcity, with zero-sum games abounding. Rather, the messianic entails a logic of abundance in which more for some means an exponential increase in more for all. Or in Paul's regular phrase: "how much more" (*posō mallon*). We might call this messianic math.

18. Warning to the Nations (11:12–24)

Here Paul already signals his conclusion, a conclusion that will give the definite answer as to whether God has rejected God's people or whether the failure of Israel to receive the messiah of Israel means that they have stumbled so as to fall. And the answer, he is signaling, is that all Israel will be included and that this is also good news for the gentiles since it means that their wealth (the promise of God) abounds or multiplies exponentially, all the more. Let's see how this works.

First, Paul indicates that because he is the delegate of God's good news, his own vocation is subservient to God's purpose with respect to

God's (original) people. He makes this clear by taking his (gentile) reader into his confidence: **Now I am speaking to you nations. Inasmuch as I am a delegate** [apostle] **to the nations, I glorify my own service in order to provoke those of my own flesh to jealousy so that I might save some of them.** Paul has a small part in what God is doing. What God is doing is provoking jealousy in Israel; what Paul is doing is provoking jealousy in *some* of them. What God is doing will result in the salvation of all; what Paul is doing is aimed at the salvation of some (not yet all).

But what is most astonishing is that the apostleship to the gentiles is really aimed at the salvation of those who are not gentiles! The mission to the gentiles is simply a sort of detour to the true mission to Israel. Paul exaggerates his own mission to the gentiles in order to save some of Israel. The gentiles aren't the point. They are the means. The potential "arrogance of nations" (the title of a splendid study of Romans by Neil Elliott) is here undercut in the most decisive way. They might suppose, as Christians have for millennia, "We got it, but they didn't. They rejected, but we accepted. They were the chosen, but now we are." Christian anti-Judaism and even supersessionism are radically undercut, made impossible, by Paul's argument here. If only Christians had read carefully! Here we may recall again the discussion between Carl Schmitt and Jacob Taubes (Taubes 51, 97–113) in which Taubes demonstrates that Paul is no supersessionist.

What of this "some" who are the remnant of Israel or who are being saved through the jealousy provoked by Paul's mission to the gentiles? Are they only a fragment? Or is the synecdochal machine going to surprise us once again?

First of all, the part is not just a part: **If their rejection means the reconciliation of the world, what will their acceptance mean but life from the dead?** If those who seem to be rejected serve by their rejection to lead to the reconciliation of the world (composed after all of those who had themselves seemed to be rejected), then their inclusion, their welcome back, can only mean the sort of thing that has been in view all along: the resurrection of the dead. What is the resurrection of the dead, after all? Is it not that all who fell by the wayside, all who were rejected, receive an unexpected future, an unanticipated life? Paul had said, **while**

we were yet enemies. Should it be any different for those we think are our enemies? For those we think of as having utterly failed to heed the claim of justice? If they cannot be included, how could we?

Now the notion of a remnant is utterly transformed from the "key" of judgment to that of redemption: **If the dough offered as first fruits is holy, so is the whole lump** [Numbers 15:18–21]; **if the root is holy, so are the branches** [Jeremiah 11:16–17]. Here the remnant intends the whole; the part includes the totality. This also helps answer the question that we noted at the very beginning of this letter with respect to its address to those in Rome: the Romans. We asked, Does this mean the faithful in Rome or the whole of Rome? And the answer is yes. For if the "some" are made holy, the whole lump is holy. We could break this out: as some are now, all will be later. But this is not the way messianic time works. Messianic time is the compression of times so that what is future characterizes the now-time. With respect to Israel the part that is faithful includes all, as well as the part that is characterized as "trespass." The "some" is bigger than the whole (for the some will also include the gentiles).

The mention of branches in this regard is not fortuitous since it announces the extended metaphor that Paul will now develop to address the idea he had broached about the gentiles being included in order to include Israel. Paul will return to the current argument at 11:25 after he has warned the pagan nations (non-Judeans) against arrogance and pride in relation to the favored people of God. Alas, it is an argument that gentiles have been all too eager to misunderstand. Or as Paul has said, quoting Isaiah and the Psalm, **having eyes they [we] are blinded.**

The discourse is about roots and branches: **But if some of the branches were broken off, and you, a wild olive shoot were grafted in among them and became a partaker of the sap of the root, do not exult over the branches.** Clearly, this means don't pretend that you are now the chosen in their place. Your only nourishment, your only source of life and fruitfulness, is still that root, the root of Israel. **If you exult, remember that you do not support the root, but the root supports you.** Don't brag about your status: **You will say, "Branches were broken off so that I might be grafted in"; that is true. They were broken off because of their unfaithfulness, but you endure only on account of your faithfulness; so don't be proud but be afraid.** One is tempted to add: be very afraid! Why fear? **If God did not spare the natural branches, neither will he spare you.** Paul wants to awaken assurance for those who are faithful, but he is also ready to provoke fear among those who may be tempted to take divine favor for granted as something that is now a possession. If we recall that the faithfulness Paul speaks of here produces justice and that injustice is itself unfaithfulness, we may see that there is indeed reason to fear. For who would maintain that the history of the people who are here spoken of as grafted into the root has been characterized by justice or mercy, above all, their justice and mercy with respect to the favored people of God?

For what is the relation of Christianity to Judaism if it is not a boasting over the branches that were cut out? And this history that bears the bitter fruit of Christian anti-Judaism, a deformity whose consequences are too horrifying even to name—Shoah, the unspeakable itself—is it not a testimony to our desire to be not branches but the very root itself? Indeed, it is the desire to tear up the root of the promise of God to Israel and to supplant this root and suppose that it is only by being grafted onto us that Jews can find the nourishment of the root. It was for this reason that the later Karl Barth could rightly suppose that Christian anti-Semitism is the unpardonable sin. It is unpardonable because it is the absolute refusal of grace, because it is this willful severance of itself from the root of God's unfailing promise to Israel.

See then the kindness and the severity of God: severity toward those who have fallen; kindness to you, if you imitate that kindness. To continue in the kindness of God is to continue to exhibit that kindness, that inclusion for the undeserving. Hardly anything is clearer in biblical faith than that the merciful receive mercy and the merciless receive no mercy: **Otherwise, you too will be cut off.**

And even the others, if they do not insist on unfaithfulness, will be grafted in, for God has the power to graft them in again. But they are not grafted into a gentile root but back into the root of Israel, where they belong. Not by becoming what we call Christians (a gentile phenomenon now) but by becoming who they "naturally" are: the favored people of Israel who are destined to faithfulness and so to justice. In this connection it is important to bear in mind something noted by Krister Stendahl, that Paul does not urge Jewish Christians to renounce circumcision or the observance of food regulations. He simply maintains that these should not be imposed upon gentiles (Stendahl 2; cf. Esler 306–307, 354–355). Paul is concerned with the eschatological incorporation of Judeans as Judeans, and how should Judean identity be recognized save through adherence to the "law"? To be sure, this adherence would be understood as that which awakens one to the seriousness of the claim of justice, so is faithful to that claim. But that is precisely what the great Jewish thinkers from Maimonides through Rosenzweig and Levinas have asserted about maintaining the particularity of Jewish identity through adherence to the laws transmitted across history. Later Paul will argue, with respect to such differences as those between Judeans and gentile believers, that each should adhere firmly to their own view and practice as a matter of conscience, but in ways that do not lead to mutual condemnation (Romans 15).

For if you have been cut from what is by nature a wild olive tree and grafted, against nature, into a cultivated olive tree, how much more will these natural branches be grafted back into their own olive tree? The image depends upon the contravention of normal or customary (natural in that sense) horticultural practice. Usually the cultivated shoot is grafted into the wild root in order to produce edible fruit. (This is the way of California vineyards, for example: native wild root stock produce less desirable grapes, so cultivated branches are grafted in to produce higher-quality grapes.) The act of God in history then is "against nature" (and here we should recall the discussion of what is "against nature" in Romans 1).

But when the cut-off branches are restored, they return to their own (*idia*) olive tree, where they (not we) belong (by nature in another sense). This image of olives is addressed to the "nations" whose potential arrogance Paul seeks to interdict. Centuries of Christian history show that he had good reason to worry. We may even reflect upon a certain history of gentile branches being cast off. From the seventh century onward, is it not the case that even the most powerful branches of what was then Christianity came to be cast off and to wither with the spread of Islam? Had Christianity itself become so self-preoccupied with its alliance to imperial power and prosperity, so arrogant with respect to its own dogmatic certitudes as itself to expel Arians and Nestorians and Monophysites, that it had become useless to the divine project of mercy and justice? Were not branches of Islam grafted on in the place of an arrogant Christianity that had forgotten a commitment to the poor? Even today when the allegedly Christian nations seek to cast suspicion upon Islam, do they not confront the implacable commitment to the poor as the strength of "traditional" (some even say, "fundamentalist") Islam?

And at the beginning of the twentieth century it is not too great a stretch to see the corrupt Christianity of the czars being overwhelmed by a Marxist-Leninist commitment to the working class. That is, a forgetfulness of justice and mercy on the part of Christianity led to many branches being cut off. But we seem incapable of learning from history, even a history that is remarkably prefigured in Paul's warning here.

Whether we restrict ourselves to the history that Paul already knew or expand this history forward to our time, we must be struck by the way in which Paul underscores what seems to be the curious ability of the divine to improvise. God (or we might say, justice) does not operate in accordance with hard-and-fast rules, by any sort of iron law of history. God (or justice) improvises, which makes this "history of salvation" so unpredictable. God promises seed, but not the firstborn. Pharaoh opposes liberation—but never mind; we can use that. Israel or some elements of Israel reject the messiah—that will only mean including the nations. Divine justice responds to what we might call the fluid situation on the ground.

But this unpredictability is at the same time utterly reliable. It has a single aim: justice that flows from mercy. This is the unchanging decree, if we may use that language, of the way justice works out in history. But because human history is itself uncoerced (otherwise, we could speak of neither justice nor mercy), justice must come to terms with obstinacy and arrogance as well as unexpected faithfulness and loyalty. Hence God is never predictable but always reliable. God improvises. History is the history of divine improvisation to the tune of justice and mercy.

And because this is so, Paul warns his readers: **For I want you not to be ignorant of this mystery so that you not use your own "wisdom."** The mystery turns out to be what I am terming "improvisation." And having our own wisdom is the gentile equivalent of Israel seeking to possess its own justice, taking it for granted that it knew what justice was. For the wisdom (*phronein*) of which Paul speaks here is precisely the supposition that we can work this out in accordance with our own knowledge, that the way of justice conforms to our "common sense," that reason alone will tell us how justice comes—in short, that it is a kind of deductive system so there are no surprises left, no ground for sheer astonishment. But the gospel, the glad-making announcement, is all about surprising us, all about taking our breath away. That is what Paul means by mystery.

19. Eucatastrophe (11:25–36)

Paul is now ready to bring this argument concerning God's history with Israel and the nations to a close. He has prepared the ground in various ways. But he may also only now be beginning to realize the full impact of his own argument. In any case it is the declaration of a "mystery," of an unveiling of what has been hidden—of a completely unpredictable yet, in retrospect, inevitable working out of God's promise to Israel as extended to the nations but by no means revoked for Israel.

So that you not have a certain wisdom [*phronein*] in yourselves, I want you not to be ignorant of this mystery. To have wisdom that comes from oneself is somehow parallel to having a certain righteousness that is based in oneself. It is to be ignorant. For the basis of justice and of wisdom must lie outside ourselves, not be deducible from that with which we are familiar or at home.

The mystery here has to do with the relation of Israel and the nations: **Hardness has happened to part of Israel until the totality [*pleroma*] of the nations enters. And so all Israel will be saved.** The relation of part to whole here has been prepared in 11:14 (dough/lump, branch/root). Part of Israel has had hardness befall it (like Pharaoh), but the aim of this hardness is that all, the totality, of the nations shall enter into the promise. And then comes another totality: all Israel. We might have supposed that Paul had said his last word about the salvation of (some of) Israel when he spoke of trying to make Israel jealous by his mission to the nations. There it was "some," but now it is "all." The rejection of (part) of Israel is simply a tool for the bringing in of all nations. And the bringing in of all nations is merely a tool for the consummation of the divine promise to Israel: **The deliverer will come from Zion; he will banish impiety from Jacob.** The citations from Isaiah 59:20–21 and 29:9 recall that when all is said and done, Jacob will receive the blessing promised, in spite of all that may happen along the winding road to this redemption.

To his gentile readers Paul says, **As regards the gospel they are enemies of God for your sake; but as regards election they are beloved for the sake of their forefathers. For the gifts and the calling of God are irrevocable.** Those who are hardened are the theme of this affirmation: they are enemies of the gospel (just as Paul had been), and this redounds to the advantage of the nations (for your sake). How then are we to regard the refusal of the messiah on the part of (part of) Israel? Quite simply as that which provides the opening for us to be the ones who hear and heed the gospel. It is precisely insofar as they are, to use contemporary categories, Jews rather than Christians that they are our benefactors.

Those who are now enemies of the gospel are nevertheless beloved. They remain forever the elect, the chosen, the singular people of God. For God does not take back God's word, God's gift, God's calling. These are irrevocable. Thus, God can be trusted. Indeed, we here confront the basis of Christian anxiety about salvation: if God can reject his chosen people, then God can reject us. This is what Paul himself had pointed to (11:22–24). But this sort of anxiety is what produces all the deformities of religion. And what produces the contrary? The assurance that "**nothing can separate us from the love of God**"—that the promise, the gift, the call of God, is irrevocable, above all for Israel and therefore also for us.

We thus emphasize that to be **beloved for the sake of their forefathers** means that Judeans are incorporated in divine salvation simply because they are Israelites, the inheritors of the promise to Abraham, Isaac, and Jacob, and for no other reason. It is not because they are better or more deserving or more observant, but simply because God promised. For this reason it is absolutely essential that we not disturb or limit this "all." But that is precisely what Western Christian exegesis has done almost from the very beginning. In doing so, in thinking only of a remnant or of those who come to be converted to a Christian religion, the whole of Paul's argument has been reduced to utter nonsense. Thus, in this now-time Judaism as Judaism remains. It is not destined to be evaporated into the universal, for then the promise to Israel would have been in vain.

Here then is the answer to the questions: **Has God rejected his people? Absolutely not** [11:1]; **Have they stumbled so as to fall? Absolutely**

not [11:11]. Paul is thus able to draw the consequences: **Just as you were once disobedient to God but now have received mercy because of their disobedience, so they have now been disobedient in order that by the mercy shown to you they also now receive mercy.** We, after all, were the enemies of God, yet we have been given the gift of the divine promise. Shall their being enemies prevent them from receiving the same mercy? On the contrary, the very fact that we receive this gift makes it evident that Israel does as well. In Paul's vision, what we may term "Christianity" is simply a long detour or parenthesis that leads to what God had intended all along: the blessing of the whole of Israel. In order to reach this goal, however, it was necessary to also include all the nations.

These two "alls" are now brought into clear focus: **For God has consigned all in disobedience in order that God may have mercy on all.** Simply all. It is just as we heard at the end of chapter 3: all are disobedient. So now all receive mercy, favor, blessing, not because it has been deserved but because it is God who has promised. Of course, there will always be those who take offense at this "all." But Eastern theology from Origen to Gregory understood that this "all" was the essence of the gospel. For Gregory it included not only all people but even Satan—just because God is God, and good news is simply and astonishingly good news.

Paul has earned his rapturous conclusion: **O the depth of the riches and wisdom and knowledge of God. How unsearchable are his judgments, how inscrutable his ways.** Beyond what could be seen, understood, or known by human imagining, God has found a way to make even disaster (catastrophe) turn into radiant consummation (eucatastrophe).

Yet even the astonishing and inscrutable coheres with what God had already intimated. Isaiah had already asked, **For who has known the mind of the Lord, or who has been his counselor?** (40:13). This shows that no one can dictate to God how it ought to turn out, or how God will act to achieve those ends. And Job had asked, **Who has given a gift to God so as to deserve repayment?** (35:7; 41:11), thereby anticipating that God gives not out of obligation but out of sheer unmeritable generosity. The freedom of God goes together with the unpredictability and reliability of God—this is what it means to say that God improvises in history so as to take into account human response without being defeated by it.

For from, through, and to[ward] **God—everything. To God the shining forth through all the ages.** Everything, all, absolutely all, is incorporated in the gracious determination of the divine. Indeed, that is the divine as such, this all-encompassing divine radiance. The point of what God is up to in the world is neither Israel nor the nations. It is, quite simply, all.

Fifth Phase

Almost from the beginning we have heard of a coming justice, a justice that comes from God, a divine justice. That this justice is "of God" means, at least in part, that it comes unexpectedly and from outside the inherited or even invented institutions that heretofore have instantiated the hope for justice. For law is the way in which the aspiration and yearning for justice have been made concrete in history. In that sense law is "holy, just, and good." But the basic institutions for establishing justice through law have failed. This is true whether we are to think of the legal foundations of the Greco-Roman world as incorporated in Roman justice or in the structures of Israelite polity focused in the law of Moses. The social orders thereby established have produced injustice rather than justice, most dramatically for Paul through their collaboration in the rejection and execution of the one who was the messiah of God—the one who embodied the call and promise of justice. By the messiah's return from the dead God had demonstrated a new and unexpected way toward justice that irrevocably turns away from the law-based quest for a just social order. In the light of this messianic alternative, it becomes clear that law could not accomplish justice because it has always already been seized upon by human incapacity and anxiety (flesh) to become, against its own intention, an instrument of injustice.

In place of this attempt to realize justice through law, the messianic project comes into being as promise and gift, as favor and generosity. It comes, that is to say, as the impossible, as life from the dead, whether from the dead bodies of Abraham and Sarah, or the dead body of the messiah, or the death-determined bodies of the old humanity.

Paul has offered a number of clarifications along the way. He has insisted that the messianic way is in a certain discontinuity with the old Adamic way in that it really breaks with the history of injustice, of settling for less than justice. So far from offering a relaxation of the claim of justice, it renders it, for the first time, truly effective. Instead of the impotent yearning for justice that always finds itself incapable of engendering what it wants and always finds itself undermined from within, Paul points to a messianic liveliness or spiritedness that characterizes loyalty to the messianic way of justice and mercy. Even now, this messianic liveliness takes shape as the capacity to endure the afflictions produced by the clash of eons as the messianic takes form in messianic societies somehow lodged within the old and increasingly hostile institutional orders of the world. The insatiable yearning for and commitment (fidelity) to justice make it possible to endure and even to exult in this affliction and to find solidarity with the groaning of the earth itself for deliverance from the weight of injustice. If there is this solidarity in suffering, then indeed there is nothing that can separate us from the love of God.

This hope against hope must be rooted in the way of God (or justice) in human history. Paul, as the apostle of Israel's God to the pagans, takes on the task of interpreting the history of Israel as a history that does not invalidate the reliability of this promise but as a history that, in fact, against all expectation, establishes the reliability of the divine promise to bring justice to the world through or by means of this people. Thus, the history recounted by Paul is a history of divine improvisation that turns opposition into unpredictable avenues for the bringing of justice and therefore wholeness for all the earth.

But what does it concretely mean that justice takes shape in the now-time or the messianic time inaugurated decisively in the resurrection of the executed messiah? The whole of Paul's argument to this point is but preparation for what lies ahead. For now Paul turns his attention to the actualization of justice in the way of life of the messianic cells that have begun to emerge in response to the messianic message. Runar Thorsteins-son, who emphasizes the connection between the moral teachings of Paul and those of the Stoics, also makes clear that what follows is no moral appendix but the point of Paul's entire argument (93).

The material of the next four chapters is sometimes dismissed as moralizing "parenesis," as a kind of appendix added on to supplement the more interesting theological discussion that has preceded it. This is perhaps inevitable if one has lost sight of Paul's main theme, which is the coming of justice and so the emergence of corporate ways of life that embody this justice and thus demonstrate that the promise of God is not mere wishful thinking. In fact, it would be better to regard all that we have read to this point as a prologue to Paul's real concern: to show how justice in fact takes shape "apart from the law." For if it does not do so, then there is no viable alternative to law-based social orders; there is no justice based upon gift that actualizes, in this now-time of the messianic, the call and claim of justice.

20. The Messianic Body (12:1–13)

What we read now is not an appendix but the point of Paul's argu-ment; it is the heart of messianic politics. Accordingly, it begins with *Therefore*:

Therefore, I appeal to you comrades through divine compassions to offer your bodies as lively sacrifice, holy and pleasing to God: your rational worship.

These words may be read as the initial summary statement for all that is to follow. "*Therefore*" links it to all that has gone before. Now we come at last to the heart of messianic politics: the justice that comes otherwise than as law.

That which is otherwise than law is thus an **appeal** rather than a command, the statement or articulation of desire and yearning, an appeal to the heart as will. It is situated in solidarity among those des-ignated here as **comrades** (brothers), most importantly as equals who address one another in freedom as well as frank openness, without dis-simulation. An appeal that is rooted in the **divine compassions** that have been made manifest in what has gone before, the forbearance, the patience, the promise, the gift of the impossible, in the solidarity in groaning for the new world of justice that leads to peace with all creation and with God.

It is an appeal to reason, to what is called here **rational worship**. The Judeans had mocked the irrational worship of the pagans who honored idols. And in this they were joined by pagan lovers of wisdom, who mocked the irrational superstitions of their own world. Paul himself had argued earlier that this irrationality of worship was deeply connected to the violence and injustice of the Greco-Roman world. But the lovers of wisdom had also found Judean forms of worship equally irrational with their temple sacrifices and odd customs. Philo had felt obliged to reinterpret the "special laws" of Moses, which could seem so odd to outsiders (what one can and cannot eat and so on), in Platonic terms in order to bring them into some conformity with reason. But what is rational worship? What is the way of honoring the divine that corresponds to right reason?

It has to do with our **bodies**. The body is the way we are in and of the world, the way we are available to one another, the way we engage the world and one another. It designates what Heidegger might call our comportment: the shape of our interaction with others, all others. It is not invisible but visible, indeed tactile. The body represents the ways we affect and are affected by one another, the ways we are vulnerable to giving and receiving pain or pleasure—the ways we can plausibly be, as Paul has earlier said, "instruments" of injustice or of justice.

The body as the interactivity of existence may be clarified perhaps by reference to the reflections of Jean-Luc Nancy, who has been the thinker most devoted to rethinking the way in which existence is being-with and thus is always, as the title of one of his books has it, "being singular plural." It is plural because always shaped in interaction with all other existents, and singular because shaped singularly, newly, differently, oddly perhaps, each time. Each body is thus singular, yet never alone but always plural. Body is that whereby we are exposed to one another. Nancy refers to this as the place of proximity as well as separation whereby we are placed in community without the merger of communion (*Inoperative Community* 60–61).

It is thus as body that we are to honor God's call to justice, in all our ways of being engaged with one another and the world. This is the "sacrifice" that is acceptable to God. This "sacrifice" consists not of the dead bodies of those who are governed by death but of living and lively ones that enter more and more fully into life, with one another and with all. The prophets had always maintained that God was not interested in sacrifices of cows or doves, not interested in days of feast and fasting, not interested in all the religious games by which God's people distracted themselves from the call and claim of justice. These religious diversions must cease so that we might learn to seek justice and love mercy. What justice calls for is precisely ourselves, our ways of being with one another. Amos had spoken for this justice when he said, "I hate and despise your feasts . . . but let justice roll down" (5:21, 24), and Isaiah had said, "This is the fast that I choose: to take the humble poor into your house" (58:5). The call of the divine has to do not with religion but with a rational way of responding to the divine, a way that governs all our interactions with one another and the world—that is, our bodies. For this we substitute the irrational worship of ceremonies and cultic sacrifices. And this, as the prophets (and some philosophers) knew, is defiance of God. It is not too surprising, alas, that translators have effaced the call for rational worship by calling it spiritual, even though Paul's word is more aptly translated as "logical." If this sounds too "humanistic," so much the better.

What we shall hear is that the rational way of honoring God is doing what honors our neighbor. The sacrifice called for is what enables us to live in solidarity with the vulnerable. It is this which is **well pleasing to God**. We should not forget that much is at stake with our bodies—with being body—for as Paul has recognized, the redemption of our mortal bodies brings with it the hope for the renewal of all creation. This renewal begins in the now-time of our bodies put forward in ways that correspond to justice and mercy.

It is this that is **holy**. For the holy is that which corresponds to the divine, set apart for it. Recall the paradox that we noticed at the very beginning when noting Paul as set apart for the universal message directed to all: to be separate in order to be available (an offering therefore) to all. So also with those Paul spoke of as holy ones in Rome: They are set apart precisely as those whose manner of life anticipates the messianic justice intended for all. They are set apart from the profane only in the sense that they are set apart from the old eon of death and violence, of cruelty and injustice.

Precisely because the body locates us in the world and is our way of being available to one another and is, as Käsemann noted, "that piece of the world that we are" (*New Testament Questions* 135), Paul goes on to say:

Do not be conformed to this age but be transforming by the making new of your mind so that you can make evident the will of God: the good, the pleasing, the fully realized [perfect]**.**

The age or eon that is yet all too present but that Paul had indicated in writing to Corinth is perishing (2:6)—because it belongs to the order of death enforced by the rule of death—does not have a grip on what is coming into being. For we live as those who have passed from death into life. Thus, we do not play by the rules of the old order: we are not conformed to it and its all too predictable regularities.

That which corresponds to the will of God is here called the good, the pleasing, the fully realized. These categories appear first of all as pagan or gentile terms. Paul has used this sort of terminology before in this letter when he spoke of those who seek glory and honor and immortality in doing what is just (2:7). And he had used similar terminology in encouraging the messianic gathering in Philippi to aspire to "whatever is true, grave, just, pure, loveable, of good reputation, if there is any virtue or praise" (Philippians 4:8). This means that Paul, in addressing pagan or Greek culture, has no difficulty appropriating the highest aspirations of that culture for purposes of his messianic project. The messianic takes these terms and their associated aspirations into itself, thereby indigenizing the messianic into the heart of the Greek aspiration.

But there is even more here, for these categories are not only those with which Greek culture would resonate. They are also not so much ethical categories as aesthetic ones. The form of life that Paul is entreating his equals (brothers or comrades) to embody is one that is good, that has a pleasing shape, that is fully realized (perfect). These are terms that could well be used to describe a fine work of art: a symphony, a painting or sculpture, a play or novel. What we might term "ethics" here shades into aesthetics.

Moreover, the well-shaped life is one that depends upon a renewed intelligence. This is not something that somehow just happens without discernment or forethought or something that can be shaped by going along with the way the world as presently constituted thinks of such things. It is a work of intelligence (*nous*) that has been made new, made innovative.

New forms of life must be intelligently fashioned so they give evidence of what God is purposing for the world. Just as God acts in and through history in ways that improvise in relation to what is happening in the world, so, too, must the lifestyle that testifies to or gives evidence of divine justice also improvise. Improvisation is not random. It is responsive and creative, and in that way, it both imitates God and gives dramatic evidence of the in-breaking of the messianic age.

One might even say that precisely this new improvisational and creative form of life is the only persuasive evidence of the messianic reality. For this reason Paul is so urgently concerned with these questions of the form, shape, or style of life of his readers. If there is to be any proof of the truth of the gospel, they must be it. Three centuries later in arguing for the plausibility of the Christian proclamation of the incarnation of the word, Athanasius could still point to the dramatically different forms of life that characterized Christian communities—their fearlessness, nonviolence, generosity—as decisive evidence of the truth of the gospel. Such a proof has become less persuasive. Perhaps this testimony is less persuasive in part because of the failure to grasp Paul's urgency in this matter, a misunderstanding fostered by supposing that the material we are beginning now to read is mere appendix. This has led to a trivial moralizing that takes the place of the actualization of dramatic signs of social justice.

In the next few sentences, Paul will offer pleas about what we might call the internal life of the community, to be followed by sentences that address the way in which this group interacts with those outside, even with those opposed to the messianic mission. What is at stake throughout is the way to shape the common or shared life of those loyal to the messianic. It is not our life alone but our life together that concerns Paul. Ethics is more like ethos. This ethos is to be shaped with intelligence and creativity to be a dramatic sign of the new that is occurring in the now-time of the messianic.

For through the gift given me I say to all among you not to think more highly than is fitting, but to think with sober self-assessment.

As it stands, this might be regarded simply as sage philosophical advice, not that different from the advice a wise Stoic might give. Indeed, there are several points at which Paul's advice intersects with that of Greek schools of philosophical wisdom. It will thus not be surprising that at the end of the second century Clement of Alexandria could devote almost his entire body of work to seeking to inculcate forms of life and thought that would resonate with that ethos.

One important difference, however, in the advice Paul is giving is that it has in view not the lifestyle of individuals as such but the form of life and thought that conduces to living together. It is this corporate exigency that makes arrogance and self-preoccupation so clearly problematic from his point of view. In virtually all of his letters Paul sounds this same theme with the same relation to the question of life together, of a shared life.

Paul writes here to his equals on the basis of the gift that has been given him. He supposes that all his readers are also gifted in a variety of ways. He does not write, therefore, from some position of exclusive right or authority but as one equal to another who has a particular gift and responsibility that governs his way of being loyal to the proclamation concerning the messianic. His advice is oddly inflected in ways that would not be at all common for the Greek philosophical ethos: **But to think of each according to the measure of faithfulness that God has distributed to each.**

We have heard much of faithfulness in this letter, but now we hear that there are many ways of being faithful. Faithfulness is not conformity with the world; it is also not conformity with one another. It is distributed within the group in diverse ways, and this diversity is to be affirmed and carefully nurtured. We might wonder, How could it be otherwise if the messianic form of life is not the mechanical application of a rule book but the improvisation of a style or form of life that answers to the new, to the messianic innovation of God? Thus, we will hear that there is more than one way of being faithful, of forming a life shaped by the spirited in-breaking of justice. As we shall see again and again in this concluding argument of Paul, much depends on this diversity of faithfulness and on finding ways to embody and affirm this diversity in community.

For as in one body we have many members, and all the members do not have the same activity, so we many are one body in the messiah, and each one members of one another.

Paul's comrades are asked to imagine themselves as a multitude of members of one whole, each with a distinct function, each a different "instrument," each a distinct part of an ensemble whose various parts are necessary to one another and to the ensemble as a whole. The singularity of each is related to the plurality of all. This is the messianic sociality that Paul sees coming into being precisely as participation in the messianic. It is by virtue of the messianic that a multiplicity becomes a sociality in which each is necessary to the whole, in which we become parts not of a machine but of a living and lively body.

One image that might help explain this is the way in which a jazz ensemble might work together. One has a saxophone, another a trumpet, another a harmonica, and so on. They are each distinctive, but they need one another and "play off" one another. Each may improvise in its own way but always in relation to the others. There is a certain democracy in that each part is important, each is necessary, each has its own voice. But it is a "social" democracy because together they achieve unexpected variations as well as unexpected harmonies, all related to a discernible pattern or melody or rhythm. Here the "melody" will be the messianic, the coming into being of justice and mercy. Because it is justice and mercy, the individual parts, the singularities, are not isolated, self-contained individuals but parts of a well-shaped whole—and essential to one another. It is in the "interest" of one that the others be different. Diversity is not an obstacle to a certain wholeness but indispensable to it.

Thus, to return to Paul's image of the body: if I am a heart, it is essential that another be the lungs; or if I am a thumb, somebody else will have to be a finger. Being all thumbs is not a good way to be a body. Moreover, it is clear that for Paul each has an active and indispensable role to play. There is no division between an active "clergy" and a passive laity. There are only active parts.

Hence, **having gifts given that differ according to the giving** [let us use them]. The singular functions or actions are themselves rooted in the generosity (gift) that comes to each differently. There is in what follows no hierarchy, nor is the list definitive or exhaustive. Rather, it is illustrative. The first point to be made is that these gifts are potentialities to be activated: **if serving then in serving, if teaching then in teaching.** There is no rule book offered for the particular function but an exhortation to "do it." The reference to prophecy at the beginning of this list may well be a reference to the task of discerning what is appropriate in a given situation and of enabling the band to act in ways consistent with the messianic message and form of faithfulness. Paul continues: **those who share in simplicity, the ones aiding in diligence, the one showing mercy in cheerfulness.** The body, we have said, is that by virtue of which we become available to others, to one another. Here Paul emphasizes the ways this messianic body engages those others outside itself. It was precisely the astonishing generosity of Christian communities in the next few centuries that served to win over larger and larger elements of the general population. In his *Rise of Christianity* (73–94), Rodney Stark uses the example of the care of the sick in plague-ravaged cities of the empire to show how Christians' selfless service to others accounted in no small measure for the outward movement and growth of these messianic communities.

Let love be sincere, shrinking from what is bad, holding fast to what is good, in brotherly friendship to one another with warm friendliness. With terms like *philadelphia* (brotherly friendship), Paul points toward a friendship of equals that is impassioned. A much later semimessianic movement would insist on the appellation of "comrades." These comrades do not share the same class position or gender (as "brothers" might lead us to suppose) but are differently enabled to be instruments or members of the messianic project.

Outdo one another in showing honor to one another. The quest for honor divides, while showing honor to another as a common aspiration unites. In the Dong Huk rebellion in Korea at the beginning of the twentieth century, the bow of obeisance reserved by Confucian culture for the king became the way that each person of the ragtag groups of peasants and slaves greeted one another, honoring the divine in each, even the lowliest. Similarly for Paul, the competitive character of the Roman social order is turned on its head: instead of competing for honor, they compete to show honor to the other, every other.

In zeal, be unflagging; in spirit, be burning, serving the lord; in hope, rejoicing; in affliction, enduring; in prayer [yearning],

persistently continuing; for the necessities of the saints, sharing; hospitality [friendly welcoming] **seeking.** Although I may have rendered this passage a bit awkwardly, the point is to show that it has a nearly poetic character. The terms of affliction and endurance, of persistence, hope, and rejoicing we have encountered before (5:3–5, 8:32–35). All of this is now animated with zeal and spiritedness. All seems to aim at those expressions of sharing and welcoming that imitate the generosity of the divine, the messianic. Responding to the needs of the other, welcoming the wandering stranger—all of this suggests how the divine love and generosity take concrete shape through the messianic body.

21. Overcome Evil with Good (12:14–13:7)

Bless those who persecute you; bless and do not curse them. The inner generosity of the new society reaches outward to those who oppose, even persecute, this fledgling messianic society in order to bless rather than curse. Here and a few sentences later, we have a vigorous emphasis upon the love of the enemy, even the enemy in a position of power such that they are capable of persecution of the vulnerable body taking messianic shape in their midst. The response of the faithful to the persecutors is not a mechanical tit-for-tat but is surprising, creative, and in that way spirited and lively. A few decades later, the narrative ascribed by tradition to Matthew will present a similar perspective in more detail: turn the other cheek, go the second mile, and so on. It is critical, however, if we are not to have an unrealistic picture of how the messianic body takes shape in the world of the old eon to note that this is accompanied by persecution. The community does not separate itself from the world, but the world draws the dividing line by means of persecution. The "body" is separated from the "age" only by the opposition of the age. As body, the messianic intends the inclusion of all, but the age reacts to this inclusiveness through persecution. Thus, we have the irony that precisely the inclusivity and solidarity of the body come to set it apart from the age, "separate it" as the messianic or the holy.

Within the new social reality there is to be a remarkable mutual attunement: **Rejoice with the rejoicing, weep with the weeping, be**

attuned to one another. It is this mutual sympathetic attunement that makes the improvisation of the members result in a harmony.

Don't be arrogant but seek out the lowly; never be self-centered. These are not merely high-sounding ideals or idealistic platitudes. They depict the way any concerted living together takes shape. The mind-set that Paul is encouraging is characterized by a sort of intentional "downward social mobility." He had also encouraged this in Philippi when he urged his readers to imitate the mind-set of the messiah (Philippians 2:5). This seems to have been reflected in his determination to earn his living as a common laborer in the lower-class occupation of stitching together animal skins to make tents or market awnings (an occupation he may have learned when on the run from the authorities in Thessalonica) rather than accept as his "due" the financial support of his hearers. And it is reflected in his self-characterization as a slave. Those who are the adopted heirs of God orient themselves toward the lowest in imitation of the messiah. This is the surprisingly countercultural lifestyle of those who participate in the messianic. This is all quite different from the post-Pauline encouragement of those who are themselves on the lower rungs of the social order (women, children, slaves) to comport themselves in a servile way toward their social betters. For here, Paul is exhorting all in the community to associate themselves with the humble, the humiliated, rather than to look out for their own advantage. Needless to say, husbands telling wives to submit or slave owners telling slaves to be humble is simply flying in the face of the messianic transvaluation of all values.

Moreover, this living together aims outward to include rather than to exclude. **Repay no one evil for evil, but provide only good things toward all people. Insofar as it depends upon you, seek peace with all.** The justice that takes shape here is not retributive or distributive but creative. It seeks to bring about now the messianic goal of peace that flows from justice, a justice that flows from generosity. That the goal is peace is already entailed in Paul's greetings to the community: **generosity and peace from God** (unconditional generosity is the beginning and the means; peace is the goal).

How is peace with those who oppose the messianic to be achieved? **Beloved, not avenging yourselves, but rather making space for wrath; for it has been written, "Vengeance is mine; I will repay, says the**

Lord" [Deuteronomy 32:35]. **No, if your enemy is hungry, feed him;
if he is thirsty, give to drink, for by so doing you will heap burning
coals upon his head.** While some of the imagery here presents commentators with difficulty, the general drift is clear enough and is quite
radical. Indeed, it goes further than what we later find in the Sermon on
the Mount, since it specifies what it means to love not only the neighbor
but also the enemy: give food; give drink. The citation from Deuteronomy
is deployed to indicate that the fate of the unjust is to be left to God.
Although Paul speaks of wrath, he does not actually say the wrath "of
God." We have already pointed out this shift in terminology in chapter 8.
In any case we have seen from the first chapter that the notion of wrath
is regularly tied to systematic injustice. Once again the idea is that the
justice practiced by the community is unpredictable because it does not
conform to worldly notions of justice. Instead, it is creative, innovative.
Käsemann guesses that the reference to **burning coals** may be a reference
to an Egyptian penitential ritual (*Romans* 349), but no certainty seems
possible about the allusion. What seems involved is that the surprising
action of the messianic community aims at the transformation of the
unjust or, perhaps failing that, leaves them without any pretext or excuse
for their unjust behavior.

The general perspective that governs relationships with opposition
is this: **Do not be conquered by evil but rather conquer evil by goodness.** To give in to evil, to imitate it or to respond with reprisal, is to be
overcome by it. We become "the evil we deplore." But the band of messiah
followers in Rome can conquer evil by its own manifest and surprising
goodness. The idea here is not to escape from the evil or to be passive with
respect to it but to turn the tables on it and in that way conquer it so that it
is won over to the good. The messianic community becomes a body of the
messianic, for in this way as well it imitates the action of the divine, who
"while we were yet sinners . . . while we were enemies," yet loved us—
and sets out to win humanity over to the good by showing only goodness,
astonishing goodness, toward all. Thus, the corporate body that is the
evidence of the messianic in the world is to overcome all evil by doing only
good toward what until now has been an instrument of injustice.

The relation to the persecutor (12:14) and to the unjust (12:18–21) must
be borne in mind if we are to have any hope at a reasonable interpretation

of the sentences that follow concerning "higher authorities" (13:1–7). One of the chief ways in which Paul's perspective has been distorted in the history of theological and ecclesiastical interpretation is through the separation of segments of his argument from their context. This has been true with respect to the severing of Paul's talk of the coming of justice through faithfulness rather than compliance with legal structures in such a way as to eliminate the claim of justice altogether. We have also seen this sort of distortion arising when Paul's discussion of God's way with Israel is separated from its context in order to develop a non-Pauline doctrine of double predestination. Something similar has often happened with respect to the next few sentences of Paul's argument, sentences that seem to refer to an unquestioning obedience to political authority, an authority that takes the place on earth of God's own rule.

While this fragment of Paul's argument has often been cited in a politically reactionary sense, it has also been appropriated in somewhat progressive ways. At the beginning of the modern era Hobbes and Spinoza could see here a basis for the laicizing or secularization of the state that would affirm its independence from competing religious dogmatisms, thereby laying the foundation for the separation of church and state. And others could cite the connection between authorities and the enforcement of the good as a rationale for opposing authorities when they manifestly opposed the good. Despite these alternative ways of understanding the import of this segment of Paul's argument, neither they nor the more common uncritical celebration of state authority has usually taken the context of Paul's argument into account.

If any sense is to be made of these sentences, they must be kept firmly in relation to the overall thrust of Paul's argument in Romans (that justice comes not through adherence to the law but through faithfulness to the messianic event) and to the more immediate context that emphasizes that the messianic follower—though persecuted by the world—still seeks to overcome evil with good and, as Paul will go on to say, that the "world" as we know it is disappearing with the arrival of the messianic reality. While the sentences having to do with "authorities" may fit rather awkwardly within their context (giving rise to the plausible view that they may be the interpolation of a later follower of Paul), it is the context that must provide the way toward a plausible interpretation of them.

**Let every soul be subject to superior authorities. For there is not author-
ity except by God, and those in existence have been ordained by God. So
the one resisting authority has opposed the ordinance of God, and the ones
who oppose will receive judgment to themselves. For the rulers are not a
terror to good work but to the evil. But you want not to fear the authority?
Do good, and you will have praise from it. For he is a servant of God** [divine
servant] **to you for** [the sake of] **the good. But if you do evil, fear, for he bears
the sword not in vain; for he is a servant of God, an avenger for wrath to
the one who practices evil. Therefore it is necessary to be subject, not only
because of wrath but also because of conscience.**

If we are to take the whole of Paul's argument seriously, we will have to
begin by understanding these phrases in relation to the whole. For example, we would have to be clear that this should not be read as taking back
Paul's radical critique of the injustice of the imperial system in the first
chapter. Recall that there he had indicted the politics of Rome as manifestly incapable of administering justice, since the Roman ruling class was
characterized by a thoroughgoing opposition to divine justice. In 1 Corinthians he had suggested that it was precisely "the rulers of this age" who
"had crucified the lord of glory" (2:8) so were to be regarded as "perishing"
(2:6) with the onset of the messianic reality inaugurated in the messiah.
Some have therefore supposed that Paul is not referring at all to imperial
authorities but to the low-level magistrates with which the community
might ordinarily come in contact. This is the perspective, for example, of
Ernst Käsemann (*Romans* 354). Others have supposed that Paul is referring not to civil authorities but to the officials of the synagogues within
which the messianic groups would meet (Nanos 291–336). In the nature
of the case, since we are reading texts so far removed from our own time
and culture, texts not addressed to us, there will always be an irreducible
multiplicity of plausible interpretations of such matters.

In any case, those who suppose themselves to be "authorities," whether
"religious" or "political," whether lower magistrates or higher imperial
authorities, would be only too ready to suppose that all (every soul) ought to
be obedient to them as those who are appointed by God or who administer
justice in the name of the divine law. Thus, it is likely that several of these
phrases could be cited more or less verbatim from the self-justification of
those who present themselves as wielding authority in a social body. I think

that it is probable that many of these phrases do come more or less directly from the authorities themselves. Paul's readers in Rome would recognize in these words the very words of the authorities. The question is what becomes of these words when they are inserted into Paul's messianic perspective. We have already learned that such self-justification of legal authorities must be taken with a substantial helping of salt. For it is not the case that those who face persecution, for example, will uncritically agree that these authorities are **God's servant for your good** or are always and everywhere **a terror not to good conduct but to bad**. They have not forgotten that authorities that claim this for themselves have been the ones to condemn and to execute God's own messiah and who are at least complicit in the persecution of the messianic cells that have been forming within the empire.

To remind ourselves of Paul's indictment of the law and of those who administer "justice" in the name of the law is also to remind ourselves of the other side of Paul's argument about the law—it is, in regard to its reference to justice itself, **holy, just, and good**. Could it be that Paul is doing something similar with respect to the authorities? Certainly this would help align this passage with what we have been reading. The "authorities" are those who act on behalf of the law and thus "administer" justice as it is encoded in the law. Apart from this legal function related to the question of justice, there are no "authorities" in the sense being written about here. (Paul is not writing about academic authorities, for example.) Thus, precisely insofar as the law is holy, just, and good and precisely to that extent, the authorities are **God's servant for your good**. Just as the law is holy, in the sense that it is derived from and aims at the divine claim of justice, so also and in the same way, the authorities may be servants of the good. (We recall that in Romans, Paul has abandoned the suggestion made in Galatians that the law comes not from God but from Moses through intermediaries.)

But Paul and his readers also know that authorities are not so benign. They, like the law, are corrupted by injustice. For this reason it has been necessary to speak of comportment in relation to (unjust) persecution, comportment that aims at overcoming evil with good, which involves concrete ways of doing good even to the enemy. This doing good aims at provoking the enemy to renounce bad behavior (coals of fire) or at least to deprive the enemy of an excuse to continue in its animosity.

There is another sense in which authorities are **instituted by God** or **appointed by God** consistent with Paul's earlier argument. It has to do with Paul's appropriation of the prophetic tradition's view of the arrogant empires that threaten Israel with destruction. They are regarded as **instruments of wrath** not because they themselves are just but because they serve to punish the injustice of Israel itself. Paul had said, citing prophetic tradition, **What if God, desiring to show wrath and to show his power, endured with patience the instruments of wrath that were themselves to be destroyed?** (9:22). Here he says concerning the authority: **He is the servant of God to execute wrath on the one who practices evil** (13:4). What is invoked here is the world-historical function of "imperial" authority that serves, despite its own arrogance and injustice, to awaken the sense of the awesome claim of justice. Of course, neither for the prophets nor for Paul does this mean that God favors these authorities. On the contrary, they are already consigned to destruction just when they are at the apex of their power. For the arc of history aims not at wrath and destruction but at mercy and salvation. And this messianic aim is accomplished not by unjust instruments of wrath but by the just instruments of the messianic itself.

Thus, the reference to the ways in which the authorities legitimate their own authority may be understood to be deeply relativized by the messianic context within which this self-understanding is cited. What Paul is doing here may be consistent after all with what he does in 1 Corinthians in his discussion of the relation to existing institutions like marriage and business and religion: the "as not" (*hos me*) that, without engaging in a frontal assault on existing social institutions, nonetheless robs them of their force, their ability to determine the identity of the subjects who operate within them. This is what Žižek has termed "uncoupling" (*Fragile Absolute* 127–129), and Agamben has insisted that the "as not" renders all such classifications "inoperative" (*Time* 28). Agamben notes: "The only interpretation that is in no way possible is the one put forward by the Church, based on Romans 13:1, which states that there is no authority except from God, and that you should therefore work, obey, and not question your given place in society. What happens to the *as not* in all this?" (33). Of course, what has happened is that a fragment of Paul's discourse has been isolated from the context of his argument as a whole in order to render that entire discourse harmless so far as the world is concerned.

Does what Žižek termed "uncoupling" operate here? **Therefore also pay taxes, for they are divine servants attending constantly to this particular thing; render to all what is owed: taxes to those to whom they are due, tribute to whom tribute is due, fear to whom fear is due, honor to the one due honor.** The question of tax and tribute is especially emphasized, together with what may well be a rather sardonic reference that the authorities may be chiefly concerned with revenue. Of course, for ordinary people in the Greco-Roman world, the authorities would be far more aptly characterized as seeking to extract money than to administer justice. This issue is also treated in the Gospels, written some years after Paul. There we find the desire to distinguish the messianic movement from a mere tax revolt—hence the question in the synoptic Gospels about paying taxes to Caesar or in Matthew concerning paying the temple tax. In each case, what transpires is that a sentiment along the lines of "let them have their damned money" is combined with the radical undermining of the claims of the authorities to legitimacy. That undermining is accomplished in the Gospels by the call to render to God what is due to God (namely, the very loyalty that the imperial coin ascribes to Caesar).

Here that subversive gesture occurs in a rather different way. Paul has just said to **give honor to the one due honor**, but he had already said to the messianic group that they should compete to give honor to one another, thereby undermining the whole system of seeking honor. Honor is to be given away rather than claimed. The giving of honor to the authorities is actually undermined from within by the fact that the same honor is shown to everyone else. On the one hand, the authorities receive the honor they crave, but on the other hand, that honor is deprived of the significance it was supposed to have by being distributed promiscuously, to all. While the Gospels undermine the ideological significance of taxes by reference to what is due to God, Paul undermines the ideological significance of honoring the authorities by reference to what is due to the fellow human.

The messianic politics of Paul, then, does not entail a taking over of the state and its functions. This was certainly a much debated issue in the emergence of the nineteenth-century messianic movement associated with Marx, Engels, and Lenin. On the one hand, there was the view that the capitalist state would simply self-destruct on account of its manifest self-contradiction. On the other hand, there was a flirtation with the capturing of the state through a violent revolution more or less patterned on the French Revolution, which had ushered in the capitalist state. In either case it was supposed that with the coming of the new and just society, the state would "wither away." For Paul, the state is essentially irrelevant to messianic politics. There is no point in an attempt to assume state power, for it belongs to an order that is no longer pertinent: it has a past, but no future. Indeed, in a remarkable group of essays titled *The Idea of Communism*, Alain Badiou and a number of other contemporary Marxists renounce the dream or nightmare of an assumption of state power. This is one of the ways that a Marxist or "post-Marxist" political thinking converges with the Pauline project. In the now-time, the state or empire is engaged in the same way all other institutions are engaged: as if not. But that does mean offering it its due in taxes and so on, doing good in order to win over evil, rather than engaging in the counterforce of revolt that the state knows only too well how to deal with. Here as elsewhere, the aim is to take the world by surprise—the messianic surprise of love. Or, as he has already said, seeking where it depends on us, to be at peace with all.

22. After the Law (13:8–14)

The radicality of this approach is further demonstrated in the way Paul seems to take back the entire logic of giving what is due or owed (tax, tribute, fear, honor) with this advice: **Owe nothing to no one except to love one another; for he who loves his neighbor has fulfilled the law.** The entire economy of debt is here being undercut. Of course, love is not the payment of a debt. It is the excess, the "how much more" that is the very character of divine justice. The law is here relativized by being both abolished and exceeded all at once. And this is also precisely what has happened to the authorities. The honor they crave has been radically shared out and is thereby deprived of any ideological significance. The love that is "outside the law" is also and at the same time not against the law (insofar as the law aims at justice) but beyond its dictates. It overthrows the law of what is due by doing what is not due. It thereby "overcomes evil with good."

The reflections of Derrida on what he calls a duty beyond debt may help clarify the stakes of what Paul is wrestling with here. Speaking of an appropriate, even necessary, gratitude, Derrida writes: "Pure morality must exceed all calculation, conscious or unconscious, of restitution or reappropriation. This feeling tells us, perhaps without dictating anything, that we must go beyond duty, or at least duty as debt; duty owes nothing, it must owe nothing, it ought at any rate to owe nothing" (*On the Name* 133). This language is eerily similar to Paul's, even though Derrida makes no reference in these discussions of duty beyond debt to Paul or an "indebtedness" to Paul (Jennings, *Reading Derrida* 96–108).

For "you shall not commit adultery," "you shall not kill," "you shall not steal," "you shall not covet," and whatever other commandment is summed up in "you shall love your neighbor as yourself." Jacob Taubes has pointed out that here Paul's perspective is rather more radical than the one attributed in the Gospels to Joshua/Jesus, who added: "Love the Lord your God with all your strength." There is here no "love of God" that can be set against the love of neighbor. Taubes writes: "No dual commandment, but rather one commandment. I regard this as an absolutely revolutionary act" (53). Opposing the love of God to the love of neighbor is precisely what Jesus's/Joshua's opponents had done in suggesting, for example, that healing (love of neighbor) could just as well wait until after the Sabbath (loving God). Although Paul's formulation is far more radical than that attributed to Joshua, it does correspond pretty well to the messianic practice as recorded in the gospel narratives to be written much later.

It is characteristic of Paul that neither here nor elsewhere does he supplement his exhortation by appealing to the teachings of the messiah. Moreover, when he does cite the commandments, he refers not to the "religious" or God-oriented ones (honor God alone, Sabbath, etc.) but only to what might be termed the "interhuman commandments," those that have to do with not wronging the neighbor, the other human being. This is the very heart of the divine justice, the messianic justice, with which Paul is concerned. Moreover, here Paul is attending to the commandments not as enshrining a particular legalism but as intending justice. What is really at stake is not a question of not violating one of these laws but of what violates the neighbor.

Levinas has attempted to clarify a similar perspective in claiming that one can honor God only in the face of the other, the other whose claim of regard is the claim of the divine: "The supernatural is not an obsession for Judaism. Its relation with divinity is determined by the exact range of the ethical" (*Difficult Freedom* 49). Thus, a separate honoring of God that bypasses the need of the other, the neighbor, is simply impossible.

The "commandments" identified here, while couched in terms recognizable from the traditions of Israel, are common to Judeans and gentiles and in some form or other are common to all cultures (with each culture exhibiting variations on what exactly is covered by the prohibition). Similarly, versions of the exhortation to look out for the interests of one's neighbor seem also to be common to all cultures, again with important differences in how this is to be understood. From Paul we already know that this "love" or concern for the well-being of the other extends also to the enemy so is without restriction. It is this unrestricted commitment to the welfare of all without exception that marks the messianic exigency of a sociality beyond or outside law. The messianic is therefore a radical humanism that aims at a certain universalism.

Love does no evil to the neighbor; therefore the fulfillment of law is love. If as Hobbes believed, law (and the state) has the purpose of limiting the damage done by interhuman aggression and violence, the war of each against all, then love, which does not do evil to the other, has no further use for law (and the state). It is abolished in principle (as Marx and Lenin supposed would be true with the advent of the new sociality of humanity). If the law aims at a certain negative justice (limiting the damage by measuring violation, as Paul has suggested), it has nonetheless proven itself incapable of establishing a positive justice. Moreover, it has been captured by anxiety (sin) so as to become a force of injustice. Thus, it is only love that can accomplish even the negative function of the law and the state. Paul has just indicated that the "authorities" exist to restrain evil. But he had also earlier pointed out the way in which the social order of Rome not only did not restrain but actually fomented injustice (something similar had occurred in relation to Mosaic law as well). Thus, the law is no longer serviceable, nor can it be made serviceable. Even the negative function of the law can be accomplished only through that which is outside the law—love.

Giorgio Agamben has shown that Jewish, Christian, and Islamic messianic perspectives contemplate the end of the law and ask what then happens to law. It becomes, he says, an object of childlike play or, what amounts to the same thing perhaps, simply an object of study. This play— or this study—he reminds us, is not justice itself but is the gateway, the entrance into justice. When law has lost its "proper" function, it becomes inoperative in its original use but becomes usable for imagination (*State of Exception* 63). To a certain degree, this is what already occurs with the law in Talmudic study. Neither is it made into a univocal prescription nor is it discarded (on the ash heap of history, as certain Marxists said about bourgeois institutions), but it becomes the fount of endless study or play.

That Paul's perspective is determined precisely by this messianic consciousness is made evident in what he next says: **And then this: knowing the time [*kairos*], that now is the hour for you to be raised from sleep. For now the salvation is nearer than when we believed: the night passing away; the day has drawn near.** The now of messianic time is a moment when it is still dark, still obscure (so a time of danger and affliction), yet it is also the time when the day approaches precisely in and as this darkness. Thus, the meaning of the present darkness is transfigured as approaching day, just as the meaning of creation's groaning had been transfigured as birth pangs.

The metaphor of being raised from sleep echoes the metaphor of being awakened from among the dead. The now-time thus becomes already characterized by the anticipated resurrection. It is an awakening from the sleep (*hypnos*) of the current age that has also been characterized as the dominion of death. This awakening is occasioned by the drawing near of that salvation (for all flesh) that had been the subject of the messianic announcement.

The theme of wakefulness or alertness as characterizing the appropriate consciousness of messianic time is also present in the Gospels, where it is associated both with the requisite alertness in the time of affliction and travail (Mark 13:33–37) and with the unheeded injunction to the disciples as Jesus enters into his agony in the garden prior to being arrested (14:38).

Levinas has characterized the ethical relation to the other as entailing a certain insomnia, which maintains a constant state of alertness to the coming and to the need of the other (*Of God* 59). In Pauline discourse, this insomnia is also a historical political insomnia, one that awakens in the darkness of the present to shake off the drowsiness of the present age and to discern signs of coming light.

This sense that the time is growing shorter, that the wholeness for which we hope is rushing toward us, is the indispensable horizon for Paul's work and thought. We may be less sure, we who live some two millennia later. Can we still live with this sort of insomnia, this same wakefulness? Have we not, rather, dozed off? We may, however, wonder whether it is really possible to live toward justice without the sense of impendingness, without the sense that the coming of what we hope for is not far off. Agamben suggests that messianic time is "the time that remains between time and its end" or "not the end of time but the time of the end" (*Time* 62). This figure gives its name to his commentary on Romans: *The Time That Remains.*

Let us then cast off works of darkness and put on the weapons of light. As regularly happens in Paul, the indicative (the salvation is nearer, the hour of awakening) becomes the imperative to conduct oneself in accordance with the true time, the *kairos* of approaching light. Earlier Paul had spoken of being instruments or weapons of injustice or of justice. Here justice is linked to light, the approaching daylight of the messianic time that heralds the radiance or shining forth of messianic consummation. The weapons of light would appear to refer precisely to the comportment that vanquishes evil with good, so is not passive but active in its surprising ways of engaging "the enemy" with a disarming goodness as well as with the capacity to endure affliction and even to exult in it.

Let us conduct ourselves [walk] as becomes the day, not in reveling and drinking bouts and in beddings and in outrageous excesses, not in strife and jealousy. These depictions of nighttime activity do not correspond to the ways in which the members of the messianic movement in Rome might be thought plausibly to comport themselves but echo depictions of the behavior of the elites in Rome who are familiar to us through more or less contemporary histories of the time. In this allusive way, Paul distinguishes the comportment of the messianists from that of the "authorities" who are immersed in darkness. The discerning reader will then be reminded of the characterization of the apex of Greco-Roman society in Paul's opening indictment.

But put on the leader, Joshua messiah, and make no provision for the flesh to gratify its desires. The readers are exhorted to so identify with the executed and resurrected messiah that this becomes their way of appearing to the world; in this way they become weapons or instruments of justice and of light in the midst of a society of injustice and darkness. The new sociality that is coming into being is thus itself messianic, both in its state of affliction and in its active love of the neighbor. It so assimilates itself to the messiah as to be the body of the messiah, the way that the messianic becomes visible as well as vulnerable—and also victorious in the midst of the death-dominated present age.

While many interpreters have linked the "passions of the flesh" with the revelings, beddings, and so on of the previous sentence, passions of the flesh for Paul have far more to do with enmity, jealousy, and those behaviors that arise from what Levinas termed an "allergic reaction to the other" (*Totality and Infinity* 51). That this is precisely what Paul is concerned about is evident from the issues to which he immediately directs the attention of his readers—the question of welcome.

If we pause to look back over the way we have come, we may be struck by a remarkable consistency in the direction of Paul's argument. He had earlier suggested that the new life outside the law stood in a fundamental contrast to life under law and sin. Indeed, he had faced the question of **continuing in sin** as what it might mean to be outside the law (6:1, 15) and had answered with a number of analogies of transformation: death to life, passing from one owner to another, being liberated from marriage by the death of a husband. He had encouraged his hearers, [Do] **not to let sin exercise dominion in your mortal bodies to obey their passions** (6:12). He had also spoken of the flesh and of our liberation from the self-preoccupation that flesh entails. What has been added here, however, is a positive description of the new life, the lively life, of those who have passed from death to life, of those for whom death lies in the past rather than the future. And this is precisely the perspective that he has now made concrete. He is weaving a very intricate web here, and it hangs together with a remarkable, even if not "predictable," consistency.

23. Welcome: The Messianic Sociality (14:1–15:13)

How are we concretely to **put on the leader Joshua messiah,** and in what way does this exclude a provision for the appetites of the flesh? Above all, these questions aim to make evident how a new social reality comes into being, one that instead of enmity exhibits commitment to the other, to one another. The argument that Paul makes in the following sentences has to do with this new politics, this new sociality, that exhibits justice beyond the law.

In order to be clear about this, it is helpful to recall the sociality or, rather, antisociality that Paul had described at the beginning of his letter: **they were filled with all injustice, flesh-obsessed, covetousness, evil, full of envy, murder, strife, guile, malignity, gossipers, slanderers, god haters, insolent arrogant, boasters, inventors of evils . . . foolish faithless, heartless, ruthless.** That is the social (dis)order within which the new sociality is to take shape, one constituted through a renovation of mind-set that will demonstrate or embody the aim of divine justice.

Again, we cannot stress too much the way that, for Paul, this takes the shape of a sociality, a way of being related with one another. It is therefore a kind of politics. But it is a politics that is beyond the law, beyond the coercion that the law entails, one that is spirited to invent or improvise the concrete forms of love. And this has to do above all with welcome. **Welcome the one weak in faith, not for disputes over opinions,** Paul writes. Welcome is the openness to the other, the one who is different, the one who is therefore by no means the same. The very difference of the other makes the other other, and thus this difference is itself the possibility of a welcome of another.

Here we touch upon the most basic feature of a messianic politics, a polity that instead of closing itself to the other, the stranger, the different, actually welcomes the advent of the other as distinctly other. Derrida writes that justice "is the affirmative experience of the other" (*Negotiations* 104) and that justice "is the experience of the other as other, the fact that I let the other be other" (105).

To see what is at stake here, we may reflect on the character of the polities we know. In general, they seek to make clear the distinction favoring those who are the same, our citizens over theirs, nationals over aliens.

Think of the basic political struggles, for example, in Europe: Who is French? Who is German? Is a refugee from Algeria French? What of one from the Ivory Coast? Is someone from the Bahamas English? Or from Nigeria? Is someone born in Turkey German? Or is someone born in Albania Italian? The great stresses in the national political life of the so-called nation-states have typically had to do with the stranger. Often the polity is one of exclusion, sometimes of assimilation or integration, which demands of the newcomer to become as we are, hide the differences. But what differences are to be hidden or excluded? Are the differences of language, custom, food, observance, religion, and so on to be excluded or hidden? What is hard to imagine is a welcoming of difference as difference, of otherness as otherness. And this, we may even say, is the basic question of a cosmopolitan sociality, one that does not impose uniformity but welcomes difference. Derrida notes that in the face of the contemporary issues of right of refuge and of the undocumented and so on, what is called for is a quite different international law, a quite different cosmopolitanism of welcome, of hospitality (*Adieu* 101).

Paul will be dealing with this order of question in his argument. It is therefore with a question that bears directly on the question of the instantiation of justice. The form that this question takes for Paul here and elsewhere (in 1 Corinthians 8, for example) is the difference, as he puts it, between those who are weak and those who are strong. Weakness is identified with a set of scruples or restrictions, while strength is identified with the absence of such scruples. Thus, one who has and obeys a number of rules about how to be faithful is regarded as weak, while one who seems on principle to be more or less indiscriminate is said to be strong.

We note first that this is to a degree counterintuitive, since it is more often thought that those who are very strong in faith are precisely those who observe more restrictions. We may think, for example, of the prestige of the anchorites of the early Christian world who abstained from a variety of foods and a number of activities, including sexual ones. Precisely these disciplines were regarded as badges of strength, especially of spiritual strength. And there would seem to be a certain connection to some of Paul's rhetoric here, as they seem to be those who, as Paul has said, take no thought for the lusts or desires of the flesh. It would be easy to provide further examples since Christianity came under the spell of ascetic movements of the ancient world. These disciplines seek to provide a way of demonstrating that one was not conformed to the world but transformed. And this continues into modernity with holiness movements and the like. Thus, the first move that Paul makes here is one that is itself counterintuitive, associating strength with what looks like laxness, and weakness with what looks like rigorous discipline.

We should be aware that this is a question that occurs regularly in Paul: 1 Corinthians 8 and 10 are concerned with a similar set of issues, although in that case it is directed to the question of eating food that is part of the celebration of civic deities. The so-called Jerusalem Council imposed an abstinence from this practice upon gentile or pagan Christians according to Acts 15:20, but Paul seems willing to accept greater liberty among the Corinthians in this regard. This serves as the background to the sorts of issues to which he turns attention in Romans. Here it is not a question of meat that has been dispensed from the temple of other gods as part of civic ceremony but, rather, it would seem, of certain forms of ascetic discipline chosen to signify a messianic difference.

One confidently eats anything; another, being weak, eats only vegetables. What is this apparent difference of "faith," and why is one weak and another not? In the first place, how is eating only vegetables a sign of faithfulness? Already in pagan practice there was a possibility of principled vegetarianism. It is not clear that this was a possibility in Judaism, although this is sometimes debated. Certainly we may recall that Adamic humanity, before the Fall and until the time of Noah, was supposed to refrain from eating meat. Is this eating of meat not itself a sign of violence? Today can we not see the terrible reality of the meat industry with its utter disregard for the animate life of the animal, for what makes an animal precisely animal—its animation, its freedom of movement. On this question, Jacques Derrida has presented some rather compelling arguments from a philosophical perspective (*Animal* 25). There may well be very good reasons for adopting vegetarianism as a sign of messianic faithfulness.

And what of those who disregard such restrictions? They may, of course, have simply not given the matter any thought. But they may also be persuaded that all foods are the good gift of God and therefore accept all with gratitude.

Why are the former weak in faithfulness? Perhaps because they suppose that faithfulness consists in rules and regulations, so seem nearer to the compliance with the law from which the gift of the divine has set us free. Meanwhile, those who eat anything are not anxious. Above all, they do not place limits on the gifts of God, they do not regard them with suspicion, and so on. (Perhaps also in the background here is the way in which eating and not eating certain foods was made to be the mark of religious difference by which Israel distinguished itself from the pagans. Nevertheless, this is not the primary issue with which Paul is dealing.)

Paul is by no means concerned to resolve the dispute in terms of deciding which is right. This also is quite remarkable. For it is the work of what is often called ethics to make this judgment, as it is the work of politics, or of law. But this is precisely what Paul will not do. Instead, Paul will insist that these very important differences remain side by side. The eater is not to despise the noneater, and the noneater is not to judge the eater. Whether in despising or in judging, what each seeks is the elimination of difference. This is precisely what Paul does not want, for in this elimination of difference, whether as despising or as judging, is found the true or greater violence.

The basis of not despising or judging, but in fact welcoming, is this: **For God has welcomed him**. That is, what the divine has done already, as the inauguration of a messianic politics, is to welcome the other, including, of course, my other. That is to say, the other person or other community, whether this otherness is expressed by the absence or presence of scruple, is one who has already been welcomed.

Who are you to pass judgment on the servant [or household member] **of another? That one stands or falls** [in relation] **to his/her own lord; that one will stand because the leader enables him or her to stand.**

The term "servant" simply indicates one who is a member of the household of a lord. It may be translated as "servant," "client," or even "adoptee." Any of these have been prepared for in the arguments that Paul has advanced before. Thus, he has spoken of himself as a slave of the messiah and of his readers as slaves of justice. The point seems to be that one who is a slave belongs to the other and can be disciplined or commanded only by the one to whom he belongs. I have no rights with respect to the one who belongs to another. This belonging to the leader marks the limit of my interference with the friend, sibling, or even fellow servant. That the other person belongs to another prevents my assimilation of him or her. It is thus the other's freedom from my judgment, my accusation. And this is especially so since the lord of the other can make sure that the other stands and does not fall.

In a way, this is the inviolable secrecy of the other: the other belongs to someone other than myself. We might be inclined to say that the other person belongs to himself or herself rather than to another, a third. Is this as effective a way of ensuring the other person's independence from me? It is also likely that Paul has in mind here not only other persons but other cells or communes of messiah followers that have developed different views about how to practice the messianic justice to which they are committed.

One judges a day to be above others; another judges every day [to be the same]. **Let each be persuaded in his or her own mind.** The special regarding of particular days is a mark of a certain piety. This was true of Roman or pagan piety as well as of Judean piety. And it is today true also of Christian piety, and Muslim piety, and so on. In fact, the dividing of days into "holy" and "profane," together with particular inclusions or exclusions concerning food, is the invariable way in which religion, or what we call religion, distinguishes itself. What could be more important than determining how one ought to observe special days in honor of the tradition, or of the gods? In the world of the old eon, governed by law—perhaps especially religious law—these differences of opinion and practice have been the occasion of an astonishing amount of violence and bloodshed.

It is critical that Paul feels that there is no need to declare for another what is right here. However, he does not say that this is a matter of indifference: **Let each be persuaded in his or her own mind.** Decide for yourself what is good, and do what you decide to be good. But make no rules, no laws here. Invent no religion to which you will seek converts and from which you will exclude unbelievers. This is extraordinarily difficult: to insist that this is something that is not a matter of indifference but also to say that it is not a matter to cause division or separation.

The one who observes the day, to the leader, the one eating, to the leader; for each gives thanks to God. And the one not eating, to the leader abstains, and gives thanks to God.

Here then is the basic principle: Give thanks. What matters is whether what we do or don't do is an expression not of anxiety but of thanksgiving, and so of gratitude. In this way the doing or not doing is oriented to the messianic as gratitude to God. Gratitude is what marks the orientation to the gift and produces justice as a gift or on the basis of gift. Turning away from gratitude is a turning away both from God and from justice, as Paul had emphasized early on in this letter when indicting gentile civilization as being characterized as knowing God but without honoring or giving thanks to God. It is becoming clear that Paul is opening up considerable latitude for what I have been calling improvisation with respect to the forms of life that may honor God and arise from and aim at thanksgiving.

None of us lives to him- or herself; no one dies to him- or herself, for if we live, we live to the leader and if we die, we die to the leader; whether we live or die, we belong to the leader.

Here all is placed in a much more decisive context. Far more dramatic than the difference between eating or not eating a certain food or observing or not a particular day is the difference between life and death. But even in this difference, living or dead, we belong to another. We live or die in the direction of, or in orientation upon, another.

Before, Paul could deploy the alternative of living or dead to mark a frontier: before alive to sin, dead to justice, and so on (chapter 6). But now this frontier, the last and most intractable border, is all but erased: **For to this end the messiah died and lived, in order to be leader of both the dead and the living.** Note that the death and resurrection of the messiah are here related to the question of abolishing the division between the living and the dead and thus of abolishing division as such. For the messiah, who can be lord or leader of both the dead and the living, can certainly be lord of both the eating and the noneating, the observant of days and the nonobservant.

This is not said in such a way as to make us individuals or monads or isolated subjectivities. Rather, we are of or to another, and we are this precisely as we are incorporated into the messiah. In what may have been his first letter to a messianic community (1 Thessalonians), Paul had felt compelled to deal with the apparent separation between those who had died in the messiah and those who were yet alive. The issue there had been an intolerable rupture in the solidarity of the community. It was in this connection that he spoke of the essential equality of the living and the dead in the messiah. Here the social character of the messianic, which overcomes the distinction between the living and the dead, is redeployed to effect solidarity among those groups who have fundamentally different views about what faithfulness to the messianic might mean in practical terms. Being possessed by the messiah or the messianic makes us free to make up our own minds and free not to interfere with the other doing the same.

Why do you judge your own comrade [brother]**, or why do you despise your own comrade** [brother]**? For we will all stand before the divine tribunal.**

Here it seems to me that we could go back and maintain that the belonging to the household of which Paul spoke earlier is to be understood in terms of the adoptive relation celebrated in chapter 8. The one who eats what I do not is precisely my sibling who has received the same adoption that I have received and under the same condition: by sheer unmerited and undeserved (and undeservable) generosity. Each must stand before the divine tribunal, and there we know that there is justice. It is a justice, however, that does not condemn but welcomes.

To emphasize this point, Paul cites Isaiah 45:23, a text that also shapes what is called the Christological hymn of Philippians 2:10–11. The Isaianic passage has in view the eschatological victory of God in which all nations and creatures join in praise of God. In the course of Christian doctrinal reflection, this will be taken to authorize the incorporation of the messiah into the divine as understood in Greek philosophical terms. But it may also be noted that the tendency of Paul's thought is to identify the divine with the messianic in such a way as to prepare the way for a messianism that absorbs the divine, rather than the other way around.

Each will explain himself [or herself] **to God, so then let us then no longer judge one another but rather decide** [judge] **not to trip up or hinder a comrade.**

The only judgment is the good judgment of not judging one another—of not putting our opinions and practices in the way of another in such a way as to make him or her agree with us on pain of exclusion or condemnation. How could it be otherwise if the power of law to condemn has been broken? There is then no law, but there is still conscience, and here not my own conscience is decisive but the conscience of the other and this is not to be damaged but treated with all respect and tenderness.

This is the turning point in the argument. Until now, it has been simply that there is to be an end to that judging and condemnation or even contempt that rends the fabric of sociality, especially in matters that may be termed "religious." But now we seem to go further, in a direction already prepared by the quote we have read. This is at least the case for those who know how Paul deploys this trope in Philippians, since there it serves the purpose of indicating how believers are to renounce their own privilege to accommodate the weaker, just as the messiah or the Son has done.

As difficult as what Paul has already suggested is to put into practice, what follows is far more difficult. It is to not offend the other or cause the other to stumble, especially the weaker. Here Paul accepts the principle of "the strong": **I know and am persuaded in the leader Joshua that nothing is unclean.** This is the very basis of the possibility of a mission to the nations, the pagans, those who are after all "unclean." This is even narrativized in the later Acts of the Apostles in terms of Peter's vision, which leads to his decision to baptize Cornelius. Paul himself had had to grapple with Peter's ambivalence in this regard according to Paul's account in Galatians. There he strenuously defended the freedom that pertains to the messianic.

The difficulty is that this freedom with respect to scruple can itself cause damage to the conscience of the scrupulous, that is, to one who thinks something is unclean. In 1 Corinthians, Paul had likewise warned against harming those who had a more tender conscience with respect to meat that had been used in cultic ceremonies in pagan temples (chapter 8).

Paul decides the Galatians case rather differently: no circumcision, no succumbing to the scruples of others. But the cases are different. Here it is not that the weak are attempting to impose their scruples on me, but I am attempting to impose my lack of scruples on them. But this may do violence to them. It may injure them. **If your comrade is being injured by what you eat, you are no longer walking in love.** If my comrades decide to imitate my freedom but without confidence, without clarity in their own mind, then they may do what they think or feel is wrong. And then they have in fact violated their own conscience; they have acted without faith or confidence and thus have "sinned." This flaunting of a freedom from scruple, then, is not love for the other, not a care for what is in the interest of the other. It can seem to **destroy one for whom messiah died**.

It should be clear that we are caught here between irreconcilable imperatives: on the one hand, the imperative of an openness to all (including all foods and so on) and, on the other hand, a love for the other that sacrifices even the privilege of faithful freedom. For if I yield to the conscience of the weak, I am in danger of imposing a law; but if I do not, I am in danger of violating her or his conscience. There is here a seeming aporia.

So do not let what is good to you be spoken of as evil.

There is no program by which I can act here without responsibility, without negotiating the unconditional, the nonnegotiable. This is precisely the character of a properly ethical decision, as Derrida has so carefully explained: "Negotiation is always negotiation of the nonnegotiable" (*Negotiations* 304); "one must negotiate the nonnegotiable" (325). This is also the reason that the ethical ultimately requires improvisation rather than rules. There can be no way that accomplishes both aims of this dilemma perfectly, so there can only ever be improvisation.

It can never be the case that rules about eating and drinking can become the condition of the reign of God. The only condition here is **justice and peace and joy in holy spirit. He who thus serves messiah is acceptable to God and approved by humanity.** It is here that we become responsible, where there is a kind of aporia. But we are responsible not only for ourselves (for we must explain ourselves to God) but for our neighbor as well. **So let us pursue what makes for peace and for strengthening one another.**

Neither rules about eating and drinking nor freedom from those same rules should become the reason for dividing the new messianic sociality. **Do not for the sake of food destroy the work of God.** This work is precisely the bringing into being of a justice without or outside the imposition of law, a justice impelled by love. **Everything is indeed clean, but it is wrong if one stumbles over eating. It is good not to eat meat or drink wine or do anything that makes your comrade stumble.** This is a concrete attempt on Paul's part to show how love for the neighbor and the welcoming of the other takes shape in an emerging messianic sociality.

The faithfulness or the faithful manner of life that you have according to yourself, have or hold in relation to God or before God. Blessed is the one who does not judge [condemn] **himself or herself in what he approves. But the one who eats with conflict or against his or her own judgment has been judged because it does not come from confident faithfulness. All that does not proceed from confident faithfulness is sin.**

This is rather difficult, but it seems to me that the test here is not a rule or law but free confidence and loyalty. If what I do leaves me in internal conflict about what is right, about whether I am being faithful, then I am still in that position of being divided and anxious, so am not within the sphere of free and happy adoption that rests on gift. This does not mean that what I do is decided for me by a programmed response dictated by rules. On the contrary, as Derrida notes, "There is no decision without the undecidable. If there are no undecidables there is no decision. There is simply programming, calculation" (*Negotiations* 31). The messianic form of life is improvisational. This improvisation, however, is oriented not to what pleases me but toward another: to the lord, to the neighbor. And this double orientation is in fact single, for the messianic is precisely the openness to and care for the other.

This is precisely what Paul argues: **We the strong** [or empowered] **ought to bear the weakness of those who are not strong** [or empowered] **and not please ourselves.** Note that the terminology of "weak" and "strong" is rather too static to get at what is going on here. What is at stake is the power (*dunamis*) of faithfulness, the greater of lesser degrees of such empowerment. The measure of our faithfulness is not how empowered we are but the extent to which that empowerment is placed in the service of the less empowered. **Let each of us seek to please the neighbor for the good** [of the neighbor] **with the aim of building up.** The aim of pleasing the neighbor isn't to leave the neighbor alone but to also empower the neighbor and thus to build up the body.

Paul argued in 1 Corinthians that this is the true mark of power: it appears as weakness for the sake of the other. There he had spoken of the message concerning the cross and of the way it seemed both foolish and weak yet was the power of salvation. Here that "theology of the cross" is made, perhaps even more clearly than in 1 Corinthians, into the principle for the development of a messianic sociality.

For even messiah did not please himself. As in 1 Corinthians and Philippians, the point of recalling the messianic event is that it should serve as a pattern for our dealings with one another. To underscore this point, Paul cites Psalm 69:9: **"The insults of those who insult you have fallen on me."** The psalm gives voice to the one who is insulted because of his faithfulness to God, who bears the reproaches directed against God. But notice the transfer that occurs here. The messiah receives the reproaches directed against the weak, the ungodly, the enemies of God—who bears a condemnation as outlaw that by rights should be directed to us. Once again Paul is not interested in a speculative theory of atonement. The point is that just as he bore with our weakness, so we, too, ought to bear with the weakness of our neighbor.

The citation of the psalm leads Paul to maintain that the written (the law, the prophets, the psalms, and so on) has the function of teaching us, of enabling us to be faithful. **Whatever was written previously was written to instruct us.** This is not, of course, a theory of the inspiration or even of the authority of the written but rather an assertion of the pragmatic usefulness of the written, in particular of the texts of Israel. Paul's view is quite different from the one that will come to prevail: that all must have a Christological interpretation. Instead, the point of rereading or of appropriating the previously written is that **by steadfastness and by the encouragement of the written we may have hope**. Thus, the written, when read within the context of endurance (that is, the context of affliction, suffering, or persecution), strengthens the reader toward hope. The function of the text is to awaken hope and thus to orient the reader toward the messianic consummation set in motion by the messianic event associated with Joshua messiah. This is a far cry from later ideas that the function of the text is to impose laws, either for thought (doctrine) or for moralism. The text is to be read as encouragement toward hope. Several times in the course of this letter, we have heard Paul connecting affliction, endurance, and hope. What is added here is that the written has the function of enabling this perseverance toward hope, this confidence in the promise of God.

It is important to note that by bearing the weakness of the other, we are enabled to bear together so to endure and to have hope. The love that has been directed to us is directed through us to the neighbor, and in that way both we and the neighbor are able to stand. It is this that testifies to the overcoming of the world of enmity, the antisocial disorder of everyone for himself or herself. In this way we are enabled truly to hope (together) for the overcoming, the transforming, of the world—and thus for the accomplishment of the justice to come.

And the God of endurance and of counsel [comfort, advocacy] **give to you the same thing so that you may think among yourselves in accordance with the messiah Joshua. So that with one voice and one harmony you may make shine forth the God and Father of our leader, Joshua the messiah.**

The aim of the new form of sociality that is constituted through the love of the neighbor expressed concretely as the welcome of the other is the praise, the glorifying of God. It is the togetherness of what is basically different that is this glorifying. It is the bearing with one another, the welcoming of the other, and the concern for the other in and through such great differences that is the shining forth of God, of that God who is the father of the one to whom we are oriented in life and death: the messiah Joshua. The basic sense of "glorifying" here is that it causes this divine to appear, to shine forth, or is itself this shining forth within the darkness, that heralds the dawn of the divine radiance or shining forth itself.

Welcome one another, therefore, as messiah welcomed us, so that the divine may shine forth.

It is this welcoming of the weak by the strong, of the strong by the weak, of the different that remains different, that echoes the act of God in messiah Joshua and is that which testifies to the power of God in weakness and the victory of God over injustice. In this way the divine radiance shines forth into the world.

Although some commentators have understood the distinction between weak and strong as applying to the difference between gentile and Judean members of the messianic cell in Rome, this is quite dubious in my judgment because of some of the specific differences indicated (drinking wine or not, being vegetarian or not, neither of which distinguishes Judeans and gentiles in this or any period), and because of the deployment of weak and strong that Paul has seemingly also applied in 1 Corinthians to indicate differences among pagan or gentile messianists concerning the distribution and consumption of meat deriving from cultic celebrations in pagan temples. Up to this point in the text I am in agreement with Thorsteinsson (91–92).

However, Paul does want to make use of the pattern of the action of God relative to Israel's messiah in order to indicate the importance of not pleasing oneself but attending to the requirements of the weaker neighbor. This now allows him to return to a theme that has permeated this letter: that the good news concerning the messianic establishment of justice is first for the Judeans and then also for the pagans. This theme, announced several times early in the letter, became the subject of his lengthy argument concerning the incorporation of all of Israel into the messianic salvation by means of a sort of detour though the pagans, occasioned in part by the rejection of the messiah by (some of) his own people. He is now able to combine these approaches in a way that justifies his confidence in the salvation of both Judeans and pagans.

For I say messiah had become a servant [*diakonon*] of circumcision for the sake of the truthfulness of God, in order to confirm the promises pertaining to the "fathers" and the nations to make the divine mercy shine forth.

The text may be translated in a variety of ways, but something like what I have ventured helps make it clear that Paul understands the promise to the patriarchs to be a promise that expressly reaches out to the nations or pagans. That the messiah becomes a servant of the circumcision thus confirms the priority of Israel as God's chosen people while at the same time makes clear that the favoring of Israel comes to fullest expression in the extension of the messianic effect (justice and thus salvation) to the pagan nations.

In contrast to the extended argument of chapters 9–11, which dealt with the actual rejection of the messiah on the part of the Judean authorities and indicated that even this rejection would have the effect not only of including the gentiles but also "all Israel," here Paul implies that that rejection was by no means essential to the divine "plan" or intention. It was, rather, as I have indicated, a case of improvisation that responded to historical contingency (the rejection) in such a way as to accomplish the original goal both in spite of and by means of that rejection.

Here Paul is emphasizing an even more basic perspective that the divine promise had always been a promise to Israel concerning the incorporation of the gentiles. The significance of this is that on this most basic level, it is not the case that the messiah "had to die." Rather, if we were to extrapolate from Paul's argument, it would be fair to say that God has been able to turn what would appear to be a drastic setback into an instrument to serve the original divine intention. To demonstrate that God has done what God promised to Israel—and to the nations as well—Paul introduces a chain of citations from the written testimonies of ancient Israel.

As it is written, "Therefore I will confess you among the nations and sing praises to your name" [Psalm 18:49], **and again he says, "Rejoice, O nations, with his people"** [Deuteronomy 32:43], **and again, "Praise the Lord, all you nations, and let all the peoples praise him"** [Psalm 117:1], **and Isaiah says, "The root of Jesse shall come, one who rises to rule the nations; in him the nations will hope"** [Isaiah 11:10].

The selection of texts (Psalms, Torah, and Prophets) is consistent with what Paul has done at other points in this letter when calling upon the testimony of "the written." Whereas he had before cited texts that seemed to confirm the unfaithfulness of Israel, he is now able to bring to bear texts that emphasize the promise to Israel. Accordingly, the tone is not that of accusation or lament but of glad rejoicing. The passage from Isaiah is decisive in that it connects the messianic hope of Israel to the root of hope for all the nations of the earth: **"in him the nations will hope."** Earlier Paul had maintained that the true function of the written was to undergird hope, and with this chain of passages he demonstrates that hope for Israel and hope for the nations is the same hope, rooted in the promise to Israel.

It should be clear from this perspective that there can hardly be any justification for a "Christian" mission to the "Jews." Paul is a Judean with a mission to the gentiles: to proclaim the good news that Israel's messiah is also the messiah for the gentiles and that this is precisely in conformity with God's promise to and through God's chosen people. The promise is not that pagans can become Judeans, nor is it that Judeans can become "Christians" (nor still less that the Judeans should become gentiles), but that God is faithful to God's promises to Israel in such a way as to include all the nations (and, as we have heard, all of Israel as well). The relation between Jews and Christians in the very different circumstance in which we find ourselves today should be one by means of which we can mutually incite one another to hope and do so in terms of a commitment to justice that welcomes one another. In our own time, the way in which Jewish thinkers like Levinas and Derrida incite us to think justice and welcome of the other anew, as well as the ways in which Jewish thinkers like Scholem, Benjamin, and Taubes incite us to think anew in the key of messianicity, testifies to the significance of this pattern of relationality. Whether Christian thinkers can similarly be "servants of the circumcision" remains to be seen. If so, it would justify Paul's confidence that hope for the nations does not abrogate but substantiates Israel's hope as well.

Accordingly, Paul can conclude: **May the God of hope fill you all with joy and peace in faithfulness, so that you abound in hope by the power of holy spirit.** The One whose word of promise turned Abraham and Sarah to hope against hope, whose promise to Israel cannot be defeated even by Israel's rejection, and whose messiah cannot be defeated even by shameful execution is indeed the source of hope, the God of hope as Paul suggests. And this hope is the ground of exuberance, perhaps in a certain sense irrational exuberance—joy. For already in the life of a welcoming sociality, we are able to see a sort of anticipation of the ultimate peace or harmony that is the goal and consummation of the divine justice.

The mark of spirit or spiritedness is a certain exuberance that is not solitary but eminently social, a rejoicing together that makes the anticipated peace not a pacification but an exultant harmony of multiple voices, each distinctive but "in tune" with one another in a way that can be characterized only as love, a love that accomplishes what law cannot: justice that endures for each and all.

Coda

24. Paul's Messianic Mission (15:14–33)

In this concluding section of Paul's argument, he will return to where he began in the preface to the letter, explaining the rationale for his desire to come to Rome (14–24) and why he is not coming immediately (25–32). This conclusion, together with the introduction, gives further clarity regarding what may fairly be termed Paul's "political agenda" or "messianic politics."

At the beginning of this letter Paul had written: **For I long to see you that I may offer some spirited gift to you.** In the meantime he has provided something of a down payment on this spirited gift through his treatment of the messianic justice of which he had claimed he was not ashamed. While aware of his own responsibility as an apostle and his own gifts as an interpreter of the glad proclamation, he had maintained that his coming was in no way an imposition of apostolic authority but that his purpose was **that we may be mutually encouraged through one another's faithfulness, both yours and mine.** He seeks, that is, a relationship of mutual encouragement, the sort of relationship he has been emphasizing in the concluding sections of his argument about the new sociality he sees coming into being in the messianic now-time. Now at the end he emphasizes this mutuality: **I myself have been persuaded about you, comrades, that you yourselves are full of goodness, having been filled with all knowledge** [*gnosis*] **and so are able to instruct one another.**

In this way he suggests that they, too, have important knowledge, that he is not presuming that they have nothing to offer, either to him or to one another. **But on some points I have been bold as a reminder to you through the favor given me from God.** In a way he is claiming that he has been simply reminding them of what they presumably already know, although his way of explaining these things may be somewhat different from what may have been familiar to them.

The ground of his boldness in this regard was earlier rooted in his apostolic responsibility, but here he substitutes "liturgical" language to much the same end, explaining that the favor or gift that has been granted him enables him **to be a** *leitourgon* **of messiah Joshua to the nations**. The *leitourgon* is not a professional priest but a citizen who plays a role in the public dedication of a project that benefits the public good. What he dedicates or offers up (sacrifices) is **the glad-making proclamation of God**, which he had at the beginning specified as a proclamation concerning Joshua messiah. His work then is lifting up—as in a sacrificial offering—of this proclamation to the end that the **offering of the gentiles may be acceptable, made holy by holy spirit**. Here Paul uses cultic language to express a public and even political responsibility—his work among the nations—just as he had used similar language to speak of all offering up their bodies as a living sacrifice or a rational worship. What seems evident is that Paul makes use of familiar pagan cultic language to give expression to his mission as well as to the form of just life that he supposes characterizes the life of the messianic sociality. This is not a giant leap, since the pagan *cultus* was itself a sort of civil religion deeply embedded in the public and political life of the *polis*. In any case, the goal is that these messianic groups for which he has a certain responsibility should be in conformity with the aim of God in history that, as we have seen, has to do with the beginnings of the actualization of messianic justice.

In messiah Joshua therefore I have pride in the things of God, although I will not speak of anything but what messiah worked through me for the adherence of the nations, by word and deed, by power of signs and wonders, by the power of holy spirit. Paul exults in the way his service to the messianic event has been effective thus far among the nations due to the way he has been used by the messiah and empowered by spirit. At the beginning he had spoken of his work as a delegate or apostle to **bring about the adherence of faithfulness . . . among all the nations**. He now exults over or takes a certain pride in the efficacy of his work to this point. The "signs and wonders" likely refer to the extraordinary ways in which he has thus far escaped peril (cf. 2 Corinthians 12:11–13:11; he uses similar language about signs and wonders in 2 Corinthians 13:12) and to the ways in which persons in a variety of towns and cities have responded affirmatively to his message and been formed into new messianic vanguards.

Certainly it is to this formation of cells of messianic loyalists that he immediately refers: **So that from Jerusalem around to Illyricum I have filled up the good news of the messiah.** The trajectory described by Paul is a sort of semicircle beginning in Jerusalem and going through Syria into Turkey and Greece, and then into what was once Yugoslavia, thereby bringing him close to what is now Italy. He has thus traversed the eastern half of the Roman Empire, filling it with the proclamation concerning the messiah. Indeed, he will say that he now has **no longer any space for work in these regions**. Obviously, it is not Paul's task to "Christianize" the empire. This can scarcely be said to have already been accomplished. What, then, can it mean that he has run out of room? We may suppose that at this time there may be messianic cells of at most a few dozen folk in perhaps fewer than a score of towns and cities in the eastern half of the empire. What can it mean that he is basically done here? How does this count as fulfilling the messianic mission?

Here it is important to recall the synecdochal logic with which Paul has been operating. A part not only stands for but also entails the whole of which it is a part. The first fruits—to use a cultic reference—entail the entire harvest. This is particularly true of the messianic "vanguard" that Paul has been establishing in places like Corinth, Philippi, Thessalonica, Galatia, and Ephesus. Insofar as these messianic cells are sufficiently well established in manifesting the new just sociality in the midst of the towns and cities of this half of the empire, it is time for Paul to move on. Here we might recall Stanislas Breton's observation that Paul seems condemned to a "perpetual transit" (52).

In an analogy offered by Frederick Engels at the beginning of *On the History of Early Christianity*, Paul is like the early leaders of the social democrats who launch cells of workers among the proletarian masses of the cities and towns of Europe and leave the rest to them—and to history's inevitable triumph. Now, of course, what Paul is doing is somewhat different. His is an explicitly messianic movement that supposes that God's purpose of a truly just social order has been inaugurated in the messianic event of Joshua's mission, execution, and resurrection. I recall Steve Biko in South Africa saying that it is not a matter of organizing a movement to bring about liberation but of preparing people for the liberation that is coming. Something like that is going on here it seems. If there are communities of generous welcome that exhibit a new sort of justice outside the law within the empire, then this is enough to demonstrate that the days of that empire are truly numbered.

Paul is not alone in this mission. Thus, he is **eagerly striving to announce the good news not where the name of the messiah is already heard, so that I don't build on a foundation that belongs to another, but as it is written: They shall see who have never been told of Him, and they shall understand who have never heard of Him** (Isaiah 52:15). Paul's point is that his is the work of going into so-far-untouched territory to launch new cells. He has no ambition either to correct or improve, still less to administer, the work that others are already doing. He goes only where no one else has gone before in the messianic mission of announcing God's proclamation concerning the messiah.

Of course, as we have seen here and know from the other letters, he is not interested simply in giving people the right ideas but in enabling them to become mini-societies of messianic justice. He has no particular interest in cult or even the fine points of doctrine but in forms of social life that reflect the coming justice of God.

It is this work that has been completed in the eastern half of the empire. But for this to be truly and effectively a counterimperial movement, it is necessary to move on to the western half, the part that is not Greek but "barbarian," as he had said at the beginning. Now he makes this a bit more explicit: **Since I have long yearned for so many years to visit you, I hope in traveling on to Spain to see you and be sent on by you if it may be possible and to be refreshed by you.** Paul hopes to find in Rome a sort of blessing and encouragement to move into the next urgent phase of his mission. His way of phrasing this seems designed to prevent the Romans from supposing that he is coming to exercise any sort of authority over them. He is, rather, seeking partnership with them on his way onward. This letter seeks to suggest why they might indeed welcome this traveling delegate and approve of and perhaps even facilitate in some way (perhaps through the provision of translators or places of hospitality along the way) his mission.

On reading this, one might suppose that Paul is immediately coming to Rome. He has spoken of a long-deferred deep desire to see the Romans, and he clearly has an urgent mission if he is to go on to Spain in the short time that he may believe remains before the consummation of the messianic reign (**the time has grown short**, he has said). He has now finished his work in the east that has previously prevented him from moving on. But there is one more thing to do first, something that for Paul trumps even the urgency of his eschatological mission.

But now I am going to Jerusalem to serve the saints. Wherever Paul is writing this letter from, he is headed not toward but away from Rome. What motivates this strange deviation or detour? Why turning away again from the "saints" of Rome to those of Jerusalem? **Macedonia and Achaia** [Greece] **thought it good to make some contribution for the poor of the saints in Jerusalem.** Of this collection we read considerably more in 2 Corinthians 8 and 9. Reading those chapters makes it quite clear that for Paul it was an extraordinarily important thing.

In spite of the importance Paul attaches to this collection of support destined for Jerusalem, it is not obvious what precisely was entailed thereby. We know that Paul has had his troubles with the "saints" in Jerusalem. He gives some account of this in writing to the cells in the region of Galatia. But there Paul also maintained that the only condition set for the mission to the gentiles by those in Jerusalem was that those entrusted with this mission, especially Paul, not forget the poor. Paul has here just referred to the poor who pertain to or are the concern of the saints in Jerusalem. Briefly, I suppose that the following is at stake here. The community in Jerusalem was characterized, according to Acts, by a Pentecostal communism. All gave all so that it might be distributed to (all) the poor. This is a policy that we read of twice in Acts, in chapters 2 and 4, the first two times that we are told of the community receiving holy spirit. Keeping the poor in mind is something utterly crucial to this community, so crucial that it becomes, according to Paul, the condition for agreeing to the mission to the gentiles. In this way, the gentile or pagan communities would dramatically reflect the will of the God of Israel that the welfare of the poor be the measure of the justice of the whole society. It is this consistent theme of the law and the prophets that comes to be dramatically enacted in Jerusalem. If pagan communities imitate this polity, then they will give clear and unmistakable evidence of loyalty to the messiah of Israel.

Paul may have invented, or stumbled upon, or improvised, a way to "up the ante" on this expectation. Not only would pagan communities imitate this polity or politics but they would actually contribute to the ability of the saints in Jerusalem to serve the poor of Jerusalem, thereby strengthening the witness of the Jerusalem community in Jerusalem itself. Since Jerusalem was the site of both the execution and resurrection of the messiah, this would indeed be a dramatic sign of the truth of the gospel of God concerning that messiah and evidence of the coming reign of messianic justice. Instead, therefore, of paying the temple tax expected from all Judeans in diaspora to support the temple in Jerusalem, the pagan devotees of the messiah of Israel would be contributing to the building of justice that begins with attention to the weak, the humiliated, the impoverished—in Jerusalem itself.

Paul explains about the cells in Macedonia and Achaia: **They were happy to do it and are indebted to them, for if the nations have come to share their spirited things, then they should also be of service to them in fleshly things.** We recall that the gospel is for the Judeans first and then the Greeks. This sharing from the Judeans to the pagans in the messianic proclamation now redounds to the Judeans in the form of concrete material assistance, what Paul does not hesitate to call **fleshly things**: things, that is, that serve or minister to the weakness of the human, the necessities of life. In this way, the historical progression he had sketched in the movement of the glad proclamation from the Judeans to the gentiles—in part through the rejection of the proclamation by (some of) the Judeans and then culminating in the salvation of all Israel—is now enacted in a partial, preliminary, yet extraordinarily concrete way in the collection destined for the poor of the saints in Jerusalem.

It is on this fleshly service that Paul places extraordinary priority, for he must do this before he can continue on his urgent business in and beyond Rome. **When therefore I will have completed this and sealed to them this fruit, I will be on my way through you to Spain.** The "fruit" here is the first fruits of the mission to the gentiles or pagans, the material evidence of growing solidarity in mission among all who belong to the messiah. It is this, then, that will complete his work in the eastern half of the empire and permit him to move on to complete what remains of his mission: **And I know that when I come I will come to you in the fullness of messianic blessing.** Paul will then have good reason to know that his mission is indeed the sign of the messianic blessing in which both Israel and the nations will rejoice.

But this final task is not without its very real dangers. **I beg you comrades, through our leader Joshua messiah and through the love of the spirit, to strive together with me in prayer to God for my sake, that I may be delivered from the unbelievers in Judea and that my service to Jerusalem may be acceptable to the saints so that in joy I may come to you through the will of God and find rest with you.** The danger from those who do not (yet) adhere to the good news is not imaginary. After all, Paul was himself one who persecuted the early community. He may have been one who regarded the gospel concerning a rejected and executed messiah to be blasphemy, deserving of death. Thus, he knows all too well the danger that may arise from the zealous defenders of a certain law and order, a certain tradition, even a certain patriotism. He then begs the Romans to be in solidarity with him in yearning for his deliverance from this real and present danger. In this way they already become his partners in his mission.

We do not know to what extent Paul's contribution for the poor of the saints of Jerusalem produced the desired result. It seems likely that it did. But we are informed by Acts that Paul was less fortunate with respect to escaping the ire of the Judeans generally. The result was Paul's imprisonment, which may have greatly delayed his journey to Rome, but in what Paul must surely have recognized as another surprising bit of improvisation on the part of divine agency, it was precisely that opposition and imprisonment that eventually ensured his arrival in Rome—under military guard. It would only confirm his assurance that God improvises in and through history to advance the messianic promise.

The God of peace be with you all.

Ultimately, peace is the goal of Paul's messianic politics—not, as we have seen, the peace of pacification but the peace of diversity rejoicing in harmony. There is indeed no other politics that is worth striving for or to which it makes sense to seek to be faithful.

25. Traces of the New Sociality (16:1–27)

The material that we encounter in Romans 16 has been a source of considerable controversy. Some Pauline scholars have regarded the entire chapter as a fragment (perhaps somewhat altered) of another letter of Paul's that came to be attached to the letter to the Romans after losing its original context. The body of the letter of Romans suggests that Paul is a stranger to the group or groups of messiah followers in Rome, while this material suggests Paul's deep acquaintance with groups there and with groups who are heading for the destination of the letter. Thus, many have suggested that this might actually be a letter of greeting from Paul to another community where he might plausibly have known many people because of his prior residence there: Ephesus, for example (as Käsemann suggests).

However, a rather plausible case can be made that the letter to those in Rome had been occasioned by the end of the expulsion of Judeans, including Judean "Christians," from Rome, which permits not only the arrival of Paul in Rome but also the return of Judean messiah followers to Rome. Accordingly, the letter would be commending these and their associates, who had in the meantime become friends or associates of Paul and who would precede Paul in coming to Rome. Thus, Paul's emphasis on the relation of Judeans and pagans would come to a head in (and perhaps have been motivated by) the desired mutual welcome of returning Judean messianists to Roman messianic communities that had in the meantime become largely pagan in membership. This is an argument that Jewett ably puts forward.

Disputes of this sort admit only of more or less plausible reconstructions. In this case, the difficulty is increased on account of the appearance of passages that seem quite puzzling from the standpoint of the letter as a whole. For example, the doxology of Romans 16:25–27 seems to have in view not the togetherness of Judeans and gentiles that Paul has argued for in the letter (and that the offering to Jerusalem makes concrete) but a divine plan aimed exclusively at the gentiles. Thus, Jewett is able to label this whole doxology as supersessionist in character (997–1002). In addition, much of the terminology (though not all) seems to be borrowed from phrases more familiar from late first-century documents, including post-Pauline documents like 1 Timothy and Ephesians. Similar puzzlement attaches to the warnings in Romans 16:17–20a, which in spirit seem to flatly contradict the irenic position of Paul's desire that those of different opinions "welcome one another" (in addition to language about crushing Satan under your feet, which may have echoes of the deutero-Pauline 2 Thessalonians).

In this concluding section, I will not attempt to adjudicate these scholarly disputes but will deal with two issues germane to the themes of my reading of the argument of Romans as a whole. One concerns what it might mean for the perspective I have offered that the texts of Paul are subject to significant alteration in the decades after their writing and, indeed, in the decades after Paul's death. The other consideration concerns what can be gleaned from the names in the lengthy greetings that constitute the bulk of this chapter concerning the sort of sociality and thus polity or politics that Paul's mission is bringing into being. It will turn out that these are in fact related questions.

What is to be made of an apparent grab bag of names of persons who are to be received or welcomed or to whom the writer sends greetings? In most cases we have no other knowledge of the persons named than what the writer suggests about them in the names and designations provided in this letter. However, considerable attention to the provenance of names as well as reflection on the wording that Paul uses in connection with them actually yields a rather helpful outline of Paul's friends and associates and thus of the character of the new sociality that Paul has been laboring to foster.

This material opens with the commendation of a certain Phoebe and includes the names of several other women who appear as Paul's associates and as persons of some distinction among the messianic cells in the empire. Phoebe is designated as a sort of "patroness" (not, as some suppose, simply a "helper"). That is, she appears to have the means to give some material support to messianists who are associated with her.

We next encounter Prisca (or Priscilla) and Aquila, who we are told have a "house" in which a messianic cell meets. We are not told whether they are husband and wife, brother and sister, or related in some other way. In Acts 18, we are informed that they are husband and wife who had left Rome and engaged in the same trade as Paul (tentmakers). They have placed themselves in harm's way in order to rescue Paul from some great danger, most likely in Corinth or in Ephesus. It is notable that the woman (Prisca) is mentioned first, in contrast to the way in which Acts makes Aquila the lead character. Next, after Paul's beloved Epaenetus, we have Mary or Miriam, who is distinguished by her labors among the recipients of this greeting. This is followed by Junia and Andronicus, who are not designated as persons whom the apostles honor but as apostles themselves. There has been a long-standing attempt to disguise Junia's female identity and her apostolic role because of the supposition that a woman could not be an apostle.

Already at this point, we see that women were regarded as very important collaborators and leaders in the messianic mission. In addition, we have the women companions Tryphaena and Tryphosa, who as laborers in the lord are designated as leaders in messianic groups. Further, there is the mother of Rufus, who is also called the writer's (adoptive) mother. Among the five leaders of what may be a distinct cell in 16:15, two are women (Julia and the sister of Nereus). Overall, the impression given here is of leadership in the messianic communities or cells that appears to place male and female on a completely equal footing.

This gender equality in leadership of messianic communities is not destined to last much beyond Paul. Indeed, in the light of this and other indications in the Pauline correspondence we can guess that the prohibition of women speaking in the assembly in 1 Corinthians 14:33b–36 is an interpolation designed to claim Paul's authority for an anti-Pauline innovation. This will in turn mean that the gender of important apostles like Junia will be changed by both copyists and translators until the latter part of the twentieth century, when Christianity begins to free itself from its denial of gender equality.

Yet a further trace of the messianic sociality Paul envisions relates to the way in which we find names of Judeans and Greek gentiles intermingled among the leaders that are named here. Jewett (953) offers a useful table for organizing the names as Greek, Judean, and Latin, with possible ethnic identities attached. The majority of the names (nineteen) are of Greek origin, although two of these may suggest Jewish identity (Andronikos and Herodion). Eight are of Latin derivation, although Jewett suspects Jewish identity among four of these (Aquila, Junia, Rufus, and his mother). The difficulty has to do with ways in which slaves (and former slaves or freedmen) take names from the household of their owners, thus making identification imprecise.

Whatever the difficulties in assigning ethnicity on the basis of names, what does emerge from this list of greetings and commendations is a remarkable coming together of Judean and gentile adherents to the messiah. Moreover, if we were to accept the disjunction of Greek and barbarian that Paul employs early in the letter to those in Rome, then the non-Greek but Latin names of some of these persons might indicate the presence among the gentiles of persons of "barbarian" origin (to which we might add Persis, whose name suggests Persian or Parthian origin).

The new sociality that Paul and his companions and collaborators are fostering, therefore, is one that cuts across preexisting cultural, linguistic, and even religious identities (as we have seen in Romans) to constitute a sociality based not on such identities but on a shared commitment to the messianic project and mission. This does not mean that these preexisting cultural identities are abolished, but they are rendered "inoperative" or nondeterminative, as Agamben has suggested (*Time*), or that those who are called into the messianic project are "uncoupled" (Žižek, *Fragile Absolute* 123–130) from those identities that might separate them or set them against one another.

We may notice two entire "congregations" or cells that appear to be constituted by slaves: those belonging to Narcissus and those belonging to Aristobulus. The Greek only indicates that they are of or belong to the aforementioned men, who are referred to neither as leaders nor as belonging to cell groups. Translators have often inserted the supposition that those who are greeted are family members of the aforementioned worthies, but there is no indication that they are members of the family or even that they are of the household. Rather, the natural supposition is that those of Narcissus are among his slaves; the same would be true of those of, or belonging to, Aristobulus. We thus have two cell groups formed among (some of) the slaves of slave-owning persons of some power who themselves have no relation to the messianic movement.

In addition, we are told of two other groups: the "brothers" (or comrades) who are led collectively by Asyncritus, Phlegon, Hermes, Patrobus, and Hermas; and the "saints" led collectively by Philologus, Julia, Nereus, his sister, and Olympas. We have here first an indication of a sort of collective or shared leadership that Jewett thinks would be characteristic of what he calls "tenement churches" (as distinguished from the "house churches" that might be formed in the homes or apartments of more prosperous members of the community). All the names listed here indicate probable slave background according to Jewett, suggesting either that they are slaves or freed persons of low status.

Other names that seem to suggest slave or former slave status include Herodion, Ampliatus, Urbanus, Stachys, and Trypania. There are others of whom slave status is not indicated by their names or other epithets, including Phoebe, Rufus and his mother, and Prisca. At the very least, we learn that messianic cells were often formed among the lowest groups of society and that some were groups composed entirely of slaves belonging to particular masters, whereas others may have included slaves and freed persons with collective leadership. More prosperous persons, either of free descent or manumitted from slavery, also formed communities or cells. What this set of greetings envisions is that both within and among these groups there should prevail an unreserved welcome and an intimate fellowship. In this way they give dramatic testimony to the coming of a new messianic justice, already taking shape now in the slums and apartments of the cities of Rome.

On account of something like a cult of personality that has grown up around the name of Paul, it is important to notice the way in which Paul's labors are never solitary. He works among companions and insists upon the bonds of affection and collaboration that unite him with others. Here, for example, several persons are called Paul's beloved: Epaenetus, Ampliatus, Stachys, and Persis (the one female in this number!).

One way a strong sense of collaboration is emphasized is Paul's identification of persons as "coworkers"—for example, Prisca, Aquila, and Urbanus. This is one of Paul's frequent uses of this term that also appears in Philemon, Philippians, and other letters. In addition, Paul identifies persons as fellow militants (usually translated as fellow soldiers), as fellow prisoners, and so on. In general, Paul supposes that all are or may be fellow laborers, companions in the messianic project. Badiou suggests that this emphasis of being coworkers is an important marker of the egalitarian character of Paul's mission: "Where the figure of the master breaks down come those of the worker and equality conjoined. All equality is that of belonging together to a work" (*Saint Paul* 60). Hence, one of the characteristic features of Paul's diction is the use, and perhaps invention, of so many compound terms in Greek prefaced with *syn-* (*co-*).

While some have supposed that the standard form of organization of early cells was the house church (or perhaps better, apartment church), with the owner or renter offering support for common meals and perhaps having some leadership in those cells (here, for example, Phoebe or the "house" of Prisca and Aquila), other forms of organization are identified by Jewett as "tenement churches," with a more communal style and collective leadership (here those who are slaves of Aristobulus and Narcissus as well as the two collectives with five leaders identified in verses 14 and 15).

It appears that Paul does not insist on any particular "polity" concerning the difference between house churches or tenement churches. Rather, he seems to be nonchalant about how these groups are formed so long as they embody among themselves the love that is his aim and demonstrate this same love, generosity, and hospitality in the relations between these groups.

Whether one agrees with those like Jewett, who place these leaders and cell groups in Rome, or with those like Käsemann, who incline toward locating those who are to be greeted in Ephesus, it is possible to glimpse (as through a glass darkly) something of the astonishing character of the messianic sociality that Paul and his associates have fostered. Groups may be led by women or men or both together; they may be inaugurated by men or women or both together. Roles played out in these communities depend not on gender but on the particular gifts of those who launch and lead such messianic cells.

Moreover, groups that are predominantly of pagan origin and composition and groups that are primarily of Judean origin are yoked together, overcoming ethnic and religious divisions. Some groups are constituted wholly or primarily of slaves, others of mixed slave and freed persons, and others led by free patrons who may enjoy full citizenship. Thus, there is a great diversity of class, gender, and ethnic "location," even if primarily associated with the urban underclass.

All of these are to greet one another with the "holy kiss," a greeting generally reserved for intimate members of the same family. Thus, there is to be a remarkable intimacy among members of the same cell and between members of different cells, composed of different sorts of people, united in messianic hope and in the project of living out already in the now-time a form of life in dramatic contrast to the old social order out of which they have been called.

We have noticed in this range of names the tendency in later copyists of the text (as well as translators) to reduce the range of Paul's astonishingly inclusive polity. The countercultural inclusion of women among the most prominent members and leaders of communities came to be covered over as emergent Christianity assimilated itself to safer patriarchal norms of imperial (and later) social order. Less marked, perhaps, but also noticeable has been the reduction in the togetherness of persons of different ethnic and cultural origin and of class location. The radically egalitarian sociality onto which these greetings provide a window appears to have been compromised quite early.

The very fact of this set of compromises, however, testifies to the radical political significance of the Pauline messianic project. The compromises themselves seek to make this project more politically palatable within the social order that was inadvertent host to these vanguard cells of a new sort of humanity, a new sort of politics.

Now we can see a similar process at work in the "interpolations" that were signaled earlier. These interpolations need to be seen within the wider framework of a general tendency to modify and perhaps deradicalize Paul's letters. Moreover, we have the widely recognized phenomenon of passing off other documents as from Paul that appear to have a completely different character from those letters now agreed to be genuinely Pauline. These texts (deutero-Pauline and Pastoral) are certainly not without value in their own right, but they also show an unmistakable tendency to reduce the Pauline inclusivity in decisive ways.

We may also note the struggle over Paul that occurs in the light of history in the case of Marcion. It is generally agreed that Marcion sought to create a gentile Christianity in Rome that severed its tie to the root of Judean texts, society, and practices. In this attempt, he adopted and revised the Pauline letters. Galatians he may have found acceptable, but Romans (and he was in Rome) provided certain challenges. Among the changes made by Marcion is the elimination of chapters 15 and 16. The Judeans named in chapter 16 are thereby erased from Marcion's history of Christian beginnings. The concluding doxology that emphasizes the gentile mission to the exclusion of Israel seems to have been composed under Marcionite influence. The doxology sees the "mystery" of God as the inclusion of the gentiles as opposed to the letter that understands the inclusion of the gentiles as a detour on the way to inclusion of all of Israel.

The translators' erasure of slave communities by making Aristobulus and Narcissus into "fathers" whose families are Christian (rather than as slave owners, some of whose slaves form messianic cell groups among themselves without permission or patronage) also serves to mitigate or erase the radical character of messianic sociality, of the messianic politics of Paul.

What can we learn from this? One thing is that the letters them-selves were a kind of political dynamite that had to be handled with care. Moreover, "Paul" becomes the name of a receding authority figure whose ideas must be adapted and whose name must be appropriated by those who sought to maintain the relevance of Pauline views in many respects, without the dangers that would be associated with the messianic project.

Here let us take up Derrida's astute reflections on autoimmunity to clarify this political reality. In his reflections on the "democracy to come," which serves for Derrida as a way of orienting a decidedly political hope, an orientation toward the call and claim of justice, he is led to wonder about the ways in which democracy may undermine itself from within in the unceasing quest to transform any actually existing democracy toward greater inclusivity or in the attempt to maintain or preserve itself (*Rogues* 36). One side of this problem would be the question of whether a democratic ethos must welcome or give place to antidemocratic views and movements. The point is that this is fundamentally an insoluble double bind. If democracy in the name of democracy silences opinions that in some fundamental way oppose democracy, then it has already attacked its own democratic values. But if it does not constrain antidemocratic movements, then it may very well find itself overwhelmed by them and again lose itself.

In the Pauline case, if Paul's egalitarian experiment were to grow unabated, then outside forces would surely seek to destroy it—with likely success. If the movement compromises with those forces, it may survive but will have lost what was most distinctive about itself. Or again if, in the name of the messianic project, alternative views about how to actualize that project under existing imperial conditions had been silenced, then what of the principle of **welcome one another . . . but not for disputes about opinions**? Paul insists in this letter on the mutual welcoming of those with fundamentally different opinions. To say, for example, that only the "strong" (let's say feminists) are right and others must not be allowed to express their views or to gain influence would undermine the democratic project from within. If, on the other hand, those antidemocratic views are not only expressed but for a variety of reasons gain influence or even control, then once again the messianic project is fatally compromised. And of course, it is not an equal struggle, since those who prefer a more autocratic or narrower sociality have no compunctions about excluding those of a different view. Thus, the struggle is always unequal, and democratic or inclusive views always succumb precisely on account of their democratic ethos.

But wait. If this were all there is to be said about the matter, then the struggle would be without hope—indeed, it would be impossible to see how the struggle might be waged in the first place, let alone continued. What awakens the desire for this new sociality? In our case, it may be these compromised texts themselves. The insertions and redactions that serve to render Paul's texts more palatable, and perhaps less explosive, in later or different contexts also preserve the texts, together with the explosive potential they still bear. The writing of letters in Paul's name that answer to a different, less egalitarian, ecclesial context does so at the price of claiming and maintaining the authority of these more subversive texts. The very attempt to claim Paul's authority for these compromises still underlines and perhaps even increases Paul's authority, and thus the capacity of his less authoritarian and more socially (as well as theologically) radical voice to still be overheard. That is, the attempt to preserve or construct authority for these less radical positions runs the risk of allowing the messianic politics a chance to break out again. The antidemocratic impulse has its own autoimmune crisis, or as Derrida notes, "We now know that repression in both its psychoanalytic sense and in its political sense—whether it be through the police, the military, or the economy—ends up producing, reproducing, and regenerating the very thing it seeks to disarm" ("Autoimmunity" 99).

The very attempts to protect the messianic project fatally compromise it. But even as thus compromised, and indeed sometimes perverted into its very opposite, it still sparks here and there that hope that continues the struggle against all forms of domination and division. These texts have never been rendered completely harmless to the existing social order. Their explosive potentiality still awakens a hearing, an aspiration, a loyalty to the call and claim of messianic justice. Those who have contained the texts have preserved them. That which seeks to render them harmless has not erased them or completely silenced them. So they still may be read, their audacious claims may still be deciphered, and they may still awaken hope and an unflinching fidelity—and the struggle begins again.

One of the many names of this struggle is that of democracy. In writing of the meaning of democracy, Derrida notes that there have hardly ever been any philosophical friends of democracy and points to Nietzsche, whose contempt for democracy is as strong as (and perhaps fueled by) his animosity toward Paul, especially the "Pauline perversion that turns weakness into force" (a reference to 1 Corinthians 1–3). Derrida continues: "More than any other form of democracy, more than social democracy, or popular democracy, a Christian democracy should be welcoming to the enemies of democracy; it should turn them the other cheek, offer hospitality, grant freedom of expression and the right to vote to antidemocrats, something in conformity with a certain hyperbolic essence, an essence more autoimmune than ever, of *democracy itself*, if 'itself' there ever is, if ever there is a democracy and thus a Christian democracy worthy of this name" (*Rogues* 41). Thus, the Pauline messianic project can even be identified as "democracy itself," a democracy that, of course, has never existed but always remains a democracy to come—or, as Paul had called it, "divine justice."

Bibliography

Agamben, Giorgio. *The Open: Man and Animal.* Translated by Kevin Attell. Stanford, CA: Stanford University Press, 2004.

——. *The Sacrament of Language: An Archaeology of the Oath.* Translated by Adam Kotsko. Stanford, CA: Stanford University Press, 2011.

——. *State of Exception.* Translated by Kevin Attell. Chicago: University of Chicago Press, 2005.

——. *The Time That Remains: A Commentary on the Letter to the Romans.* Translated by Patricia Dailey. Stanford, CA: Stanford University Press, 2005,

Althusser, Louis. *Lenin and Philosophy and Other Essays.* Translated by Ben Brewster. New York: Monthly Review Press, 2001.

Aristotle. *Politics.* In *The Basic Works of Aristotle,* edited by Richard McKeon, translated by Benjamin Jowett. New York: Random House, 1941.

Augustine. *City of God.* Translated by Henry Bettenson. New York: Penguin, 1972.

Badiou, Alain. *Ethics: An Essay on the Understanding of Evil.* Translated by Peter Hallward. London: Verso, 2001.

——. *Saint Paul: The Foundation of Universalism.* Translated by Ray Brassier. Stanford, CA: Stanford University Press, 2003.

Barth, Karl. *Church Dogmatics.* Vol. 2, *The Doctrine of God,* pt. 2. Edited by G. W. Bromiley and T. F. Torrance. Translated by G. W. Bromiley et al. Edinburgh: T & T Clark, 1957.

——. *The Epistle to the Romans.* 6th ed. Translated by Edwyn C. Hoskins. New York: Oxford University Press, 1968.

Benjamin, Walter. "Critique of Violence." In *Reflections: Essays, Aphorisms, Autobiographical Writings,* edited by Peter Demetz, 277–300. New York: Schocken, 1978.

——. "Theological-Political Fragment." In *Reflections: Essays, Aphorisms, Autobiographical Writings,* edited by Peter Demetz, 312–313. New York: Schocken, 1978.

——. "Theses on the Philosophy of History." In *Illuminations: Essays and*

Reflections, edited by Hannah Arendt, 253–264. New York: Schocken, 1968.

Boers, Hendrikus. *The Justification of the Gentiles: Paul's Letters to the Galatians and Romans*. Peabody, MA: Hendrikson, 1994.

Breton, Stanislas. *A Radical Philosophy of Paul*. Translated by Joseph N. Ballan. New York: Columbia University Press, 2011.

Calvin, John. *Calvin's New Testament Commentaries*. Vol. 8, *Romans and Thessalonians*. Edited by David W. Torrance and Thomas F. Torrance. Translated by R. Mackenzie. Grand Rapids, MI: William B. Eerdmans, 1960.

Caputo, John. *The Prayers and Tears of Jacques Derrida: Religion Without Religion*. Bloomington: Indiana University Press, 1997.

Caputo, John D., and Michael Scanlon, eds. *God, the Gift, and Postmodernism*. Bloomington: Indiana University Press, 1999.

Cicero. *The Republic and The Laws*. Translated by Niall Rudd. Oxford: Oxford University Press, 1988.

Cohen, Shaye J. D. *The Beginnings of Jewishness: Boundaries, Varieties, Uncertainties*. Berkeley: University of California Press, 1999.

Critchley, Simon. *Faith of the Faithless: Experiments in Political Theology*. London: Verso, 2012.

Derrida, Jacques. *Adieu: To Emmanuel Levinas*. Translated by Pascale-Anne Brault and Michael Naas. Stanford, CA: Stanford University Press, 1999.

———. *The Animal That Therefore I Am*. Translated by David Wills. New York: Fordham University Press, 2008.

———. "Autoimmunity: Real and Symbolic Suicides." In *Philosophy in a Time of Terror: Dialogues with Jürgen Habermas and Jacques Derrida*, edited by Giovanna Boarradori, 85–136. Chicago: University of Chicago Press, 2003.

———. "Before the Law." In *Acts of Literature*, edited by Derrick Attridge, 181–220. New York: Routledge, 1992.

———. "The Force of Law: The 'Mystical Foundations of Authority.'" In *Acts of Religion*, edited by Gil Anidjar, 228–298. New York: Routledge, 2001.

———. *The Gift of Death*. 2nd ed. Translated by David Wills. Chicago: University of Chicago Press, 2008.

———. "Justices." Translated by Peggy Kamuf. *Critical Inquiry* 31.3 (Spring 2005): 689–721.

———. *Negotiations: Interventions and Interviews, 1971–2001*. Translated by Elizabeth Rottenberg. Stanford, CA: Stanford University Press, 2001.

———. *Of Spirit: Heidegger and the Question*. Translated by Geoffrey Bennington and Rachel Bowlby. Chicago: University of Chicago Press, 1989.

———. *On the Name*. Edited by Thomas Dutoit. Translated by David Wood, John P. Leavey Jr., and Ian McLeod. Stanford, CA: Stanford University Press, 1995.

————. *The Postcard: From Socrates to Freud and Beyond.* Translated by Alan Bass. Chicago: University of Chicago Press, 1987.

————. *Rogues: Two Essays on Reason.* Translated by Pascale-Anne Brault and Michael Naas. Stanford, CA: Stanford University Press, 2005.

————. "A Silkworm of One's Own." In *Acts of Religion*, edited by Gil Anidjar, 309–355. New York: Routledge, 2001.

————. *Specters of Marx: The State of the Debt, the Work of Mourning, and the New International.* Translated by Peggy Kamuf. New York: Routledge, 1994.

Derrida, Jacques, and Anne Dufourmantelle. *Of Hospitality.* Translated by Rachel Bowlby. Stanford, CA: Stanford University Press, 2000.

Derrida, Jacques, and Elisabeth Roudinesco. *For What Tomorrow . . . : A Dialogue.* Translated by Jeff Fort. Stanford, CA: Stanford University Press, 2004.

Dio Cassius. *Roman History.* Translated by Earnest Cary. Loeb Classical Library. Cambridge, MA: Harvard University Press, 1924.

Douzinhas, Costas, and Slavoj Žižek, eds. *The Idea of Communism.* New York: Verso, 2010.

Elliott, Neil. *The Arrogance of Nations: Reading Romans in the Shadow of Empire.* Minneapolis, MN: Fortress Press, 2008.

————. *Liberating Paul: The Justice of God and the Politics of the Apostle.* Maryknoll, NY: Orbis Press, 1994.

Engels, Friedrich. *On the History of Early Christianity.* In *Karl Marx and Friedrich Engels on Religion.* Atlanta: Scholars Press, 1964.

Epistle to Diognetus. In *The Apostolic Fathers: Greek Texts and English Translations of Their Writings*, 2nd ed., edited by Michael W. Holmes, translated by J. B. Lightfoot and J. R. Harmer. Grand Rapids, MI: Baker, 1992.

Esler, Philip F. *Conflict and Identity in Romans: The Social Setting of Paul's Letter.* Minneapolis, MN: Fortress, 2003.

Foucault, Michel. *The Courage of Truth: Lectures at the College de France 1983–1984.* Translated by Graham Burchell. New York: Palgrave Macmillan, 2011.

Gregory of Nyssa. "An Address on Religious Instruction." Edited and translated by Cyril C. Richardson. In *Christology of the Later Fathers*, edited by Edward R. Hardy, 268–325. Philadelphia: Westminster, 1954.

Heidegger, Martin. *The Phenomenology of Religious Life.* Translated by Matthias Fritsch and Jennifer Ana Gosetti-Ferenci. Bloomington: Indiana University Press, 2004.

Hobbes, John. *Leviathan.* Edited by J. C. A. Gaskin. Oxford: Oxford University Press, 1996.

Horsley, Richard A., ed. *Paul and Empire: Religion and Power in Roman Imperial Society.* Harrisburg, PA: Trinity Press International, 1997.

Irenaeus of Lyons. *Against Heresies.* Translated by Alexander Roberts and James

Donaldson. In *The Ante-Nicene Fathers*, vol. 1, edited by Alexander Roberts, James Donaldson, and Cleveland Coxe. Grand Rapids, MI: William B. Eerdmans, 1885.

Jennings, Theodore W. *Plato or Paul? The Origin of Western Homophobia.* Cleveland, OH: Pilgrim Press, 2009.

———. *Reading Derrida / Thinking Paul: On Justice.* Stanford, CA: Stanford University Press, 2006.

———. *Transforming Atonement: A Political Theology of the Cross.* Minneapolis, MN: Fortress Press, 2009.

Jewett, Robert. *Romans: A Commentary.* Minneapolis, MN: Fortress, 2006.

Kahl, Brigitte. *Galatians Re-imagined: Reading with the Eyes of the Vanquished.* Minneapolis, MN: Fortress, 2010.

Kant, Immanuel. *The Metaphysics of Morals.* In *Practical Philosophy*, translated by Mary J. Gregor. Cambridge: Cambridge University Press, 1996.

———. *Religion Within the Limits of Reason Alone.* Translated by Theodore M. Greene and Hoyt H. Hudson. New York: Harper & Row, 1934.

Käsemann, Ernst. *Commentary on Romans.* Translated by Geoffrey Bromiley. Grand Rapids, MI: William B. Eerdmans, 1980.

———. *New Testament Questions of Today.* Translated by W. J. Montague. London: SCM Press, 1969.

Lacan, Jacques. *The Ethics of Psychoanalysis.* Edited by Jacques Alan Miller. Translated by Dennis Porter. New York: W. W. Norton, 1992.

Levinas, Emmanuel. *Difficult Freedom: Essays on Judaism.* Translated by Seán Hand. Baltimore: Johns Hopkins University Press, 1990.

———. *God, Death, and Time.* Translated by Bettina Bergo. Stanford: Stanford University Press, 2000.

———. *Of God Who Comes to Mind.* Translated by Bettina Bergo. Stanford, CA: Stanford University Press, 1998.

———. *Totality and Infinity: An Essay on Exteriority.* Translated by Alfonso Lingis. Pittsburgh, PA: Duquesne University Press, 1969.

Locke, John. *A Paraphrase and Notes on the Epistles of St. Paul to the Galatians, 1 and 2 Corinthians, Romans, Ephesians.* 2 vols. Edited by Arthur W. Wainwright. Oxford: Clarendon, 1987.

Marion, Jean-Luc. *God Without Being: Hors-Texte.* Translated by Thomas Carlson. Chicago: University of Chicago Press, 1991.

Marx, Karl. *Contribution to a Critique of Hegel's Philosophy of Right.* In *The Marx-Engels Reader*, 2nd ed., edited by Robert C. Tucker. New York: Norton, 1978.

Miranda, Jose Porfirio. *Marx and the Bible: A Critique of the Philosophy of Oppression.* Translated by John Eagleson. Maryknoll, NY: Orbis, 1974.

Nancy, Jean Luc. *Being Singular Plural.* Translated by Robert D. Richardson and Anne E. O'Byrne. Stanford, CA: Stanford University Press, 2000.

———. *Dis-enclosure: The Deconstruction of Christianity.* Translated by Bettina Bergo, Gabriel Malenfant, and Michael B. Smith. New York: Fordham University Press, 2008.

———. *The Inoperative Community.* Edited by Peter Connor. Minneapolis: University of Minnesota Press, 1991.

———. *Noli me tangere: On the Raising of the Body.* Translated by Sarah Clift, Pascale-Anne Brault, and Michael Naas. New York: Fordham University Press, 2008.

Nanos, Mark. *The Mystery of Romans: The Jewish Context of Paul's Letter.* Minneapolis, MN: Fortress, 1996.

Niebuhr, Reinhold. *Moral Man and Immoral Society: A Study in Ethics and Politics.* New York: Scribner's, 1932.

Nietzsche, Friedrich. *Daybreak: Thoughts on the Prejudices of Morality.* Edited by R. J. Hollingdale. Cambridge: Cambridge University Press, 1997.

———. *The Twilight of the Gods and The Anti-Christ.* Translated by R. J. Hollingdale. London: Penguin Books, 1990.

Plato. *Laws.* 2 vols. Translated by R. G. Bury. Loeb Classical Library. Cambridge, MA: Harvard University Press, 1961.

———. *Republic.* 2 vols. Translated by Paul Shorey. Loeb Classical Library. Cambridge, MA: Harvard University Press, 1935.

———. *Statesman. Philebus. Ion.* Translated by Harold North Fowler and W. R. M. Lamb. Loeb Classical Library. Cambridge, MA: Harvard University Press, 1925.

Royce, Josiah. *The Problem of Christianity.* Chicago: University of Chicago Press, 1968.

Rubin, Gayle. "The Traffic in Women: Notes on the 'Political Economy of Sex.'" In *Toward an Anthropology of Women,* edited by Reyna Reiter, 157–185, 198–200. New York: Monthly Review Press, 1975.

Spinoza, Baruch. *Theological-Political Treatise.* 2nd ed. Translated by Samuel Shirley. Indianapolis, IN: Hackett, 2001.

Stark, Rodney. *The Rise of Christianity: A Sociologist Reconsiders History.* New York: Harper, 1997.

Stendahl, Krister. *Paul Among Jews and Gentiles.* Philadelphia, PA: Fortress Press, 1976.

Stowers, Stanley K. *A Rereading of Romans: Justice, Jews, and Gentiles.* New Haven, CT: Yale University Press, 1994.

Suetonius. *The Twelve Caesars.* Edited by Michael Grant. Translated by Robert Graves. New York: Penguin, 1979.

Tacitus. *Annals.* Translated by A. J. Church and W. J. Brodribb. Chicago: Encyclopedia Britannica, 1952.

Tamez, Elsa. *The Amnesty of Grace: Justification by Faith from a Latin American Perspective*. Translated by Sharon Ringe. Nashville, TN: Abingdon, 1993.

Taubes, Jacob. *The Political Theology of Paul*. Translated by Dana Hollander. Stanford, CA: Stanford University Press, 2004.

Thorsteinsson, Runar. *Roman Stoicism and Roman Christianity: A Comparative Study of Ancient Morality*. Oxford: Oxford University Press, 2010.

Žižek, Slavoj. *The Fragile Absolute, or Why Is the Christian Legacy Worth Fighting For?* New York: Verso, 2000.

———. *The Puppet and the Dwarf: The Perverse Core of Christianity*. Cambridge, MA: MIT Press, 2003.

Index

Cultural Memory | in the Present

Eyal Peretz, *Becoming Visionary: Brian De Palma's Cinematic Education of the Senses*

Diana Sorensen, *A Turbulent Decade Remembered: Scenes from the Latin American Sixties*

Hubert Damisch, *A Childhood Memory by Piero della Francesca*

José van Dijck, *Mediated Memories in the Digital Age*

Dana Hollander, *Exemplarity and Chosenness: Rosenzweig and Derrida on the Nation of Philosophy*

Asja Szafraniec, *Beckett, Derrida, and the Event of Literature*

Sara Guyer, *Romanticism After Auschwitz*

Alison Ross, *The Aesthetic Paths of Philosophy: Presentation in Kant, Heidegger, Lacoue-Labarthe, and Nancy*

Gerhard Richter, *Thought-Images: Frankfurt School Writers' Reflections from Damaged Life*

Bella Brodzki, *Can These Bones Live? Translation, Survival, and Cultural Memory*

Rodolphe Gasché, *The Honor of Thinking: Critique, Theory, Philosophy*

Brigitte Peucker, *The Material Image: Art and the Real in Film*

Natalie Melas, *All the Difference in the World: Postcoloniality and the Ends of Comparison*

Jonathan Culler, *The Literary in Theory*

Michael G. Levine, *The Belated Witness: Literature, Testimony, and the Question of Holocaust Survival*

Jennifer A. Jordan, *Structures of Memory: Understanding German Change in Berlin and Beyond*

Christoph Menke, *Reflections of Equality*

Marlène Zarader, *The Unthought Debt: Heidegger and the Hebraic Heritage*

Jan Assmann, *Religion and Cultural Memory: Ten Studies*

David Scott and Charles Hirschkind, *Powers of the Secular Modern: Talal Asad and His Interlocutors*

Gyanendra Pandey, *Routine Violence: Nations, Fragments, Histories*

James Siegel, *Naming the Witch*

J. M. Bernstein, *Against Voluptuous Bodies: Late Modernism and the Meaning of Painting*

Theodore W. Jennings Jr., *Reading Derrida / Thinking Paul: On Justice*

Richard Rorty and Eduardo Mendieta, *Take Care of Freedom and Truth Will Take Care of Itself: Interviews with Richard Rorty*

Jacques Derrida, *Paper Machine*

Renaud Barbaras, *Desire and Distance: Introduction to a Phenomenology of Perception*

Jill Bennett, *Empathic Vision: Affect, Trauma, and Contemporary Art*

Ban Wang, *Illuminations from the Past: Trauma, Memory, and History in Modern China*

James Phillips, *Heidegger's Volk: Between National Socialism and Poetry*

Jean-Luc Marion, *Being Given That: Toward a Phenomenology of Givenness*

Theodor W. Adorno and Max Horkheimer, *Dialectic of Enlightenment*

Ian Balfour, *The Rhetoric of Romantic Prophecy*

Martin Stokhof, *World and Life as One: Ethics and Ontology in Wittgenstein's Early Thought*

Gianni Vattimo, *Nietzsche: An Introduction*

Jacques Derrida, *Negotiations: Interventions and Interviews, 1971–1998*, edited by Elizabeth Rottenberg

Brett Levinson, *The Ends of Literature: The Latin American "Boom" in the Neoliberal Marketplace*

Timothy J. Reiss, *Against Autonomy: Cultural Instruments, Mutualities, and the Fictive Imagination*

Hent de Vries and Samuel Weber, eds., *Religion and Media*

Niklas Luhmann, *Theories of Distinction: Re-Describing the Descriptions of Modernity*, edited and introduced by William Rasch

Johannes Fabian, *Anthropology with an Attitude: Critical Essays*

Michel Henry, *I Am the Truth: Toward a Philosophy of Christianity*

Gil Anidjar, *"Our Place in Al-Andalus": Kabbalah, Philosophy, Literature in Arab-Jewish Letters*

Hélène Cixous and Jacques Derrida, *Veils*

F. R. Ankersmit, *Historical Representation*

F. R. Ankersmit, *Political Representation*

Elissa Marder, *Dead Time: Temporal Disorders in the Wake of Modernity (Baudelaire and Flaubert)*

Reinhart Koselleck, *The Practice of Conceptual History: Timing History, Spacing Concepts*

Niklas Luhmann, *The Reality of the Mass Media*

Hubert Damisch, *A Theory of /Cloud/: Toward a History of Painting*

Jean-Luc Nancy, *The Speculative Remark: (One of Hegel's bon mots)*

Jean-François Lyotard, *Soundproof Room: Malraux's Anti-Aesthetics*

Jan Patočka, *Plato and Europe*

Hubert Damisch, *Skyline: The Narcissistic City*

Isabel Hoving, *In Praise of New Travelers: Reading Caribbean Migrant Women Writers*

Richard Rand, ed., *Futures: Of Jacques Derrida*

William Rasch, *Niklas Luhmann's Modernity: The Paradoxes of Differentiation*

Jacques Derrida and Anne Dufourmantelle, *Of Hospitality*

Jean-François Lyotard, *The Confession of Augustine*

Kaja Silverman, *World Spectators*

Samuel Weber, *Institution and Interpretation: Expanded Edition*

Jeffrey S. Librett, *The Rhetoric of Cultural Dialogue: Jews and Germans in the Epoch of Emancipation*

Ulrich Baer, *Remnants of Song: Trauma and the Experience of Modernity in Charles Baudelaire and Paul Celan*

Samuel C. Wheeler III, *Deconstruction as Analytic Philosophy*
David S. Ferris, *Silent Urns: Romanticism, Hellenism, Modernity*
Rodolphe Gasché, *Of Minimal Things: Studies on the Notion of Relation*
Sarah Winter, *Freud and the Institution of Psychoanalytic Knowledge*
Samuel Weber, *The Legend of Freud: Expanded Edition*
Aris Fioretos, ed., *The Solid Letter: Readings of Friedrich Hölderlin*
J. Hillis Miller / Manuel Asensi, *Black Holes / J. Hillis Miller;
    or, Boustrophedonic Reading*
Miryam Sas, *Fault Lines: Cultural Memory and Japanese Surrealism*
Peter Schwenger, *Fantasm and Fiction: On Textual Envisioning*
Didier Maleuvre, *Museum Memories: History, Technology, Art*
Jacques Derrida, *Monolingualism of the Other; or, The Prosthesis of Origin*
Andrew Baruch Wachtel, *Making a Nation, Breaking a Nation: Literature
    and Cultural Politics in Yugoslavia*
Niklas Luhmann, *Love as Passion: The Codification of Intimacy*
Mieke Bal, ed., *The Practice of Cultural Analysis: Exposing
    Interdisciplinary Interpretation*
Jacques Derrida and Gianni Vattimo, eds., *Religion*

Made in the USA
Coppell, TX
17 January 2020

14617500R00150